Foregrounding
Ethical Awareness
in Composition
and English Studies

Foregrounding Ethical Awareness

in Composition

and English Studies

edited by
Sheryl I. Fontaine and Susan M. Hunter

New Perspectives in Rhetoric and Composition

CHARLES I. SCHUSTER, SERIES EDITOR

Boynton/Cook Publishers
HEINEMANN
Portsmouth, NH

Boynton/Cook Publishers, Inc.
A subsidiary of Reed Elsevier Inc.
361 Hanover Street
Portsmouth, NH 03801-3912

Offices and agents throughout the world

Library of Congress Cataloging-in -Publication Data

Foregrounding ethical awareness in composition and English studies / edited by Sheryl I.
    Fontaine and Susan M. Hunter.
        p.   cm.
    Includes bibliographical references.
    ISBN 0-86709-443-5 (acid-free paper)
    1. English philology—Study and teaching—Moral and ethical aspects. 2. English
language—Rhetoric—Study and teaching—Moral and ethical aspects. 3. English
language—Composition and exercises—Moral and ethical aspects. I. Fontaine, Sheryl I.,
1955–   . II. Hunter, Susan, 1948–   .
PE66.F67 1998
420' .7—dc21   97-49097
                                                                                                        CIP

Series editor: Charles Schuster
Cover design: Darci Mehall
Manufacturing: Louise Richardson

Printed in the United States of America on acid-free paper
02   01   00   99   98   DA   1   2   3   4   5

Contents

Acknowledgments

We thank the contributors to this volume for their interest in "foregrounding their ethical awareness" and for many, thoughtful revisions they undertook in response to our questions. We are also grateful to Chuck Schuster for his support of this project, his enthusiasm for our ideas and plans, and his confidence in their value to readers. Finally, we thank Richard Boyd for his good humor and helpful advice, Jeff Adams for his unwavering support and critical perspective, and David Fontaine-Boyd for his honest interest in the collaborative work we do.

1

Ethical Awareness
A Process of Inquiry

Sheryl I. Fontaine
Susan M. Hunter

Ethical Awareness Emerges
in Our Professional Discussions

In creating the premise and collecting the essays for *Foregrounding Ethical Awareness in Composition and English Studies,* we have found ourselves in the shadow of philosophers and scholars who have, for centuries, examined, criticized, and lauded "ethics" (see Weaver 1953, Faigley 1992, Porter 1993, and Jarratt 1991). Yet perhaps because of its frequent and enduring place in history, *ethics* has become a word that is easily tossed off, as if it had a single, shared meaning: "Her behavior was unethical;" "That action is a breach of ethics;" "Children today have no ethical grounding." And in addition to the assumptions about meaning that arise around any persistent language—particularly language that refers to emotions or judgments—how the word *ethics* has been used and what it is meant to suggest has taken on different shades of meaning in relation to the historical, philosophical, and even the personal and professional moments in which it has been used. These shadings are apparent in the various ways in which ethics has been applied by Composition and English Studies scholars in the current postmodern context wherein the value of static foundational assumptions has been challenged (Porter 1993, 216).

This is not to say that we can identify a progressive shift in the way ethics has been understood or used or that "old" uses have been condemned and replaced. Not only is the evolution of language far too idiosyncratic for us to document a clear-cut progression, but a progression that replaces one meaning with another would deny the value that earlier meanings carry. And even as the understanding of ethics has evolved, important contemporary arguments continue to begin with Aristotle's notions, postulating that ethics is the moral element in character from which is generated the reciprocated wish of individuals within a community for the good of others (Clark 1994). We propose instead to distinguish between ways that ethics has informed the work of Composition and English studies scholars and ways in which it has informed the reflections of the authors in this collection.

Two particular positions that ethics has held and continues to hold in disciplinary discussions are, first, as a fixed set of standards and, second, as a particular kind of response one hopes to create in others. In both of these positions, the application of ethics serves to sharpen the focus on another topic or issue, providing an important foundation to support the examination of a variety of topics and the particular conclusions about these topics that writers hope to reach.

Consider the first position: ethics used as a set of standards or a carefully defined system whose application guides behavior. For instance, the ethical standards may be intended to guide student behavior, as in Sandra Stotsky's detailed discussion of "Writing as Moral and Civic Thinking" (1992). Stotsky, who, as many thinkers do, equates the terms *moral* and *ethical*, outlines a "system of categories and . . . principles that . . . constitute one such conceptual framework that may help scholars explore the moral dimensions of academic writing and assist teachers in fostering their students' responsibilities as writers" (1992, 799). Both student and faculty behavior are targeted by the numerous articles and letters to the editor that define ethical rules by which to police plagiarism (e.g., *Council Chronicle* 1994). The behavior of writing center faculty and administrators has been the focus of a series of columns in *The Writing Lab Newsletter* (Pemberton 1993–1997) and a recent article in *WPA: Writing Program Administration* (Clark and Healy 1996). And in an obvious and important attempt to create and apply ethical standards, professional organizations that represent Composition and English studies have developed a "Statement of Professional Ethics" (MLA 1992) and a task force to examine the ethical responsibilities that guide faculty behavior (NCTE Committee on Code of Professional Ethics). Each year, more conferences, special sessions, and calls for papers continue to extend the application of ethical standards to professional behavior.

In the aforementioned instances, the goal is to apply an ethical code so as to control or guide behavior in students' writing, in the classroom, in the office, in our departments and programs, at professional meetings, and so forth. The ultimate focus, then, is on applying ethics *to something else*. Moreover, it is the something else and the writer's desire to change or control it and then monitor its adherence to the system that appears to have provided the impetus for the initial discussion. Application of an ethical system provides the method by which to achieve the goal.

A second position from which ethics informs Composition and English studies is as a basis to construct an environment within which students and others become aware of important contradictions and conflicts that will, in turn, contribute to the emergence of an ethical exigency from which to act. Consider

Christy Friend's essay on "Ethics in the Classroom" (1994), or Cynthia Selfe and Richard J. Selfe's discussion of the computer classroom in "The Politics of Interface: Power and Its Exercise in Electronic Contact Zones" (1994), or Martin Jacobi's "Professional Communication, Cultural Studies, and Ethics" (1996). Friend demonstrates how she uses particular readings and assignments to create an environment in which carefully orchestrated contradictions and conflicts will "create the kind of pluralistic forum essential to nondistributive ethical deliberation" (1994, 564). That is, she hopes to awaken in her students an ethical sensibility regarding the topic she has introduced into the simulated case study (1994, 564). In a similar manner, but regarding a different issue, Selfe and Selfe urge English teachers not to reduce the maps of computer interfaces to "simple, uncomplicated spaces" (1994, 500). By meeting their ethical responsibility to create a learning environment that "acknowledge[s] the complications and contradictions inherent" in the virtual spaces and "work[s] toward their unconcealment" (1994, 500; 501), teachers, the authors seem to suggest, will promote ethical self-reflection about computers and their use in education and the workplace. Jacobi, too, argues that it is necessary to promote ethical self-reflection among students preparing for careers in professional writing so that they can be "citizens first and business people second" and "challenge corporatist assumptions" (1996, 124).

Consider, as well, attempts by professional organizations to create environments in which to contemplate ethical issues: the MLA co-sponsored Conference on the Role of Advocacy in the Classroom (1995) and the collection of essays that resulted from it (1996), the CCC Caucus on Intellectual Property and Composition Studies, the Bard Conference on "Teaching Ethics" (1996), the NCTE 1997 Convention theme "Language as Moral Action," and the call in Fall, 1996, for papers for a special issue of *PMLA* on "Ethics and Literary Study." The officially sanctioned voices that represent each of these organizations ask their members to do what teachers have asked their students and other teachers to do in the classroom: to reflect specifically about what constitutes an ethical responsibility in the profession at large.

Again, discussion is held, not on ethics, but on whatever primary issue the authors or the organization has introduced. That is to say, the authors' goal is to create an environment that will encourage students or teachers to experience an ethical response to, in these instances, writing about dying (Friend 1994), using the computer (Selfe and Selfe 1994), and teaching in the literature or writing classroom. These discussions include the implicit recommendation that pointing out contradictions and conflicts is always a valuable means for raising ethical sensibility. However, for the most part, their focus of attention remains highly context-specific.

A third position—the one that ethics assumes in this collection of essays—provides no particular system nor promotes any particular environment and reflects the current postmodern context. From this position in the midst of postmodern epistemology, ethics is no longer a "static body of foundational principles, laws, and procedures" but a "mode of questioning" (Porter 1993, 218) that foregrounds ethical awareness and provides a lens through which to reexamine any variety of issues. The goal of foregrounding such an awareness is not to change behavior in a predetermined manner, but to see what may not have been seen before, to resist complacency and reconsider what had, heretofore, seemed acceptable. So, as belief in fixed ethical systems has been questioned, what has emerged is an ethical awareness that values the process of measuring ethical behavior, the importance of the individual, and the particularity of each situation. Such an awareness moves outside of systems and standards. Rather it is a critical, active component of each individual within the system, one that fosters inquiry and articulation (see Howie 1987, Young 1990). That is, the privileging of the individual ethical awareness takes the emphasis off resolution and allows an emphasis, instead, on ethics as a process of inquiry. Without a system for guidance, individuals must always be ready to examine the values they enact in their professional lives, accepting Nel Noddings's charge to achieve "a deep understanding of the ethical and social problems that abound in [our] fields and in the environments surrounding [our] professional work . . . to explore intelligently questions concerning [our] obligation not only to clients and society but to [ourselves] as developing human beings" (1994, ix).

For example, in their own work, Gesa Kirsch and Joy Ritchie foreground ethical awareness within the context of their shared interest as feminist Composition researchers. They begin by "consider[ing] how [they] might revise [their] definition of ethics based on caring, collaborative relationships with [research] participants" (1995, 21). Such a definition provides them with a process by which to develop and "suggest changes in research methods and forms of writing to meet these ethical demands." But in the end, they have not reached a conclusion. They are only able to "propose a reexamination of the goals and implications of research in a further attempt to examine an ethical stance in our work" (1995, 21). And so, while Kirsch and Ritchie make some particular application of their revised definition of ethics, they also demonstrate a new way to think about research and the position of the researcher. Their work does not end with a list of categories or advice on how to make others more ethically aware. Instead, they leave their readers and themselves with a means by which to engage in a "continuous, on-going scrutiny of our motivations and methods" (1995, 24).

Similarly, Gregory Clark (1994) and Mary Traschel (1995), speaking about the writing classroom and the writing center, respectively, use either a "relational ethics" or a "nurturant ethics" to reexamine and revalue the work in both places. Clark proposes that teachers no longer can seek to "rescue community" in the classroom by consensus building. Instead, he wishes to "direct us toward a broader and broadening concept of community, one founded upon the relations of mutual regard that emerge from a shared project of enabling the equal participation of differing others" (1994, 70). Traschel urges "writing center workers and indeed compositionists as a whole" to resist traditional notions of an "ethics of care" as "women's work," a view that limits and devalues the work that is done in centers across the country (1995, 34). The "nuturant ethics" that she describes not only would be "a necessary first step toward establishing the legitimacy of writing centers" (1995, 34), but also would allow writing center workers to "actively participate in the project of establishing a more 'perfect world' where our identities as caring individuals and serious professionals join forces as equals in the human quest for a unified self" (1995, 43). Neither Clark nor Traschel wishes to bring a conclusion to the discussion of classroom community or of writing-center pedagogy and scholarship. Rather, they seek to provide a way to open, expand, and reconsider each.

As these writers illustrate, once an awareness of ethics has been foregrounded, it provides a process of inquiry into valuable questions: How shall teachers prevent the "rhetoric of the discourse community" from seeming "to support democracy in principle, yet . . . undermine it in their practice [?]" (Clark 1994, 612–74); "How do [researchers] both affirm the importance of 'location' and yet understand the limitations of our ability to locate ourselves and others?" (Kirsch and Ritchie 1995, 7). Though this ethical awareness is one that Composition and English scholars may have had for some time, it has not always been in the forefront of our minds, providing a resource for inquiry and reflection. Members of Composition and English studies—ourselves included—find themselves turning their attention to questions that require taking stock of their values and their obligations to one another, to students, and to the profession, advancing an ethical awareness through which they might reconsider their behaviors as classroom teachers, writing program or writing center administrators, qualitative researchers, or promoters of electronic literacy.

In reading the literature we have cited and examining professional developments from the past five years or so, we find a conceptual shift in the way ethics has informed the discipline: from creating and providing systems that ensure ethical behavior, to creating environments that will promote the awareness necessary for ethical reflection, to providing an epistemology to which the essential qualities of ethical exigency are central—from teaching ethical behavior to adopting an ethical awareness. As the essays in this collection will demonstrate, ethics now provides a lens through which to view our professional activities and relationships and a process of inquiry by which to examine our professional activities and relationships.

Why Has Ethical Awareness Moved to the Foreground?

To begin answering why ethical awareness has moved to the foreground, we need, first, to analyze the disciplinary and epistemological circumstances that have brought ethical awareness to the foreground in classrooms as well as in professional discussions. Composition studies is well-enough established to merit what Joseph Harris calls a "revisionary look" (1994, 7). Indeed, in the past five years, we can trace a disciplinary movement toward self-reflection and reassessment that is not driven by, but occurs in the context of, postmodern epistemology. This disciplinary critique, characterized as it is by a self-conscious concern for, among other things, the effects of social and cultural context, is a process that necessitates the posing of ethical questions. When teachers and researchers start reassessing the kinds of activities they are involved in with particular people at particular times and in particular places, issues of relationship, power, authority, and obligation come to the foreground, issues that are ethical in nature.

Some touchstone books and articles in this disciplinary movement offer points at which ethical awareness appears to be emerging. For example, *Taking Stock*, the title of Lad Tobin and Thomas Newkirk's collection (1994), represents an initial step in reconceptualizing a defining paradigm within Composition studies. In this collection, writing theorists resituate writing process theory and pedagogy of the 1970s and 1980s in terms of contemporary questions about context: how gender, race, class, culture, and the teacher's reading process influence composing processes and how new technologies may transform them. The self-conscious move of "taking stock" and the act of contextualizing theoretical positions and pedagogical choices that Tobin and Newkirk promote in their collection will likely lead to the kinds of questions that foreground ethical awareness and to using that awareness as a process of inquiry.

Joining the writing theorists represented in Tobin and Newkirk's collection in the same self-critical, self-reflective turn of "taking stock," Stephen M. North and Andrea A. Lunsford and Lisa Ede chose to look back on the disciplinary moments when their influential positions about the writing center and the role audience plays in theories of composing, respectively, were published. Ten years after its publication, Steve North "revisited" his oft-cited "idea" of the writing center to amend four of its major tenets by contextualizing and resituating them (1994). Likewise, in reconsidering their 1984 *CCC* essay, "Audience Addressed/Audience Invoked: The Role of Audience in Composition Theory and Pedagogy," Lunsford and Ede attempt "to illuminate some of the ethical responsibilities and choices implicit in [their] earlier work" (1996, 177). Their concern in 1996 with the situatedness of writer and audience, of teacher and student—with difficult questions they admit that they chose not to pursue in 1984—is a manifestation of ethical awareness.

The climate of disciplinary reassessment that explicitly takes into account context and situation has stimulated the foregrounding of ethical awareness. Indeed, the disciplinary movement toward self-reflection and reassessment has recently resulted in at least one explicit connection to ethical awareness among researchers in particular. *Ethics and Representation in Qualitative Studies of Literacy* (1996), edited by Peter Mortensen and Gesa E. Kirsch, provides critical reflections on the ethical dilemmas that qualitative research methods such as ethnography and case study entail.

If we speculate about why, at this particular time, ethical awareness has moved to the foreground of disciplinary concern in Composition and English studies, we find some answers as well in postmodern critiques of the ways individuals have conceived of ethics as fixed sets of rules to be applied across the board, regardless of context. The situations of a contemporary world—including academia and the classroom—can no longer be accounted for within the confines of previously accepted ethical systems. Anticipating the most extreme conclusion, ethicist Edith Wyschogrod refers to the "death event" of the postmodern world, a world whose inhabitants' behavior not only has sent it on a spiral toward destruction, but which can, most certainly, not be controlled with pre-postmodern systems of ethics (1990, xiii). Investigations of pedagogical and scholarly issues are adopting what Zygmunt Bauman identifies as a "postmodern ethical perspective"; that is, a perspective that recognizes that what one does as a professional "may have profound, far-reaching and long-lasting consequences, which [one] can neither see directly nor predict with precision," and that members of the profession must conduct themselves ethically without the guidance of commonly agreed and commonly observed ethical rules (1993, 2; 17). In philosophy and epistemology, traditional systems of ethics that apply a fixed set of principles to the resolution of all problems are giving way to postmodern systems of ethics that reject the universality of any set of principles and offer new definitions and new terms. Nel Noddings has argued that the motivation to be moral is guided, not by a fixed set of principles, but by humans' natural caring for one another (1984, 4). Likewise, Iris Marion Young (1990) describes ethics as a public process through which conceptions of justice can be articulated in varied, changing ways. In fact, feminist studies of the 1980s have taken root and now blossom in an awareness of ethical issues and an acknowledgment that universalizing, fixed systems do not adequately describe the ambiguity of the moral and ethical choices made daily in our professional lives (see Card 1991, Tronto 1993, and Welch 1990).

In each definition and explanation that we have cited here, the authors shift from a previously accepted, relatively uncomplicated, and clear-cut understanding of ethics to one that is more complex in that it acknowledges the importance of context and the value of permitting different approaches to assist in different situations. The goal of ethical systems, then, is no longer to evaluate or solve situations or to focus on resolution and completion; instead the goal of ethical systems is to clarify, diagnose, and structure situations (see Howie 1987, xiv). The scholars we have cited recognize the ambiguity of moral choices and, because they share a concern with valuing difference, they necessarily argue for an ethical habit of thought and relationship that is not universalizing; they argue for an ethical system that is always in process.

Ethical awareness has moved to the foreground in Composition and English studies at least in part because the postmodern, epistemological climate gives rise to both disciplinary reassessment and context-sensitive judgment. Further, when he defines "ethics as the central concern for postmodern subjectivity,"

Lester Faigley notes that "postmodern theory . . . uncover[s] networks of relations of power, how these relations are constituted, and how we do and do not think about them" (1992, 24). And, as James E. Porter claims, when one is composing, ethics "provides . . . a heuristic for exploring competing values" (1993, 207). The authors in *Foregrounding Ethical Awareness in Composition and English Studies* can be seen to merge these two views of ethics into an ethical awareness that has become a lens or a process of inquiry through which to scrutinize professional issues and relationships.

The Purpose of This Collection

Shifting within a process of inquiry used by a discipline necessarily affects the topics of inquiry to be valued. Given the foregrounding of ethical awareness we have postulated here and the conceptual shift that seems to have accompanied it, we invited scholars and teachers in Composition and English studies to write about their special interests. While we did not limit the topics they might investigate, we did ask them to actively foreground this ethical awareness, to view a topic through the lens of ethical awareness, gaining the perspective this process of inquiry provides. Two levels of inquiry seem to surface within the discipline and are evident in the work of the authors collected here. The first level, some of which we have already described, focuses on large historical and pragmatic issues: What is it about the current situation inside English and Composition studies that makes such an awareness of ethics exigent? How is it that the once-unquestioned ethical systems have recently become inadequate? Can there be new paradigms that emerge from these inadequacies? What ethical tensions arise when new systems of ethics emerge and, as a consequence, values and obligations are doubted and redefined?

The second level of inquiry that emerges from the foregrounded ethical awareness that we have described is a broad-ranging but practically-grounded discussion of significant ethical dilemmas as they occur across English and Composition studies—in student/teacher relations, technological advances in the classroom, the development of writing-across-the-curriculum programs, curricular decisions, research design, graduate student training, and the structure of the profession.

We have organized the essays in *Foregrounding Ethical Awareness in Composition and English Studies* into three conceptual sections that tie together the questions the authors raised. In Part I, "Reevaluating Contemporary Pedagogies," Paul Connolly, Janet C. Fortune, Frances V. Condon, and Marguerite H. Helmers reevaluate various components of contemporary pedagogies: identifying ethical problems that arise within the pedagogical strategies and perspectives that are most highly touted as democratic; avoiding ethical risks from the empowering nature of the electronic classroom; and questioning the advocacy of literary criticism.

In Part II, "Competing Obligations," William E. Smith, Sheryl I. Fontaine, Olivia G. Castellano and Cherryl Armstrong Smith, and Devan Cook find themselves faced with allegiances to more than one group and more than one vision in the academy. For instance, teachers and administrators negotiate the competing obligations to students, institutional missions, and profession that arise in discussions of writing standards and program assessment. Researchers face the conflict between accomplishing their own professional goals and respecting the integrity of the students who participate in their research. And teachers and program administrators struggle between preparing the graduate students they mentor and exploiting them as underrespected and undercompensated members of a department.

Essays in the final section, "Professional Evolutions," consider ways in which developments and changes in the world outside the English department create ethical conflicts close to home. Richard Fulkerson, Linda S. Bergmann, Susan M. Hunter, and Pat Belanoff examine a wide range of professional practices, beliefs, and institutions that must evolve in light of the social and economic conditions that threaten them. These authors consider the purposes of doctoral education in a weak job market, conflicting ideologies in writing across the curriculum, the differing values of intellectual property held by those in Composition studies and others in the university and corporate America, and calls for external assessment that raise questions about the reality of how writing teachers assign grades.

Because of this renewed and repositioned ethical awareness that has occurred in Composition and English studies, it has become incumbent upon each one of us to view his or her agency in the profession and in the classroom from this ethical vantage point. Solutions to the situations and questions in this collection can emerge only if we are all mindful of our personal and professional ethical awareness, of how it informs and influences our understanding of the questions, and of how we can use it to anticipate and respond to the yet undefined issues that we will face.

Works Cited

American Association of University Professors. 1990. "Statement on Professional Ethics." *Policy Documents and Reports.* Washington: American Association of University Professors. 75–80.

Bauman, Z. 1993. *Postmodern Ethics.* Oxford: Blackwell.

Blau, S. 1996. "Convention Theme: Language as Moral Action." *Call for Program Proposals.* Urbana, IL: NCTE, 1996.

Card, C., ed. 1991. *Feminist Ethics.* Lawrence: University of Kansas Press.

Clark, G. 1994. "Rescuing the Discourse of Community." *College Composition and Communication* 45: 612–74.

Clark, I., and D. Healy. 1996. "Are Writing Centers Ethical?" *WPA: Writing Program Administration* 20. 1–2: 32–48.

Faigley, L. 1992. *Fragments of Rationality: Postmodernity and the Subject of Composition.* Pittsburgh: University of Pittsburgh Press.

Franklin, P. 1995. "What Does Academic Freedom Really Mean?" *MLA Newsletter* 27(3): 5–6.

Friend, C. 1994. "Ethics in the Writing Classroom: A Nondistributive Approach." *College English* 56.6: 548–67.

Harris, J. 1994. "CCC in the 90s." *College Composition and Communication* 45: 7–9.

Howie, J., ed. 1987. *Ethical Principles and Practice.* Carbondale: Southern Illinois University Press.

Jacobi, M. 1996. "Professional Communication, Cultural Studies, and Ethics." *South Atlantic Review* 61.2: 107–29.

Jarratt, S. C. 1991. "Feminism and Composition: The Case for Conflict." In *Contending with Words: Composition and Rhetoric in a Postmodern Age,* ed. P. Harkin and J. Schilb, 105–23. New York: MLA.

Kirsch, G. E., and J. S. Ritchie. 1995. "Beyond the Personal: Theorizing a Politics Composition Research." *College Composition and Communication* 46.1: 7–29.

Lunsford, A. A., and L. Ede. 1996. "Representing Audience: 'Successful' Discourse and Disciplinary Critique." *College Composition and Communication* 47.2: 167–79.

Modern Language Association of America. 1996. "Special Topic on Ethics and Literary Study." *MLA Newsletter* 28 (3): 20.

————. 1992. "Statement of Professional Ethics." *Profession* 92: 75–78.

Mortensen, P., and G. E. Kirsch, eds. 1996. *Ethics and Representation in Qualitative Studies of Literacy.* Urbana, IL: NCTE.

Noddings, N. 1994. "Foreword." In *Ethical and Social Issues in Professional Education,* ed. C. M. Brody and J. Wallace, ix–x. Albany: State University of New York Press.

————. 1984. *Caring: A Feminine Approach to Ethics and Moral Education.* Berkeley: University of California Press.

North, S. M. 1994. "Revisiting 'The Idea of a Writing Center.'" *The Writing Center Journal* 15.1: 7–19.

Pemberton, M. 1993–97. Columns on "Writing Center Ethics." *Writing Lab Newsletter* 17.5–21.4.

"Plagiarism in the Classroom: Readers Explain How They Define It and How They Deal with It." 1994. *The Council Chronicle,* June, 14–15.

Porter, J. 1993. "Developing a Postmodern Ethics of Rhetoric and Composition." In *Defining the New Rhetorics,* ed. T. Enos and S. Brown, 207–26. Newbury Park, CA: Sage.

Selfe, C., and R. Selfe, Jr. 1994. "The Politics of Interface: Power and Its Exercise in Electronic Contact Zones." *College Composition and Communication* 45.4: 480–504.

Spacks, P. M., ed. 1996. *Advocacy in the Classroom: Problems and Possibilities*. New York: St. Martin's Press.

Stotsky, S. 1992. "Writing as Moral and Civic Thinking." *College English* 54: 794–809.

Tobin, L., and T. Newkirk, eds. 1994. *Taking Stock: The Writing Process Movement in the '90s*. Portsmouth, NH: Boynton/Cook Heinemann.

Trachsel, M. 1995. "Nurturant Ethics and Academic Ideals: Convergence in the Writing Center." *The Writing Center Journal* 16.1: 24–45.

Tronto, J. 1993. *Moral Boundaries: A Political Argument for an Ethic of Care*. New York: Routledge.

"We Want to Know: How Do You Define Plagiarism?" 1993. *The Council Chronicle*, November, 8.

Weaver, R. 1953. *The Ethics of Rhetoric*. Chicago: Henry Regnery Company.

Welch, S. D. 1990. *A Feminist Ethic of Risk*. Minneapolis: Fortress Press.

Wyschogrod, E. 1990. *Saints and Postmodernism: Revisioning Moral Philosophy*. Chicago: University of Chicago Press.

Young, I. M. 1990. *Justice and the Politics of Difference*. Princeton, NJ: Princeton University Press.

2

The Poet(h)ical Art
of Teaching

Paul Connolly

*I gladly return to the subject of the ineptitude of our education. Its
goal has been to make us not good or wise, but learned; it has at-
tained this goal. It has not taught us to follow and embrace virtue and
wisdom, but has imprinted in us their derivation and etymology. We
know how to decline virtue, if we cannot love it.*

Montaigne, "Of Presumption"

In November 1995 Bard College's Institute for Writing and Thinking, which I
direct, sponsored a conference on "Teaching Ethics: Texts and Practices." The
intent of the conference was to explore not only how ethical lessons may be
extracted from texts, but also how ethical practices are enacted by the social
interactions among readers of those texts. What virtues, the conference in-
quired, are formed in the culture of the classroom by the repetition of habitual
practices of reading, writing, listening, and talking together? What do students
learn from how they behave together, in the process of studying texts? If life
is strange and lonely, as Virginia Woolf imagines it in *Jacob's Room*, and yet
"in company, perhaps—who knows—we might talk by the way," exactly how
would such talk sound, and what might it be about (1923, 93)? If furthermore,
perhaps, we were studying *Jacob's Room* in class, how would we "talk by the
way" about it there, in a manner that would contribute to "the good life"?

There is little written about this, for as Montaigne noticed four hundred years
ago, the goal of education "has been to make us not good or wise, but learned":

> It has not taught us to follow and embrace virtue and wisdom, but has im-
> printed in us their derivation and etymology. We know how to decline vir-
> tue, if we cannot love it. (1965, 501)

There is, and always has been, sustained interest in the power of literary art to provoke conversation about ethics—but there has been no comparable interest in classroom practices that inculcate behavior by which students learn from what their teachers (and classmates and school systems) do, as well as from what they say. The conference at Bard on "Teaching Ethics: Texts and Practices" was designed as an expression of interest in the latter.

An article circulated at that conference pointed up a dilemma in the way we think about "teaching ethics." In a study of "Ethics of Teaching: Beliefs and Behaviors of Psychologists as Educators," researchers reported on survey data collected from 482 members of the American Psychological Association who were asked "the degree to which they engaged in each of sixty-three behaviors and the degree to which they considered each of these to be ethical" (Tabachnick, Keith-Spiegel, and Pope 1991, 506–13). What were the sixty-three touchstones of ethical behavior in the classroom? I will not list all sixty-three here, but what the teaching psychologists were asked about were: ignoring strong evidence of cheating; giving easy courses or tests to assure popularity with students; selling complimentary textbooks to used-book vendors; dating, hugging, or otherwise becoming sexually involved with students—or junior colleagues; teaching material one had not mastered; teaching in classes too large for one to be effective; "teaching under the influence of cocaine or other illegal drugs"; accepting gifts, allowing a student's "likability" to influence a grade; using profanity in class; failing to update lecture notes; criticizing all theoretical orientations except one's own; "requiring students to use aversive procedures with rats, pigeons, etc."

Aversive procedures that teachers were *not* asked about, under the rubric of ethical/unethical behavior, were any teaching practices that might have been a transparent part of their accustomed pedagogy: How is authority distributed in the classroom, and is collaboration cultivated? What are the dynamics of the classroom? How does the teacher interact with students, and students, with one another? What disciplines do the writing assignments develop? Who does most of the talking, and what is the response to interruptions or domination by one speaker—including the teacher? Forty-eight percent of respondents reported that they engaged in "teaching ethics or values to students" either "very" or "fairly" often, and eighty-seven percent judged such practice itself to be ethical. Still, there was no consideration of whether some ways of reading, writing, talking, and thinking together in the classroom are more ethical than others—ethical in the sense of nurturing the strength and judgment and self-expression of students.

It is not enough to know virtue to be virtuous. A felt desire for beauty draws us to goodness, argued Plato in the *Phaedrus*. It is the yearning for understanding and self-esteem, formed in a relationship with another person—and not the seductive display of a powerful orator—that is most conducive to the search for, and discovery of, wisdom.

Ethical Dimensions of Motives to Learn

Three motivations to learn in a classroom are the performance of the teacher, the inherent interest of the curriculum and readings, and the social dynamic of students and teacher, interacting. A teacher may be a charismatic performer—engaging, knowledgeable, articulate, "accessible" to students—or not. Texts may feel "relevant," provoking curiosity and pleasure, or they may feel "required." Students, for their part, may discover one another when the course opens them as well as its subject, or they may struggle in solitary competition, without connectedness.

Each motive to learn has an ethical dimension that can be interrogated in studying "teaching ethics." Does the teacher arrive fresh, prepared, and attentive to students, or tired, fumbling through a yellowed outline, and determined to "cover the curriculum"? Are the curriculum and its texts engaging, challenging, well balanced? Or are they facile, doctrinaire, beyond what Lev Vygotsky called "the zone of proximal development" of many students (1962, 103)? Do students participate actively in constructing their own knowledge, or is education a spectator sport, and they, but fans at the wide, wide world of learning?

Two motives to learn—teacher and texts—bring an ulterior discipline to the classroom, from beyond the community of students itself, and it is often a hortatory discipline that may prove superficial and short-lived. Phaedrus is much taken with the oratorical prowess of Lysias, for example, a rhetorician who can prove that it is best to take as lover someone one does not love. Only gradually does Socrates draw Phaedrus into quieter conversation that invites him to seek his own goodness in his own words. As for texts, not all books worth reading appeal at once to students' interests, and a demand for "relevance" is often shallow. Texts with "a lot to say" may also speak for readers, rather than drawing them out into conversation.

The "social dynamic" of a classroom community may, for its part, also be vain and fleeting; "feeling good" can become more important than working hard, and when the best of classes ends, each student is again alone. A vital part of learning, however, depends on discovering the internal discipline of any skill: what it takes to acquire excellence in playing the harp, or building a house, or behaving justly; in writing, thinking, or reading a book. The violin exacts a discipline of the musician who would hear its best music. It is an internal discipline, acquired in performance, by doing something for oneself, not by attending only to another, without action or change. Ulterior motives may inspire desire for virtue, but virtues themselves are formed in the practice of behavior that realizes grace in oneself.

In thinking about the ethics of relations that occur in a classroom, emphasis often falls on teachers or texts, acting alone, and on how these influence a class. Attention focuses on the ethical responsibility of the teacher or on the ethical power of texts, as agents of change. Equally important to notice, however, in the varied and complex subject-object relations of a classroom, is what enhances the responsibility and potency of students. What internal disciplines do students acquire as they interact with teachers, texts, and other students? What ecology of the classroom nurtures "the good" of each of its members and of their learning society?

Writing as Ethical Practice in the Classroom

As I write this essay, I am teaching a first-year seminar at Bard College called "Ways of Knowing." The course, like the College, has four divisions: mathematics and science; the arts; language and literature; and social studies. In the course's four quarters, we ask, "How do scientists make knowledge? artists? writers and readers? social scientists?" After reading Plato's *Republic*, to consider education's relation to society, in each quarter we read a theoretical reflection, on science, art, literature, social studies: Kuhn's *Structure of Scientific Revolutions*, Dewey's *Art as Experience* (1980), Birkerts's *Gutenberg Elegies*, and Stone's *Should Trees Have Standing? Toward Legal Rights for Natural Objects*. We read Montaigne's "Of the Education of Children" (1965), Woolf's *A Room of One's Own* (1929), and Dubois' *Souls of Black Folk*, as further reflections on education and as examples of knowledge making.

In each instance, students made knowledge of their own, through doing a science experiment, creating glass art (using Plexiglas and paint), writing personal essays, and inquiry into the ecology of the Bard lands. The course aims to balance formal study of "knowledge made" by others with procedural experience of "knowledge in the making." Other goals are to notice the differences between systematic study and mangled investigation, and to understand school as both a curator of tradition and a liberator of change. I tell you this as context, but I want particularly to describe two types of writing as two very different ethical practices in the classroom.

I would like writing assignments to feel open-ended and flexible—but I write a page about each, so students do not have to guess at my intentions. Students add a note to each paper, reflecting on their composing process; on the day papers are due, students respond to one another's writing; I encourage revision. I wish the whole process felt more ethical, however, in an Aristotelian sense. That is, I wish it felt as if I were engaging students in the practice of habits that would develop their virtue, their *arete*, as thoughtfully writing persons.

On the weekend that entering students arrived, Leon Botstein, Bard's president, said in a talk to them on education that "The organization of an institution suggests its priorities of knowledge." In the first assignment, the opening week of class, I asked students to read various public statements Bard makes about itself—in the College Catalogue, the Student Handbook, on its WWW site— and to analyze the organization of the college as an expression of its values.

In the second assignment, I asked students to make informal lab notes during an experiment, led by a Bard physicist, demonstrating that "the angle of incidence equals the angle of reflection" and other qualities of light in mirrors. I asked them to notice both the experiment and the culture of the science classroom—particularly the use of language, since they had read the first chapter of Scott Montgomery's *The Scientific Voice*. Then I asked them to write a formal report of the experiment, with diagrams, stating its objective, procedure, and what was demonstrated—followed by a metacognitive note reflecting on what is gained and lost in translation from informal notes to a formal report.

Before their third assignment, students had read *Art as Experience*, attending particularly to Dewey's argument that "artistic" and "esthetic" experiences are misleadingly isolated from one another. Students had also read about the stained glass of Chartres Cathedral, seen an art historian's slide presentation on medieval windows, and made glass art of their own, collaboratively, choosing sites for the pieces they made, which we visited as a class. In their third paper, I asked them to bring together Dewey's theory and their own practice of the relation of artistic and esthetic experience.

What bothers me about the assignments is that their discipline is "external," as Dewey himself would call it. "No thinker can ply his occupation save as he is lured and rewarded by total integral experiences that are intrinsically worth while," he argues, not only in *Art as Experience* (1980, 37), but also in *How We Think* (1991). Over and over, despite being on high guard, I find myself directing students' work rather than involving them in a process that will lead them to discover, and pursue, the work's internal demands. Morality's great defect, Dewey maintained, is its anesthetic quality: "Instead of exemplifying wholehearted action, it takes the form of grudging piecemeal concessions to the demands of duty" (1980, 39). My students too often work from duty. My assignments are eminently moral: They demonstrate and elicit the practice of academically acceptable behavior—analysis of data for latent values; employment of rhetoric to heighten truth claims; comparison and contrast of concepts that are similar yet not identical. But do they form character? Are they ethical?

In conversation with the physics teacher, I complained that most academic experiments demonstrate "knowledge made" and do not explore knowledge making in the "mangled" way that Andrew Pickering, a particle physicist and sociologist of science, describes scientific practice in *The Mangle of Science* (1995). Experimentation turns the key of a question in the lock of the world; what opens is knowledge. Most school "experiments" turn a key in the teacher's file cabinet, I objected—but so do my writing assignments. They are "moral," if I may use this synonym for *ethical* to draw a distinction from it, in that they deliberately attempt to raise consciousness about writing and thinking behavior that school values. But do they also form habits of the heart?

There's nothing wrong with morality, I believe, except perhaps that it is not terribly effective. "What we resent in didactic poetry is not that it teaches," Dewey writes in *Art as Experience*, "but that it does not teach, its incompetency" (1980, 346). It is what we, teachers and students alike, resent also in didactic education, is it not? Moral assignments provide training as a thinking writer, but do they also build character in the way that a more open-ended practical struggle, guided by modeling, might?

On the other hand, my students also participate each week in an informal, low-tech computer conversation that I believe is more "ethical," in the sense of forming character by habitual practice as a writer and thinker. A class disk is on reserve in the computer lab. During the week it is every class member's responsibility to put the disk in one of the lab machines and write a screen or two about the book we are reading that week, in conversation with classmates. I open the first conversation, to model both an informal register and the three things I ask those who open conversations to do: Point to passages that interest them; ask questions; wonder aloud. Each week another student opens the conversation, and a different student closes the conversation, not by reductive summary but by braiding the principal strands together lightly. Individual entries are ungraded, but one-third of the course grade depends on how well students are present in this computer conversation.

In this writing, students wrestle with texts and with one another. Sometimes the conversation is not very ethical: People write in a lazy, perfunctory way; they make inflammatory judgments that do not respect the text; or they do not listen well to others. Whatever ill can happen in oral conversation happens here also. But the occasion, the opportunity, is inherently ethical in its potential, as students write here about ideas in a public arena, most for the first time in their lives. Political philosopher Michael Oakeshott has written, "As civilized human beings, we are the inheritors neither of an inquiry about ourselves and the world nor of an accumulating body of information but of a conversation, begun in the primeval forests and extended and made more articulate in the course of centuries." He continues:

> It is the ability to participate in this conversation, and not the ability to reason cogently, to make discoveries about the world, or to contrive a better world, which distinguishes the human being from the animal and the civilized man from the barbarian . . . Education, properly speaking, is an initiation into the skill and partnership of this conversation in which we learn to recognize the voices, to distinguish the proper occasions of utterance, and in which we acquire the intellectual and moral habits appropriate to conversation. (1962, 199)

All education is an initiation into the "skill and partnership" of hearing others; into knowing when to speak and how; into the "intellectual and moral habits" needed to converse with other human beings. The object of the computer conversation is to help us to learn to think well with others about what we see differently but come to know together through this conversation, in ways that would not be possible in class alone.

I enter the conversation each week, with the students, and we discuss it occasionally in class. Students comment on one another's behavior as writers and thinkers here. It is an ethical arena, this computer conversation, in which it is more possible to be ethical or unethical than it is in my other, formal as-signments—where it is possible to be moral or immoral, conforming to my expectations as teacher, but without the engagement that involves personal struggle and change. In the computer conversation, students develop a voice and negotiate ideas with others in a more immediate way than they do in even the most loosely prescriptive assignments.

Literature as Ethical Experience

In reading, a similar distinction can be drawn between moral and ethical re-sponses to literary art. The moral response is always reasonable and seeks, be-yond initial empathetic identification, to ruminate upon, talk about, and respond externally to the art, articulating rules of moral behavior. For philosopher Martha Nussbaum, "the work of the moral imagination is like the work of the creative imagination," particularly when it operates in novelists to resist "muddlement" and wrest light from darkness by "the intense scrutiny of particulars" (1990, 148). Her praise of the moral power of literature is, however, strongly qualified:

> The literary imagination is a part of public rationality, and not the whole. I believe that it would be extremely dangerous to suggest substituting empathetic imagining for rule-governed moral reasoning, and I am not mak-ing that suggestion. In fact, I defend the literary imagination precisely be-cause it seems to me an essential ingredient of an ethical stance that asks us to concern ourselves with the good of other people whose lives are distant from our own. (1995, xvi)

Good fiction, she maintains, "gets its readers involved with the characters, caring about their projects, their hopes and fears, participating in their attempts to unravel the mysteries and perplexities of their lives. . . . In imagining things that do not really exist, the novel . . . is helping its readers to acknowledge their own world and to choose more reflectively in it" (1995, 31). Tellingly, however, the specific novel she is thinking about is *Hard Times*, Dickens's caustic social criticism of the institution of education, which has been faulted as a novel pre-cisely because it "tells" a moral that his more admired fiction "shows."

For Martha Nussbaum, literary art can be a charismatic catalyst of ethical thinking. It is, she warns, "extremely dangerous to suggest substituting empathetic imagining for rule-governed moral reasoning," but the feelings evoked by art do awaken a disposition to imagine others' lives. Art prepares us to think more ethically because it takes us out of ourselves, and it draws our attention from a generalized life to particulars. The esthetic experience is ethi-cal whenever it sensitizes us, through empathetic imagining, to what is "other" than our self.

But for Nussbaum, literary art remains always fodder for ethical reason-ing. Aesthetic experience is ultimately both *sui generis* and a potential *oppor-tunity* for ethical knowledge, but not the thing itself. The esthetic may open us to the ethical in a way nothing else so effectively can, but the full realization of art's ethical power is located, for Nussbaum, in the talk that complements and extends the experience of art.

John Dewey takes a radically different view of the matter. While he, too, praises art as the "means by which we enter, through imagination and the emotions they evoke, into other forms of relationship and participation than our own" (1980, 333), he is emphatically insistent that "art expresses, it does not state; it is concerned with existences in their perceived qualities, not with conceptions symbolized in terms" (1980, 134).

For Dewey, art is a form of thought that expresses knowledge that can be acquired in no other way. "If all meanings could be adequately expressed by words," he writes, "the arts of painting and music would not exist. There are values and meanings that can be expressed only by immediately visible and audible qualities, and to ask what they mean in the sense of something that be put into words is to deny their distinctive existence" (1980,74). For Dewey there is a distinct and profound difference between the way "reflection and science render things more intelligible by reduction to conceptual form" and the way art presents its meanings "as the matter of a clarified, coherent, and intensified or 'impassioned' experience" (1980, 290).

Esthetic experience of literature (and of every other art) may become *culturally* important, Dewey did allow, only when "'intellectual products' formulate the tendencies of these arts and provide them with an intellectual base" (1980, 345). But that is because of the way culture assigns value to knowledge, not because art is without knowledge before it is commodified as an "intellectual product." It is clear throughout *Art as Experience* that Dewey regards the aesthetic experience as having an ethical agency and end in itself. Literature is not a performative means to a discursive end. Rather it is an impassioned ethical experience in itself, which experience he distinguishes from reasoned inquiries into moral duty. "One of the functions of art," Dewey believes, "is precisely to sap the moral timidity that causes the mind to shy away from some materials" (1980, 189). He also insists, more positively, that "art is more moral than moralities,"

> For the latter either are, or tend to become, consecrations of the *status quo*, reflections of custom, reinforcements of the established order. The moral prophets of humanity have always been poets even though they spoke in free verse or by parable . . . . Art has been the means of keeping alive the sense of purposes that outrun evidence and of meanings that transcend indurated habit. (1980, 348)

Would that it were equally plausible to claim of the ethical dimension of education that it "has been the means of keeping alive the sense of purposes that outrun evidence and of meanings that transcend indurated habit."

For Dewey, an esthetic experience—and I would add, an ethical experience—is always first and foremost an experience, not moral lessons or interpretive meanings derived from that experience after the act. He understood esthetic experience—which he insisted was common within life and should not be sought only in "art products"—as the "consummation" the human organism experiences when it encounters disruption and conflict yet recovers stability in its environment:

> The rhythm of loss of integration with environment and recovery of union not only persists in man but becomes conscious with him; its conditions are material out of which he forms purposes. The discord is the occasion that induces reflection. Desire for restoration of the union converts mere emotion into interest in objects as conditions of realization of harmony. With the realization, material of reflection is incorporated into objects as their meaning. Since the artist cares in a peculiar way for the phase of experience in which union is achieved, he does not shun moments of resistance and tension. (1980, 15)

The source of esthetic experience, for Dewey, is not a power located in the art itself nor a sensibility located in the audience, but it is relational, a function of the subject-object experience in which art and audience meet and interact. Likewise, I would reiterate, the ethical is not located in a text nor in the "preaching" of a teacher but in the practice of social interaction within the classroom that shapes "good" behavior, however we define that goodness.

Literary texts may be stimuli to ethical talk in the classroom—to the articulation of the sort of "rule-governed moral reasoning" that Martha Nussbaum identifies with ethical learning—but that is talk about the reading experience, which extends understanding of it. It is not the esthetic experience itself. Such talk may inculcate an external moral habit, but it does not necessarily, by itself, form ethical virtue or character, as the lives of many ethicists could testify. Virtue is integrated first in the practical experience of the individual student absorbed in reading the book and then, perhaps, in the particular educational experiences of the way a class writes, thinks, and talks together about the book. The ethical character is formed in the ways the writing, thinking, and talking are done, not simply by the explication of moral concepts.

Performative Talk as Ethical Practice

What sort of practice of the study of literary art would teach us to "follow and embrace virtue and wisdom," as Montaigne wished, and not just know the derivation and etymology of these words? And where can we learn such practice? Through her various books relating to "caring," Nel Noddings certainly writes often about this very issue, and her recommendations are well summarized in her latest book, *Philosophy of Education*, where she identifies four major components of "moral education from the care perspective" (1995, 190–96). (Noddings decides to use *moral* as synonymous with *ethical*.) The four are

1. *Modeling:* "We have to show in our own behavior what it means to care. Thus we do not merely tell [students] to care and give them texts to read on the subject; we demonstrate our caring in our relations with them."

2. *Dialogue about caring:* "to help us and our students to reflect upon and critique our own practice. . . . As dialogue unfolds, we participate in a mutual construction of the frame of reference . . . . "

3. *Practice:* "If we want to produce people who will care for one another, then it makes sense to give students practice in caring and reflecting on that practice." (Community service comes to mind as a form of practice, which Noddings advocates, but she is also thinking of collaborative learning: "Teachers should be explicit in telling students that a primary purpose of cooperative work is helping one another—to understand, to share, and to support. The aim is not always or primarily academic learning.")

4. *Confirmation:* affirming and encouraging the best in others. "Confirmation requires attribution of the best possible motive consonant with reality." (One has to smile contemplating the complexity of that last skill!)

So much of what Noddings identifies as crucial to ethical work involves talk—but not "simply" talk. The talk she values is *performative* talk, talk that enacts a relationship, while also simply conveying information. Interpersonal talk that creates an experience with a person even as it transports meaning. Aesthetic talk. "Genuine education," Noddings concludes her book, "must engage the purposes and energies of those being educated. To secure such engagement, teachers must build relationships of care and trust, and within such relationships, students and teachers construct educational objectives cooperatively" (1995, 196).

It is not so easy to construct a syllabus for such moral education, since it is neither textual concepts nor lecture notes but the classroom dance that requires thought, and reflection on dance is accomplished in the lived moment of execution, interactively, the way a seasoned choreographer instructs a young dancer in conversation, watching her movement and suggesting, "Try this," until the teacher is satisfied and the student is dancing. Freewriting, the varied practices of writing-to-learn and of collaborative learning, and current responding and conferencing techniques all have as their goal a new social dynamic within a classroom that enhances the social learning that is possible. "What can we learn together that we cannot learn alone?" is a central ethical question to be asked in planning a syllabus. There is no good reason to come together, in this electronic age that allows us to learn certain things alone, if we are not, as Virginia Woolf hoped, going to "talk by the way."

Virginia Woolf herself has more to teach about the practice of ethics in universities, though like other "daughters of educated men," she was not allowed to attend one. "The reduction of English literature to an examination subject must be viewed with suspicion by all who have first hand knowledge of the difficulty of the art," she writes in *Three Guineas* in 1938, explaining her objection to a "vain and vicious system of lecturing" that seemed a domestic form of fascism to her (1938, 155–56). The reduction of "teaching ethics" to a testable topic is similarly suspicious, since ethical and aesthetic behavior are

equally complex arts. Cease the reduction of learning to distribution of orna-
mental pots by headmasters, Woolf advocates in *A Room of One's Own*:

> All this pitting of sex against sex, of quality against quality; all this claim-
> ing of superiority and imputing of inferiority, belong to the private-school
> state of human existence where there are "sides," and it is necessary for one
> side to beat another side, and of the utmost importance to walk up to a plat-
> form and receive from the hands of the Headmaster himself a highly orna-
> mental pot. As people mature they cease to believe in sides or in
> Headmasters or in highly ornamental pots. (1929, 110)

Write yourself into reality is her ethical advice to undergraduates: "When
I ask you to write more books I am urging you to do what will be for your good
and for the good of the world at large." Writing "all kinds of books, hesitating
at no subject however trivial or however vast" heads Woolf's ethical agenda,
and she shows students how to do it in performative language that, as Joan
Retallack describes such "poet(h)ical art" in her book of conversation with
John Cage, is capable of changing "the grammar of the way we are together"
(1996, 52). A remark by Cage in his "Diary: Emma Lake Music Workshop
1965," quoted by Retallack as epigram to their conversations, is very much to
the point of this whole essay:

> The role of the composer is other than it was. Teaching, too, is no longer
> transmission of a body of useful information, but conversation, alone, to-
> gether, whether in a place appointed or not in that place. . . . A teacher should
> do something other than filling in the gaps. . . . What we learn isn't what
> we're taught nor what we study. (1996, xiii)

Classrooms, too, can have a performative capacity to change the grammar
of the way we are together, and here again Woolf's *Room* makes (and models)
suggestions as to how: by not delivering gold nuggets of truth but "laying together many varieties of error" (1929, 3; 109); by dangling the line of thought in
the waters of inquiry and returning small fry to fatten them up (1929, 5); by turning off "that hard little electric light which we call brilliance," replacing it with
the "rich yellow flame of rational intercourse" (1929, 11). And sometimes, it
must also be said, a teacher's passion for learning may itself be transformative
of the way we are together. Woolf herself is such a teacher, and so, to give didactic lecturing its due when done well, is someone like Giuseppe Mazzotta of
Yale, a devoted Dante scholar who held several hundred of Bard's first-year students enthralled not too long ago, by his infectious enthusiasm for what he loved.

Montaigne, like Woolf (and like Cage), expresses an educational preference for tolerant, conversational learning, in "The Art of Discussion," where
he calls discussion "the most fruitful and natural exercise of our mind." In "Of
Cripples" he claims,

> All the abuses in the world are engendered by our being taught to be afraid
> of our ignorance and our being bound to accept everything that we cannot
> refute. We talk about everything didactically and dogmatically. . . . It makes

me hate probable things when they are planted on me as infallible. I like these words, which soften and moderate the rashness of our propositions: "perhaps," "to some extent," "some," "they say," "I think," and the like. And if I had to train children, I would have filled their mouths so much with this way of answering, inquiring, not decisive—"What does that mean? I do not understand it. That might be. Is it true?"—that they would be more likely to have kept the manner of learners at sixty than to represent learned doctors at ten, as they do. (1965, 788)

Montaigne's "Of the Education of Children" is likewise famous for his candid admission that "my conceptions and my judgment move only by groping and staggering, stumbling, and blundering," and for its general sentiment, quoted from Cicero, that "the authority of those who teach is often an obstacle to those who want to learn" (1965, 110).

Teaching Ethics and Teaching Ethically

So the issues of "teaching ethics" are old ones, and "to ask the hard question is simple," as Auden wrote in "The Question" (1966):

> The simple act of the confused will.
> But the answer
> Is hard and hard to remember. (7–9)

In June 1995 the Modern Language Association, joined by two dozen other learned associations of college and university teachers, sponsored a conference on the ethical issue of "The Role of Advocacy in the Classroom." Andrea Lunsford, invited by the MLA to be the participant-observer at that conference, reported in her summary reflection that the participants' consensus was that advocacy in teaching is inevitable. *When* and *how* should a teacher advocate were the worried questions, which I have come to understand as expressions of anxiety and confusion about the potential abuse of teaching authority in the classroom.

Does such a consensus form easily because of confusion over a teacher's basic authority? Ken Bruffee maintains in workshops with teachers, as well as in his most recent book on collaborative learning (1995), that a teacher's authority comes not from what s/he knows (and the degrees and titles that testify to that), though that may indeed be the source of a prerequisite authority as a scholar. Rather the authority of *teachers* comes from our ability to negotiate boundary conversations between those outside a community of discourse and those who seek admission to it. A teacher is a translator, reconciling the natural language and native concepts that students bring into the classroom with the acquired language and concepts that various "communities of discourse" have evolved to articulate their interpretations of life. Advocacy is, of course, inevitable in translation, too, but if a teacher's task is to mediate the work of students, not determine what must be done, then advocacy is of diminished concern.

In the classroom, we may have moral experiences of literature and ethical experiences, but they are not the same. School is both a curator and a liberator. It transmits made knowledge, and it teaches knowledge-making. It is often better at fulfilling its moral function of conserving and transmitting made knowledge than it is at achieving its ethical function of making knowledge within a community of individual learners. It is this educational problem, more than any "crisis of our moral system," that should be a concern. When the empathy evoked by literature becomes only the agent of moral talk, rather than a catalyst of ethical reading, writing, and thinking experiences in the classroom, then, as Montaigne says, we will learn how to decline virtue but not to love it. When we read and learn, we need to act and do, as well as undergo and receive, as Dewey observed. More writing alone, in and of itself, does not assure that—no more than the selection of "relevant" texts does. There needs to be an open-ended, mangled practice of knowledge-making, a living culture of conversation, in which ethical formation can occur.

When John Dewey thought about the experience of art in the classroom, he wrote sadly,

> It is by way of communication that art becomes the incomparable organ of instruction, but the way is so remote from that usually associated with the idea of education . . . that we are repelled by any suggestion of teaching and learning in connection with art. But our revolt is in fact a reflection upon education that proceeds by methods so literal as to exclude the imagination and one not touching the desires and emotions of men. (1980, 347)

Conversation about the experience of "teaching ethics" also easily becomes literal minded, and this may incline us to turn away from it in revolt. Some may hear a claim that texts are, or should be, in some way salvific. Others may fear that "rule-governed moral reasoning" will trail after literature like a too talkative companion exiting a good movie. Some teachers of literature may feel that their work is not to teach ethics at all. Such revolt from teaching ethics, however, like the revolt from teaching art, may actually express a desire to accomplish something fuller and more than has yet been attempted, something "touching the desires and emotions" of women and men.

In a powerful peroration to *The Needs of Strangers*, Michael Ignatieff writes: "Our needs are made of words: they come to us in speech, and they can die for lack of expression. Without a public language to help us find our own words, our needs will dry up in silence" (1986, 142). School exists to conserve and create such public language, but exhortation alone cannot achieve this. The very structure of schooling, however, is impatient with stammering ethical struggle, and is designed, instead, for a didactic economy of morals. As an opening ethical act, we may resist our own individual impatience in the classroom. But overcrowded classes, pressure to be "popular," demands of "coverage," and other practices, well beyond those sixty-three identified in the survey in the *American Psychologist*, will remain. Only slow, deep change in the

structure of schooling, relaxing ulterior disciplines and helping students to discover the internal discipline that the many goods they yearn for require, can
ultimately develop that patient, caring environment in which teaching ethics
and teaching ethically are possible.

Acknowledgment

I thank my frequent co-worker, Susan Kirschner of Lewis & Clark College,
with whom I have thought so often about these issues that I am only here re-
moving from the line what previous dangling has fattened up.

Works Cited

Auden, W. H. 1966. *Collected Shorter Poems: 1927–1957.* New York: Random House.

Birkerts, S. 1994. *Gutenberg Elegies: The Fate of Reading in an Electronic Age.*
Boston: Faber & Faber.

Bruffee, K. 1995. *Collaborative Learning: Higher Education, Interdependence, and
the Authority of Knowledge.* Baltimore: Johns Hopkins University Press.

Dewey, J. 1980. *Art as Experience.* New York: Perigee.

———. 1991. *How We Think.* Amherst: Prometheus.

DuBois. W. E. B. 1995. *Souls of Black Folk.* New York: Signet.

Ignatieff, M. 1986. *The Needs of Strangers.* New York: Penguin.

Kuhn, T. 1970. *Structure of Scientific Revolutions.* Chicago: University of Chicago
Press.

de Montaigne, M. 1965. *The Complete Essays of Montaigne.* Trans. Donald Frame.
Stanford, CA: Stanford University Press.

Montgomery, S. 1996. *The Scientific Voice.* New York: Guilford.

Noddings, N. 1995. *Philosophy of Education.* Boulder, CO: Westview Press.

Nussbaum, M. 1990. *Love's Knowledge: Essays on Philosophy and Literature.* New
York: Oxford.

———. 1995. *Poetic Justice: The Literary Imagination and the Public Life.* Boston:
Beacon.

Oakeshott, M. 1962. *Rationalism in Politics.* New York: Basic Books.

Pickering, A. 1995. *The Mangle of Science.* Chicago: University of Chicago Press.

Plato. 1993. *Symposium and Phaedrus: Plato's Erotic Dialogues.* Trans. W. S. Cobb.
New York: State University of New York Press.

Retallack, J., ed. 1996. *Musicage: Cage Muses on Word Art Music.* Hanover, NH: University Press of New England.

Stone, C. 1988. *Should Trees Have Standing? Toward Legal Rights for Natural Objects.* Palo Alto, CA: Tioga.

Tabachnick, B. G., P. Keith-Spiegel and K. S. Pope. 1991. "Ethics of Teaching: Beliefs and Behaviors of Psychologists as Educators." *American Psychologist* 46: 506–13.

Vygotsky, L.S. 1962. *Thought and Language*. Trans. E. Hanfmann and G. Vakar. Cambridge, MA: M. I. T. Press.

Woolf, V. 1923. *Jacob's Room* and *The Waves*. New York: Harcourt, Brace & World.

_____ . 1929. *A Room of One's Own*. New York: Harcourt, Brace, Jovanovich.

_____ . 1938. *Three Guineas*. New York: Harcourt, Brace, Jovanovich.

3

Ethical Awareness
and Classroom Practice

Janet C. Fortune

Making Decisions Amid Contradictions

When I temporarily left a middle school teaching career ten years ago to go to graduate school, I found that what I really needed was time to think through the confusions of a thirteen-year teaching career and to find language appropriate for talking through those confusions. I came to find that these confusions were the logical results of contradictions which occupy so much of educational discussion and practice, and in which I had been entangled both as a student and teacher for many years. The contradictions are familiar ones: studying democracy in an authoritarian setting; advocating corporal punishment while fearing the rise in societal violence; reducing important pedagogical issues to debates, as in whole language versus phonics; blaming social ills on the failures of teachers/schools while saying that parents are and must be the guiding force in children's lives; refusing to recognize adolescents as historical and potential contributors to the work of communities and families while expressing dismay at adolescents' search for meaning in their lives; preparing students for jobs that do not exist; and so on.

Contradictions and disagreements are inherent in human lives and work; the contradictions of families' child rearing are multiplied by the numbers of children and the political environment of the school. Despite this, teaching requires somehow reckoning with these contradictions and making careful decisions about how to be with children in the classroom and how to be with other teachers, the principal, and other adults concerned with the school. How teachers decide to work within these contradictions determines how children are treated, talked to, and taught in their daily school lives. In this essay, I first describe my progress toward a way of thinking about teaching that has helped

27

me reduce the tension and provide a foundation for making teaching's difficult decisions. Then, I address some of the reasons I have seen for teachers' (and I see all educators as teachers) difficulty reaching any form of clarity when reasoning through the contradictions of U. S. public education.

Over twenty years ago, one of my first public school students helped me to begin thinking through the maze of contradictions, accepting them, and changing myself and my responses. Ten-year-old Tommy came equipped with a reputation for ceaseless mischief and various forms of mayhem. As a first-year teacher, it was my turn to arrange the Christmas P.T.A. program, traditionally a big production. I convinced my teammates to paint scenery and to direct a small Christmas chorus, while my English classes wrote and performed an abridged version of *A Christmas Carol*. As I remember it, the production was a hit; no one ever dared mention that we performed acts two and three in reverse order, which put my little Scrooge in a bit of a time warp. Scrooge was exquisite; he looked remarkably suited to the part; there were giggles and glitches, I'm sure, most of which I cannot even recall.

I would not do this now, but back then I made all the directing and casting decisions. Tommy was Bob Cratchett. During rehearsals he was cavalier about his lines and disdainful of his classmates' pleas; he showed up P.T.A. night in full costume just as the curtain went up, and I was berating myself for not even thinking of casting understudies. His performance was absolutely flawless, just as his performance on all assessments was flawless. I was proud of him and resented him for seeming to be impervious to the enticements of my teaching skills and for controlling so well his relationships with his classmates. I operated from the teacher's position of determining the project, assigning the tasks, telling everyone how to do the work, and determining what was to be learned and watching for it to happen. Tommy, however, acted out of his sense of who he was and what he wanted to know, and, whether he realized it or not, a recognition that he could successfully complete any project by taking a route I did not even know about and be just fine doing it. Sometimes his path got him into trouble, but quite often, as in our Christmas play, I was uncomfortable enough to realize that he had become less important than my plans.

Tommy was endearing and infuriating, and I wanted him to respond to the classroom and to my teaching as I thought the other students did, but he, with his ten-year-old wisdom, refused. I think perhaps I wanted him to be unsuccessful so that I could believe in the efficacy of my own teaching. He had disarmed me; he had taken my institutional authority, my position in the school hierarchy, and even all my good intentions and deep love of teaching and substituted the beginning of my long process of learning to think differently about educative relationships with children.

As Tommy turned my focus toward seeing him in all his uniqueness, insisted that I know him as an individual, and shared his educational needs with me, I learned to watch each child more carefully, to speak with more precision, to wait with more patience, and to step away from the center of attention to stop interrupting their learning processes. As I read through and reflect on my notes and lesson plans from that teaching year, I know, of course, I did not always or even consistently respond with grace and patience, but I did begin to place the student, always with Tommy as a single reminder of my broader obligation to each child, at the center of my thinking about my classroom and my response to the contradictions of the school that surrounded it.

Recognizing and Respecting the Dignity of Each Student

The principle through which I made my teaching and classroom decisions changed from trying to reconcile the prevailing educational debate, from trying to find a logical position in the pedagogical research and criticisms, and from trying to blend all the opinions on curriculum design to the ethical principle of recognition and respect for the dignity of each student and of the oneness, or spirit, that binds people in responsibility for each other. As a teacher, I must have some way of deciding how to teach within the contradictions rather than leaving to chance what to do in the classroom, how to treat my students, and what is important for them to learn. I have chosen to base my decisions on an assumption of responsibility for the students who come to me and on maintaining the dignity of each student as fully human and deserving of the quality of life each of us seeks, the quality of life each of us seeks for our own children.

But, dignity and spiritual responsibility are ways of thinking about ethics that require action; to follow them I need to be able to recognize them in action in the classroom, to know how they would be manifested in the classroom every day, and to know them as tools to be used over and over. To help me be clearer in making my teaching decisions and less uneasy about effects for my students, I think of dignity and spiritual responsibility in terms of faith and, specifically, faith as defined in three ways, which serve as a kind of anchor for the actual work of the teaching day.

First, this kind of faith is in the dignity of one's self, in one's ability to form a dialogue between the behaviors of the outer world and the ethical reasoning of the inner, more reflective world. This dialogue gives each of us the courage to know that we can ground our behavior in the daily world in our ethical reasoning and reflection. When Barbara McClintock reached a particularly puzzling moment in her maize research, she left the laboratory and sat outside under a tree to think about how she could change herself so that she might see more clearly (Keller 1983, 148). The same is true here; my ability to create a classroom that maintained and nurtured the students' dignity means that I must be able to provide for and respect my own dignity and be assured that I could surely behave in ways that reflect my own ethical reasoning.

My ability to create a dialogue between my behavior (responses to the daily world) and inner reflections also helps me to be more certain that I can find and relate to that inner reflection in others, specifically here, my students. One of my guiding ethical principles is a belief in the oneness that we share that brings with it a mutual spiritual responsibility; finding and nurturing that inner "place" where reflection about ethical matters happens in me helps me to connect, and nurture in teaching, with that reflection in others. I think that the differences between us that are emphasized in relationships and institutions are actually different paths from this common core. In the classroom we certainly rejoice and celebrate our differences but always remember that we are also related through that common core. As Ross Mooney has said, "The clearer one comes to see himself, the clearer one wants to know how he is differentiated from all else, which means, in turn, how he belongs to all else" (1955, 15). If I think about this from another angle, I realize that a lack of faith in this inner core of others, specifically here, my students, implies that I hold the wisdom of deciding who can participate in this common core, which I certainly do not.

Second, this faith, which helps me to understand how to manifest the principles of dignity and spiritual responsibility is a faith in the awe and mystery of the world and in the ability to be surprised. I am speaking here of two things: a perspective toward the natural world that allows the teacher to see the presence of important and amazing things to learn, and a healthy respect for the mystery of learning and children's incredible changes as they experiment and develop. I agree with James Moffett that a complacent attitude toward the natural world precludes a teacher's ability to help learners experiment, devise, describe, and communicate: Students need to interact directly with the things of the world that prompt thoughts, the social and natural environments, from which public education actually insulates youngsters by segregating and immobilizing them in special buildings. The minds even of lower animals atrophy without plentiful stimulation. No matter how provocative a teacher or textbooks might conceivably become, they could never provide the thinking fields that real environments can (1992, 87).

While studies of the brain and pedagogical experiments are unarguably interesting, I have found them to be professionally important only to the degree that they help me to understand how these particular children can best learn and what the consequences of that learning may be. I, and other teachers, must know that the conditions for children's learning change daily, and I can never be quite certain exactly what will happen. When Barbara McClintock was asked how she could continue on one line of inquiry for two years without knowing what would come of it, she replied, "It never occurred to me that there was going to be any stumbling block. Not that I had the answer, but [I had] the joy of going at it. When you have that joy, you do the right experiments. You let the material tell you where to go, and it tells you at every step what the next has to be because you're integrating with an overall brand new pattern in mind" (Keller 1983, 125). It seems that McClintock combined a healthy respect for the natural world with the ability to free herself, her learning, from restrictions and boundaries. I might wish for stability and consistency, but what I really want is to be surprised by my students' new learning, startling insights, and ability to confound my expectations.

Third, this faith is one of courage because it compels the teacher to think about how we really ought to live our lives and what kind of world we want for our children, and then to act in ways that reflect our answers. This courage does not enable the fight against something even as concrete as hatred; it is trying to overcome the indifference and nonchalance that allow things to happen for no apparent reason and with no attention to consequences. Everyone can probably name many school and university rules or practices that make no real sense but appear to be immutable.

Camus has issued the warning that just doing something is not sufficient: "The evil that is in the world always comes of ignorance, and good intentions may do as much harm as malevolence, if they lack understanding" (1948, 124). Teaching (and, of course, not only teaching) requires asking hard questions: What does it mean to be human? What kind of world do I want children to have? What does it mean to live the "good life"? Does living the "good life" mean that someone else's children must suffer? How should I act in the face of injustice, poverty, exploitation, exclusion? Can I honestly say that what I want for my children, I want for all children? The faith in courage that I use to guide my thinking about teaching requires that I consider how my answers to these questions affect what I do in my classroom and how my teaching affects the students' realization of the "good life." When James Macdonald says, ". . . there is no assurance that the present social structures, characterized by technology, bureaucracy, and a consumer citizen's role, are the epitome of the good life" (1995, 128), he is prodding us to reflect more clearly on the kind of life we are predicting for all children.

Taking Action and Making a Commitment

Just thinking, however, is not sufficient. This courage demands more than sympathy, affection, or feelings; it is the courage of action and commitment. In this courage, dreams and thoughtful reflection partner with a commitment to plan and to follow plans through. I am speaking of the courage to address the quality of daily classroom life as well as the larger injustices that can seem so overwhelming. For example, the teacher education students with whom I study during their student teaching semester very often come to see the huge amounts of wasted time and the unchallenging classroom work in schools as a matter of courage. The student teachers wonder what wasted time and unchallenging classroom experiences say about how the school and teachers view children and the habits and knowledge they need.

Over the years, I have found students who could help me see how the ethical principles of dignity and responsibility, which I think about through the faith of personal dignity, of mystery, and of courage, are manifested in classroom practices. One of my most pleasant professional tasks has been visiting public school classrooms to observe student teachers in action. For me, this is an opportunity to play with and watch a variety of children, because I get to visit classrooms ranging from kindergarten through the eighth grade. Sometimes I get gifts of pencils, stickers, pictures, hugs, or birdseed, and occasionally I am included in a confidential talk. My talk with eighth graders John and Mike was particularly helpful.

When I came into this particular student teacher's classroom, I sat in the only available desk, which was, serendipitously, next to John and Mike. As the lesson wore on and the class was assigned seatwork, I did what I typically do: I started talking to the kids around me. To provide a context, let me briefly describe these two young men. They attend a small public Kentucky school; they ride mountain bikes to school every morning and everywhere else every afternoon. Both confessed to being pretty average students and fairly chronically behind in homework. They are best friends and agreed that *The Once and Future King* is their current favorite book, which they take turns reading aloud.

When I asked these boys what they would have me tell my education students, they did not miss a beat. They said to "be creative," because "the more interesting things there are to do, the less obnoxious people will be," and to "be nice," which they explained to mean being between their typical teachers, who either "seem to be overly concerned or don't care and are not concerned at all." They said to be "gentle with sixth graders, because all the change is confusing, and to remember that seventh and eighth graders are just figuring out what they can do."

Lesson planning brought the strongest admonition: "Don't go straight by the textbooks, and avoid worksheets." John and Mike conceded that such planning was hard, and each gave examples from difficulties with creating good Sunday School lessons; but they repeated sternly to make sure they were very clear, "We don't want to be bored; I know creating lessons is hard, but if I can do it, so can my teachers." They concluded with advice for classroom management: "Be sure to go around the classroom and don't just call on a few people"; "set rules and stick to them and do what you say"; "make the rules fair; don't set rules which make everyone in trouble, rules that make things that are just going to happen be wrong." Perhaps because of my sixteen years as a middle school teacher, I find this last piece to be my particular favorite.

If we can listen carefully to these two boys, they give some pretty good advice about what should be happening in classrooms, particularly how people should treat each other in classrooms. They ask that teachers be respectful: "Be gentle with sixth graders" and "seventh and eighth graders are just figuring out what they can do" and "we don't want to be bored." They ask for awareness of the dignity of each person in the classroom, opposing talk of students as objects to be controlled or tricked into participation through discipline schemes. They ask for authentic relationships with teachers who know their students well and who respond to the students' needs.

When John and Mike address lesson development, they ask not "to be bored," which seems only logical; they are not looking for the easy way for themselves or their teachers (remember their specific use of "creative," "interesting," "avoid worksheets," and instructions to go beyond the textbooks).

They seem to want to remove the worksheets and textbooks as impediments between them and a creative, interesting learning experience, which may be hard to construct, but they do not ask their teachers to do more than they themselves have done. John and Mike also begin a call for courage: "Don't just call on a few people," "set rules and stick to them and do what you say," and don't use rules to construct situations in which the students cannot be right.

These two boys have reminded me to consider the consequences for children of teachers' thinking through ethical teaching decisions; to ask often what our children can respect or revere in us; and, without directly saying so but through the intensity and care with which they answered my questions, to know that, as educators, we fail when we do not try to think through the confusing ethical decisions of teaching, simply because we must—we cannot—give our children less.

Entering or establishing a dialogue centered on an ethical perspective toward teaching and classroom practices is a challenge. Talking about dignity, spirit, courage, and mystery can so easily be dismissed as unrigorous, that it is less compromising and scary to avoid it altogether. The talk is challenging also because the issues and the language used to talk about them are confusing and sometimes contradictory. Although I am foggy in some ways when I think about the ethics of my teaching practices and philosophy, I have found that the clarity I do have liberates me from many of the risks of ignorant decision making and unreflective action and helps me to begin making the foggy areas more clear.

Factors That Distort the Foundation of Current Educational Discussions

I certainly do not wish for every educator to think within my framework or to reflect on classroom practices with my language. But I do wish that such thinking, reflecting, and contemplation of the contradictions of education discussion and practice would be grounded not in the illusion of facts and studies, but in some framework of humanity, relationship, acceptance, forgiveness—those things that describe us as we are and hope to be at our best, not the things we do. These things guide us in our actions rather than describing the actions that have already been. As Joseph Campbell has said, "Whenever men have looked for something solid on which to found their lives, they have chosen not the facts in which the world abounds, but the myths of an immemorial imagination" (Keen and Valley-Fox 1973, 2). As a teacher, parent, and teacher educator absolutely convinced of the efficacy and necessity of founding educational discussion and practice on those things that are most essential and important, "the myths of an immemorial imagination," I am concerned with whatever seems to distort this foundation. At this moment, there are four factors that I see as such distortions.

The current contentious educational debate is siphoning the energy and enthusiasm necessary for the hard work of education. The schools' teaching and learning energies are used up in suspicions of misspent funds, of ill-bred children, of greedy unions, and of mischievous politicians and lazy teachers. We, the public, deceive ourselves, though, by thinking that any of these debates do more than occupy us while children and teachers continue to spend their daily lives in classrooms, and we grow disheartened and lose courage. The debate is misdirected toward blaming rather than focusing on the underlying concern for the perpetuation and social progress of a culture that holds an untapped democratic promise for responding ethically to the needs of its citizens. I believe that the contentiousness of the debate is indicative of its importance and that the frustration of the debaters is a nagging awareness that the democratic promise has not been properly addressed.

The second factor that I see distorting an education founded on important and essential things is related to this heated debate. This factor is a failure to recognize that "democracy" is much more than a particular political process; democracy actually begins in respectful, life-sustaining relationships. I would even go so far as to say that democracy begins in a recognition of the sacred in everyone. Democracy, in this sense, is rooted in a sense of the dignity of each person; consequently, democratic institutions are those that best respond to the needs of their constituents. The democratic promise becomes one of personal responsibility so that, rather than blaming others or looking to some distant institution for solutions, an educational discussion focuses on building relationships between teachers, students, administrators, parents, community members.

When Wendell Berry, a Kentucky farmer and poet, speaks of the mechanization of farming and the consolidation of small farms into agricultural monoliths, he laments a production technology that requires "mechanizing consumption" and makes it "impossible to make machines of soil, plants, and animals without making machines also of people" (1977, 75). He describes the projected model farm as one that regulates access to land, to equipment, to agricultural technology, and, through control of production, to food. While these farming enterprises can potentially feed large numbers of people physically, they displace farming families and regard people as "complex, contradictory, unpredictable; they are perceived by the [agricultural] specialist as a kind of litter, pollutants of pure nature on the one hand and of pure technology, total control, on the other" (1977, 73). This technology mindset allows great distances between the human and natural worlds so that a lot that is amazing does not get noticed, and experiences with nature do not happen.

An easy, seductive reliance on technology clouds our vision so that we forget to think about consequences of using machines as intermediaries in communication or of using natural resources to feed the machines. What I fear from this mindset is a growing passion for the technology rather than an awareness of what it enables us to do: to respond quickly to human needs, to consistently monitor excessive use of resources, to teach lessons over great distances, to record stories for easy accessibility. Thinking of technology as a solution rather than a tool can potentially lead to thinking of technology as ultimately important, as one of those things that are essential and that should form the foundation of our education discussion, with unhappy consequences.

The fourth distortion of the foundation of profitable educational discussion is actually more of a reminder of a different, more sustaining way of viewing institutions. Having people congregate and spend time together is not sufficient for the construction of an institution that truly contributes to the well-being of its constituents—in other words, a truly democratic institution. The form of the institution must be comprised of people who "stand in a living, reciprocal relationship to a single living center, and they have to stand in a living, reciprocal relationship to one another" (Buber 1970, 94). Buber says that this living center, which allows the institution to serve the needs of the participants, is "the central presence of the You" (1970, 95). This I-You (I-Thou) relationship allows people to come together, recognizing and responding to the sacred in each other and treating each other accordingly.

In an institution guided by the I-You relationship, the members stand in relationship to the sacred in each other, and all members stand in relationship to a sacred, central presence composed of the sacred part of them all. When the members are all present with each other, the institution responds to their needs; when the needs are met, the institution dissolves without efforts to sustain itself while disregarding the harmful effects on its members. In this view, institutions are not immutable monoliths that far outstrip our control. They are created by the needs and relationships of individuals and change in response to the members, as schools founded on a recognition of the dignity and the sacred in each person become places where teachers and students reason, puzzle, and experiment together in ways reflective of the needs of each member (Buber 1970, 94–95).

Ethical and Esthetic Teaching

In *Art as Experience*, John Dewey discusses the relationships between means and ends in the "range of experiences" of everyday life:

> One kind (of means) is external to that which is accomplished; the other kind is taken up into the consequences produced and remains immanent in them. There are ends which are merely welcome cessations and there are ends that are fulfillments of what went before. The toil of a laborer is too often only antecedent to the wage he receives, as consumption of gasoline is merely a means to transportation. (1934, 197)

When the means are completely extraneous, or external, to the ends, the whole activity has the quality of being unesthetic, as, for example, when someone studies just to pass an examination or works simply to complete a task. When the "means and end coalesce," however, the whole activity has the quality of being esthetic; one takes the journey as much for the sake of the journey as to reach a destination (Dewey 1934, 198).

Teaching holds closely to these qualities. When the ends and means, the whole activity, are together, esthetic, clear, and wise choices have been made about the lives we want for everyone's children, and the teaching and classroom decisions reflect those choices about what is right for all children. Teaching for dignity and responsibility requires the daily practice of dignity and responsibility. Also, when the means are determined by more mechanical and unesthetic considerations, they become inconsequential and can easily be replaced by less strenuous teaching, less careful thought, and less concern for the well-being of the students. Daily practice that is considered separately from the ends of dignity and responsibility becomes governed by other, perhaps harmful or less important, things.

Creating and maintaining meaningful (educational) institutions cannot be left to chance; embracing as goals the faith and dignity of all human beings, the ability to live with surprise and uncertainty, and the courage to take action begins a dynamic process requiring certain behaviors from educators. Education that truly meets the needs of all its members must have as its foundation clear decisions about what is ultimately important and essential, combined with teaching that builds the daily life of the classroom around those clear decisions.

Works Cited

Berry, W. 1977. *The Unsettling of America Culture & Agriculture.* San Francisco: Sierra Club Books.

Buber, M. 1970. *I and Thou.* Trans. W. Kaufmann. New York: Charles Scribner's Sons.

Camus, A. 1948. *The Plague.* New York: Vintage Books.

Dewey, J. 1934. *Art as Experience.* New York: Berkley.

Keen, S., and A. Valley-Fox. 1973. *Your Mythic Journey.* Los Angeles: Jeremy P. Tarcher.

Keller, E. F. 1983. *A Feeling for the Organism.* New York: W.H. Freeman.

Macdonald, B. J., ed. 1995. *Theory as a Prayerful Act: The Collected Essays of James B. Macdonald.* New York: Peter Lang.

Moffett, J. 1992. *Harmonic Learning: Keynoting School Reform.* Portsmouth: Boynton/Cook.

Mooney, R. L. 1955. "The Artist and Our Human Need." *Journal of Human Relations* Summer: 9–16.

4

The Ethics of Teaching Composition in Cyberspace
Knowledge Making in Commodified Space

Frances V. Condon

In recent years, experts in Composition have produced a tremendous amount of work touting a revolution in the teaching of writing made possible by the advent of computers and computer technology. According to these claims, power relations are radically rewritten in cyberspace. Dominant voices (white, heterosexual, male) are reconstituted through the medium of synchronous on-line discussion as power-neutral—bearing little or none of the power and authority that their privilege accords them in the traditional classroom. Gender, race, and class, the story goes, are effaced on-line so that traditionally silenced and marginalized students are freed to participate fully and fearlessly in classroom discussion. Cyberspace is, according to some, a "reduced risk" space for conversations about racism, sexism, classism, and heterosexism. In addition, according to the literature, the authority of the teacher is transformed in cyberspace; the teacher's voice becomes merely one of many in a system of power relations arranged horizontally rather than vertically.

According to Jerome Bump, networked classrooms and electronic communications can liberate minorities by "giving back" their voices "whatever their sex, race, class, or age" (1990, 55). Continuing on this theme, in their essay "Computer Conferences and Learning: Authority, Resistance, and Internally Persuasive Discourse," writing about computer networks, Cooper and Selfe suggest that "in these spaces, writers and teachers of writing may be able to recapture, from women and other 'silenced' (Olsen) [sic] minorities, perspectives that we have lost" (1990, 858). And Lester Faigley writes, in *Fragments of Rationality*, that with the use of networked electronic communication in the classroom, "the utopian dream of an equitable sharing of classroom authority, at least during the duration of a class discussion, has been achieved" (1992, 167). If one believes the claims made for computers and electronic communication in the classroom, the technology is not merely efficient in helping students to use writing more often and with fewer inhibitions, to write more fluidly and with greater sophistication and critical acumen, the technology is, itself, liberatory and salvific.

The more exorbitant claims made by composition's technophiles are *non sequiturs* in the sense that the "conclusions" do not necessarily follow from their premises. For example, it is not true that simply because synchronous on-line conversation is possible, conversation that takes place in such electronic environments will necessarily be inclusive of traditionally silenced voices. It is not true that simply because teachers are seated at workstations with their students rather than standing at the front of the room, authority in the networked classroom is automatically redistributed. It is not true that the *de facto* practice in a networked classroom is a student-centered pedagogy. It is not true that because the computers being referred to are utilized in institutions of higher learning, issues of access are unrelated to market demand and profitability. Finally and most importantly, it is not true that justice, equality, and liberation are achieved when traditionally marginalized students are welcomed into the virtual communities of traditionally dominant classes simply because their bodies, their Otherness, cannot be seen in cyberspace.

I do not wish to argue that the use of computers in composition classrooms is, in itself, unethical. Rather, I want to point out the ways in which unbridled enthusiasm for the technologies now available to us may lead some teachers and theorists to make claims for computer technology that mask facts about the production, profitability, and principles of computer technology. If these facts were made available to students for study and critical engagement, students might become more circumspect, more critical, and more astute in their consumption and use of computers. Teachers and students alike might even be moved to work to change the conditions of production and use of computer technology.

Paulo Freire writes that "any situation in which some individuals prevent others from engaging in the process of inquiry is one of violence. The means used are not important; to alienate human beings from their own decision-making is to change them into objects" (1993, 66). There is absolutely no place for violence in the classroom. Nor is there any place for the logic of violence in the classroom, except in as much as that logic might be the object of critical analysis and critique. To take up the logic of violence (the occlusion of truth and consequent alienation of students from their decision-making processes) and to employ it, intentionally or unintentionally, as the logic undergirding one's pedagogy is unethical. An ethical pedagogy is one that enables students to do more than "master" information and skills; an ethical pedagogy enables students to arrive at a critical understanding of the information and skills that they are being called upon to know and to make informed choices about whether, how, and where to use their knowledge. In the sense that an ethical pedagogy prepares students not only to experience, but also to theorize and potentially to transform their lived realities, it is also liberatory.

Teachers who are committed to ethical, liberatory education must treat uncritical claims for the liberatory effects of computer technology in the classroom with skepticism. Ethical, liberatory teaching practices are the labor of human hearts and minds. They cannot be made more cost-effective by replacing human workers with machines. This is not to suggest that computers and computer technology cannot be helpful tools in a liberatory praxis, but rather a reminder that computers and technology are tools; they are commodities. We must be wary of any packaging of them that occludes the necessity of human labor in the work of making students conscious of and resistant to exploitation and oppression of the many by the few. This essay calls attention to the ways in which even professional writers are susceptible to the exhilaration of novelty and to remind readers, without singling out these writers as knowingly unethical, that advocacy of any nature always entails an ethical dimension.

Packaging Technology in the Language of Liberation

American compositionists are fascinated with the language of liberation. Terms such as *resistance, transformation, conscientization, empowerment,* and *liberation* abound in professional texts. Despite this fascination, however, it is not clear that there is any general agreement among compositionists about the necessity for transformation of American economic, political, and social relations. There is no shared sense of the kind or degree of change we might need in order to realize and manifest justice and equality in American society. Nor is there any widespread commitment to the political and spiritual praxis that the philosophy undergirding the lexicon of liberatory pedagogy calls for, both from those who speak of liberation and from those who hear them. It is clear, however, that in the current Composition market, liberatory rhetoric sells.

Computers and computer technology are complex commodities in that they represent the congealed labor of both First and Third World workers. At one level of generalization, it is this labor that gives computers and computer technology their value. At another level of generalization, there is a cost associated with the use in the classroom of computers and computer technology; this cost is the labor of students and teachers who use networked classrooms and electronic communication in the work of producing knowledge. Both of these forms of labor are unacknowledged in the rhetorical packaging of the technology by Composition's technophiles using the language of liberation. John Eaton, a Marxist economist and political theorist, suggests in *Political Economy* that in the markets of capitalist economies, "the value of the commodity makes itself felt as though it were a property belonging to the commodity in itself and quite independently of the human being engaged in production" (1966, 84). Marx referred to this phenomenon as fetishization, explaining that commodities are fetishized to the degree that the relations of their production are disguised. Computers and computer technology are being fetishized by their marketers in Composition to the extent that their rhetorical packaging disguises and displaces both the labor involved in the production of the machinery and software and also, more importantly for the purposes of this essay, to the extent that the labor of teaching and learning are also masked or elided by this rhetorical packaging.

Computers and computer technology are tools that may be put to a wide variety of uses. They are as accessible or, perhaps, more accessible to those who are interested in repression or are committed to the maintenance of the *status quo* as to those who are interested in liberation. Particularly given the relationship of computers to business and industry, any claims for an inherently liberatory effectivity of computers in the classroom for students who have been traditionally subjugated and marginalized must be suspect. At the very least, I want to suggest that compositionists need to think carefully and critically about the ethics involved in helping to make capitalism work better by extending the reach of multinational corporations into the institutions of education—by abstracting labor from its lived relations into its object form and marketing that abstraction as somehow inherently liberatory for student/workers.

Claims for the liberatory power of computer technology are often based on a conflation of liberation and professionalization. The premise appears to be that preparing students who have traditionally been excluded from the kinds of jobs that require computer literacy for the workplace is a liberatory practice. The necessary presupposition that supports this premise is that the reason for the exclusion of certain workers from higher-paying positions is, in the first instance, simply a lack of preparation or a lack of computer literacy and not the necessity under capitalism for a standing pool of cheap, easily exploitable labor.

Barker and Kemp, in "Network Theory: A Postmodern Pedagogy for the Writing Classroom," write that "these students [traditionally disenfranchised students] require a teaching method oriented toward advancement in business and industry" (1990, 5). Barker and Kemp call for a student-centered, inclusive, and nonhierarchical pedagogy, which, they imply, is the default pedagogy in the computer classroom. To enact a student-centered, inclusive, nonhierarchical pedagogy, seemingly one only needs to move one's students into a computer classroom. Apparently, the computers do the rest. Interestingly, although not surprisingly, Barker and Kemp advocate student-centered, inclusive, nonhierarchical pedagogy not because such a pedagogy enables students as intellectuals to read, critique, and transform the actual, material, oppressive conditions of their lives, but because "such instruction brings students into the intellectual enterprise in a real way, without transforming them into what we may misconceive to be intellectuals" (1990, 5). Seemingly, student-centered, inclusive, nonhierarchical pedagogies are good for nontraditional or minority students who have a right to a taste of intellectualism but who need not be provided with the critical skills necessary to pursue an intellectual and critical understanding of the social, political, and economic relations in which they live. By implication, Barker and Kemp seem to be suggesting that teacher-centered, exclusive, hierarchical pedagogies are still acceptable for the student elite who will continue to be class-privileged white, heterosexual men.

For Cynthia Selfe and Marilyn Cooper, networked classrooms and computer conferencing are liberatory because they somehow enable students to "develop their own ways of talking about the concepts presented in class with others" (1990, 858). According to Cooper and Selfe, students learning through computer conferencing need not fear and are not coerced to take up academic discourse by the gate-keeping process that usually attends writing-intensive courses. On-line, students can choose to accept and accommodate or reject and resist ideas and ideologies that they find embedded in academic discourse. Cooper and Selfe suggest that the electronic medium in which conferences occur has a "liberating influence."

It seems possible to read, in the logic of Cooper and Selfe, that what students are being liberated from is the necessity of learning to understand and to use effectively complex theoretical concepts that might enable them to think critically and to communicate with others about the world in which they find themselves. As Paulo Freire notes in his work with Brazilian peasants (1993), while the conditions of peasants' lives are, of course, evident to them, the systemic relations out of which those conditions arise are not self-evident. The literacy taught to those peasants by Freire and his co-workers is not merely a fluency in the written language, but also and especially a political literacy that enables the peasants to name and understand the ways in which they are oppressed. They are thereby empowered to struggle effectively for liberation from their oppression.

Coercive teaching, according to Freire's logic, would transmit an apparently value-free fluency in the written word so that the relations of production that prefigure and determine the relations of men and women continue to exist unseen and unchallenged. This is a distinction, I would argue, between coercive teaching and directive teaching that is suppressed in the rendition of the teaching story told by Cooper and Selfe. The subjectivities and subject positions of traditional and nontraditional, privileged and disenfranchised students are all written in and through dominant hegemony. The process of producing a counterhegemony in the context of either a traditional or networked classroom, of making that which had been hidden explicit and what appeared to be natural and self-evident strange, is difficult and uncomfortable for both students and teachers. A certain degree of linguistic complexity is necessary in order to communicate difficult and sophisticated concepts, regardless of the forum or medium in which they are being discussed. The onus is on teachers to help students overcome their convictions (if they, indeed, have them) that conceptual and linguistic complexity is an impenetrable barrier that prevents any possibility of comprehension.

Liberatory teaching involves teaching students to be fluent in discourses that enable critical discussion and debate about the most difficult issues of our time—exploitation and oppression. Liberatory teaching is not, I would argue, coercive but may require a certain amount of directiveness on the part of teachers. It is not surprising that students should resist understanding and using language and concepts that call into question the value and necessity of conditions about which they had not previously been conscious nor concerned. It is even less surprising that they should resist inquiring into or examining the bases of their own privilege. Teaching becomes coercive when student resistance is suppressed, ignored, or treated as if it is, itself, value-free.

When teachers make student resistance, itself, the object of study and assist students to realize that there is a relationship between student resistance and dominant hegemony, they are directing student learning. It may be that the tendency to construe this kind of directive teaching as coercive stems from the conservative impulse to argue that the Left is teaching a political agenda while the Right and Center are teaching facts and truths that transcend the political. If developments in critical theory over the last thirty years have taught us anything, however, they have taught us that claims of political neutrality are at the surface absurd and at root aimed toward the preservation of the *status quo*. Academic discourse is never apolitical and neither is student resistance. It may be that electronic communication can facilitate new kinds and degrees of political engagement for students and teachers. The extent to which such facilitation is liberatory for students, however, will be determined not by the medium (the commodity), but by the commitment with which students and teachers together engage and debate critically the concepts and philosophies that moor the lexicon of liberation. This, I would argue, is true not only in composition, but also across the disciplines.

Workspaces

In their essay, "The Politics of the Interface: Power and Its Exercise in Electronic Contact Zones," Cynthia and Richard Selfe attempt to redress some of the unthinking, uncritical claims for the liberatory power of computer technology by critiquing the construction of interfaces (Macintosh's Desktop, for example), pointing out that computers and software used by writing teachers "are never ideologically innocent or inert" (1994, 485). They write:

> In particular—given that these technologies have grown out of the predominately male, white, middle class, professional cultures associated with the military-industrial complex—the virtual reality of computer interfaces represents, in part and to a visible degree, a tendency to value monoculturalism, capitalism, and phallologic thinking, and does so, more importantly, to the exclusion of other perspectives. Grounded in these values, computer interfaces, we maintain, enact small but continuous gestures of domination and colonialism. (1994, 486)

Selfe and Selfe suggest that students and teachers spend time imagining ways in which computers and software might be altered to represent or map more inclusive and democratic realities. Their critique, while apt, is partial and, as laudable as the project of reimagining interfaces is, as a political practice, it fails to address and to challenge the lived relations that current interfaces merely reflect. Making computer interfaces more inclusive and democratic without also working to unmask, critique, and dismantle the systems out of which oppression arises will result in the improved reproduction of those systems by increasing the accessibility of previously untapped labor to exploitation.

The logic that allows Selfe and Selfe to make these claims—that reimagining more inclusive realities will somehow call more inclusive realities into being—is related to the logic undergirding claims about the liberatory power of altered spatial relations and arrangements in networked classrooms and on-line. These logics are premised on the speculation that representations of lived relations are available to be changed, while actual lived relations, the referents of representations, are inaccessible to change, either because of "social inertia," which is what Cooper and Selfe suggest, or because they exist only inasmuch as they are represented, which is the (post)modern perspective.

Both Barker and Kemp (1990) and Cooper and Selfe (1990) suggest that the altered spatial relations in networked classrooms and on-line in computer conferences radically alter the configuration of authority and power in the classroom. Barker and Kemp assert that computer classrooms offer "alternative" learning environments that, in contrast to the traditional classroom, disrupt spatial arrangements that direct students to regard the teacher as the "pivotal agent." The pivotal nature of the teacher's authority is, apparently, the product of architectural arrangements, not of institutional conventions and ideological apparatuses. According to this logic, the physical arrangement of the classroom—the spatial representation of power relations in the classroom—is the sum total of those relations.

In networked classrooms, desks or workstations are arranged in ways that more closely resemble businesses than traditional classrooms. In her essay "Computers in the Classroom: The Instruction, the Mess, the Noise, the Writing" (1990), Carolyn Boiarsky suggests that networked classrooms be arranged like newsrooms. Further, she advises that in this setting, teachers play the role of editor or bureau chief rather than teacher. The "transformation" of power relations this switch in roles necessitates is, however, not in kind, but in form. For Boiarsky, the point is not, apparently, that there should not be power differentials between students and teachers, but that the power of employers, managers, or supervisors concerned with quality control of products (in this case, student writing) is less repressive and more conducive to the emergence of "community" than the power of teachers in institutional settings.

The design of traditional classrooms, in effect, reproduces the relations of production in industrial capitalism. The computer classroom, however, reproduces the relations of production in post-industrial capitalism. The Daedalus Room at the State University of New York at Albany (before it was dismantled), for example, looked remarkably similar to an office designed for data entry and data processing. There was a station and a computer for every worker. The representative of authority—the supervisor—was not, in fact, absent, but was also at a workstation. The apparatuses of authority were also programmed into the computer; directing and constraining the choices students could make while on-line. Students took orders from the computers at their workstations in addition to their human supervisors. This conserved managerial labor and was, therefore, cost effective.

The architectural arrangement of the traditional classroom allows the teacher both to direct her students and to observe their compliance. It also allows her students to be aware of being directed and observed. The networked classroom has rendered this traditional form of surveillance obsolete. Barker and Kemp and Cooper and Selfe suggest that although teachers may be participants in computer conferences, their communications, including prompts and queries, are not spatially marked as having more authority than the communications of their students and, therefore, do not, in fact, have any more authority than the communications of their students. Students, they claim, are able to participate in computer conferences without the sense of being evaluated. The logic of these premises would seem to suggest that because teachers or supervisors can now observe and direct students or workers without appearing to do so, surveillance is not taking place and control over productivity is not being exercised. Such a suggestion is specious.

Barker and Kemp and Cooper and Selfe seem to be arguing that the networked classroom enforces a "withering away" of authority and that, in the name of student-centered teaching, which focuses on student freedom and independence, this is a desirable phenomenon. However, as Brent Harold points out,

> student-centered teaching, while it eliminates authoritarian structures, leaves intact—and in some forms may even intensify—the dullest aspect of the traditional course, and the basis of its training in status quo values and attitudes: namely, its idealism . . . the tendency to experience ideas as abstracted from the concrete, social experiences of the people holding them, as well as to abstract the people themselves from their actual classroom and other situations. (1972, 201)

The ways in which students' experiences have political implications are not self-evident. Any course that discourages students from becoming conscious of those implications "enforces on students an experience of, an apprenticeship in idealism" (Harold 1972, 204). Even though they are seated at workstations alongside their teachers, students engaged in on-line conferencing are not, in fact, free to say whatever they want in whatever manner they choose. It is not clear, however, why authority that exerts such constraint over students might be inherently problematic. Students who are privileged by proximity to social, political, and economic "norms" and who have the opportunity to write on-line without constraint are at least as likely to reinscribe the hatred in which they are inculcated (racism, classism, and homophobia, for example) and to continue to silence traditionally marginalized students as to learn from those marginalized students or from themselves, somehow, that their ideas are contingently related to the historical, social, political, and economic conditions in which they live.

Silencing, it is important to note, is not always accomplished by preventing people from speaking or writing. As even Cooper and Selfe seem aware, cyberspace enables students to ignore one another. Cooper and Selfe write that in computer conferences, students "do not have to compete for the floor and can say as much as they want to without being interrupted, although they still must be responsive to the interests of their classmates if they do not want to be ignored" (1990, 848). Ignoring what Others have to say is, however, an exercise of power, and a fairly effective one at that. Far from being inherently liberating, the technology of on-line conferencing ensures that it is just as possible as it is in the traditional classroom to subsume alternative views or the views of marginalized students in babble or for classmates and teachers to fail to address issues raised by those whom they find bothersome, offensive, or Other. Ultimately, it is lived relations, including access to wealth, privilege, dominant ideologies, and knowledges, and not spatial relations, that confer authority. Power and authority are redistributed not by technology, but through the commitment of teachers and students to painstaking interrogation of and intervention in systemic oppression and exploitation. Technology may aid in this work, but it does not do the work.

The Issue of Access

In a market economy, the production of a "need" in consumers is often as important as the production of the commodities the market supplies. As computer classrooms are integrated into the university curriculum, universities in general and compositionists in particular participate in the production of market demand. To respond to this "need" (demand) and because some students cannot afford to buy a computer for themselves, many universities have begun to buy computers that students can use. Although Cynthia Selfe raises issues of equity and access in her essay "Technology in the English Classroom: Computers through the Lens of Feminist Theory" (1990), ultimately, the market and its forces remain untouched by her analysis. After a brief discussion of "competition from foreign markets . . . the increasing savvy of the computer retail industry . . . innovative pricing schedules, equipment grants, and computer lending schemes," she writes that "Linda Stine (1986) of Lincoln University, teaches a composition course for nontraditional students in which each individual is given a 'loaner' computer for the entire semester" (1990, 133). Selfe's narrative points up several problems. The first is that loans are never given. Loans are business arrangements for which someone pays and from which someone or some organization profits. "Loaner" computers do not materialize out of thin air. They are purchased, and the cost of their purchase is either borne by the university or is, more likely, passed on to students in the form of tuition and fee increases. The second problem is that the term nontraditional here seems to refer to class, with one possible implication being that traditional students will not need to be loaned computers. If class is what is at stake, whose interests are served by masking that fact with the use of the term *nontraditional*? Finally, Selfe's citing of the practice of loaning students computers as a solution to the problem of access fails to acknowledge or address the ways in which having use of a computer for a semester does not assuage but intensifies the continuing "need" for computer access.

The existence of campus computer centers does perhaps provide some convenient access and charitable service to students who do not have computers at home. However, the conditions in which students are forced to work need to be accounted for in terms of their effect on the quality (and quantity) of writing that students are able to produce. Like most data entry and processing sites, computer centers are illuminated with fluorescent light. Students are unable to leave their terminals to stretch, use the restroom, or get a drink without either exiting their programs and taking their possessions with them or assuring that their possessions will be safe and their terminals will not be taken over by other students while they are gone. Students who rely on income from jobs rather than from parents or student loans must find ways to schedule time in computer centers during hours when the centers are open.

There is another and perhaps more worrisome issue having to do with accessibility. Networked classrooms extend the reach of multinational corporations into institutions of education. In the name of access, industries are reaching their hands further into the pockets of students and faculty alike, with the blessings of the university. Using the composition classroom to create a market for computers makes students, as consumers, more accessible to the machinations of capital. The point is not that we should (or could) refuse to use computers or that a refusal to use computers in the composition classroom might have any material affect on the exploitative practices of capital. Rather, writing teachers, particularly teachers who are interested in and committed to liberatory pedagogy, have an ethical imperative to be explicit—need to teach their students—about where computers come from and the ways in which computer use and the fostered "need" for computer access enjoins and enforces student complicity with the multinationals' exploitive use of Third World labor.

On-line Communities and the Logic of Presence and Absence

During the mid- to late 1980s through the early 1990s, many compositionists became interested in the concept of "communities" as a way of talking about inclusive, nonhierarchical teaching practices and classroom arrangements. We failed, however, to think carefully and critically about what communities are, how they operate on those who are excluded from them as well as on their members, the degree to which classroom (learning) communities can be intentional, and how the lack of intentionality in community formation might affect relations within classroom communities. We failed to account for the contradiction that dogs all university classes, real or virtual, traditional or progressive, and that certainly impinges on the possibility of classroom or learning communities in the context of the university—namely, the contradiction between the assertion or appearance of collectively conceived values and the concept of individualized success or failure as realized in the practices of assessment and grading. These problems are yet to be addressed and resolved. In the meantime, however, compositionists who are intrigued by computer technology and its applications in the classroom have used the idea of learning or classroom communities to construct a sales pitch for computer-assisted instruction.

The rising interest in communities among compositionists coincided with a more public discourse advocating communitarianism: an essentially conservative movement masquerading as liberal humanism. Communitarianism (which is related, in many ways, to social constructionism) centers around the notion that social values can and should be collectively determined in the context of communities rather than impressed on individuals or communities through the apparatuses of the state. When deployed through a purportedly apoliticized practice, communitarianism masks the reality of disparate and unequal relations by representing coherence as a natural or innate condition of community, rendering structural and systemic inequity and injustice invisible. Compositionists expressing resonances of communitarianism while advocating learning or classroom communities have failed both to theorize their own discourse and to critique the related public communitarian discourse, which both implicitly and explicitly calls for the subsumption of minority cultures in a dominant (white, male, western, European) culture.

The term *community* can be traced to the Latin root *communete*, meaning *common*, and refers to a group of any size that is held together by common bonds such as shared culture and interests and that is set apart from the rest of society. The term can also be traced to the Latin root *munere*, which refers to the building of a wall or fortification around a town. While origins do not necessarily determine ends, they can be illuminating in the sense that they may be used to guide critical inquiry into present principles and practices. What is at issue and at stake in this discussion is the way that compositionists in general and computer advocates within Composition in particular have taken up and deployed the term *community* in service of assumptions, logics, and technologies that are at least potentially more coercive than liberatory. Specifically, the claims for on-line or virtual communities in the computer classroom depend in part on unseen and unspoken exclusionary practices that computer technology makes possible.

Communities are represented by communitarians as being collectively conceived relations with collectively determined social values and a collective sense of social good. Values are embedded in the language or discourse of that community and so are continually reproduced. Literacy in this context is the acquisition of that shared discourse, through which the longevity of the community and its values are assured. The contradiction in this construction is that while values and culture are here collectively conceived, failure to assimilate or to take up community values is assessed individually and individuals are held accountable for these failures. The questions this sort of contradiction raises for classroom practice are how a class might establish collectively conceived values yet rely on individual teachers' assessments of students' assimilation or performance of values and, further, how or whether individual students could succeed or fail within a collectively established "community." This contradiction is not unique to the composition classroom (computer or traditional) but also obtains in premiere communitarian Amitai Etzioni's frightening manifesto, *The Spirit of Community: The Reinvention of American Society* (1993). Etzioni, who refers to "American minorities and women" as "enriching subcultures," argues for the supremacy of (white) Western civilization and suggests that multiculturalism, which he represents as being extremist, "undermines the shared values that help keep us together as a community of communities" (1993, 151). Etzioni implies that minorities, women, and the disabled are not now and have not actively participated in "improving their lot" and are, therefore, responsible for their own marginalization.

Both implicitly and explicitly, advocates of computer technology suggest that virtual communities are possible and inclusive of Others because the lived physical realities of their members are excluded from the lived reality of the virtual community. According to this logic, hate is either created or exacerbated by visual markers of difference. When the cues that trigger hate are invisible, hate is absent. Lester Faigley writes that "instead of being tools of repression in the skills and drills curriculum, computers joined in a network can be a means of liberation, particularly for those students who are often marginalized in American classrooms" (as quoted by Bump 1990, 49). But what precisely is the relationship between cyberspace and liberation? From what will students be liberated? Professional writer Howard Rheingold, in his *Utne Reader* article, "The Virtual Community," writes,

> Because we cannot see one another in cyberspace, gender, age, national origin, and physical appearance are not apparent unless a person wants to make such characteristics public. People whose physical handicaps make it difficult to form new friendships find that virtual communities treat them as they always wanted to be treated—as thinkers and transmitters of ideas and feeling beings, not carnal vessels with a certain appearance and way of walking and talking (or not walking and talking). (1995, 64)

The supposition that seems to be at work here is that some of us (women, minorities, the elderly, and the disabled) are oppressed not by systems, institutions, bigotries, racism, sexism, classism, and heterosexism, but by the "physical handicaps" of our own bodies (our bodies with their vaginas, their dark skin, and their age). Once freed from our bodies, we are freed from repression. On one hand, Rheingold seems to be suggesting that the minds and bodies of marginalized peoples have little to do with one another—that ideas and the material conditions of our lives are somehow unrelated. On the other hand, he asserts that the ideas expressed by marginalized peoples can garner respect on-line because no one can see our bodies there. Those who occupy positions of privilege are, in this construction, never challenged to question, abandon, or share that privilege. Liberation lasts so long as the under- or unprivileged remain on-line. The material, off-line conditions of oppression are never challenged and remain intact.

David Coogan, in an article in the *Writing Lab Newsletter* (1994), writes about his development of an on-line tutoring service at SUNY Albany. Coogan was interested to discover what would happen if the conversation of traditional face-to-face tutorials, spoken over a paper-text, took place on-line and completely in writing. He wondered "what would happen to that conversation if I [Coogan] took away speech, and took away physical presence? What would happen to the idea of a writing tutorial if we decided to make the act of writing the main event?" (1994, 3)

These are interesting questions, but they do have some troubling implications. We need, I think, to ask some additional and qualifying questions as well. What does it mean or what is the value of taking physical presence away from a student whose physical and intellectual presence in university, on campus, in the classroom, in the writing center is a hard-won right and for whom physical presence never has been and seemingly never can be taken for granted? What happens when a teacher takes speech away from a student whose right to speak in public spaces also is a hard-won right; a student whose language of origin or dialect has always been undervalued by a conservative academy and is now being entirely devalued by the radically conservative Right?

One of the presuppositions with which Etzioni (1993), Rheingold (1995), and almost all of Composition's technophiles seem to be working is that both cultural differences and the socially constructed categories of gender, race, disability, age, and sexual preference are the causes of conflict or are destructive in some way of communities and effective teaching practices. These problems can be resolved, according to this logic, either by enforcing assimilation or by making difference invisible. For Coogan (1994), it seems, these differences or categories are not reinscribed in students' texts, so that doing away with "physical" difference (as if that were possible) leaves the teacher and the student with "pure" text. In contrast, I would argue that students and their texts do not need to be nor can they be liberated from difference. Students do need to be liberated from—to liberate themselves from—oppressive social conditions, which capital justifies by fostering and exploiting fears of difference. Students who labor under the illusion that "pure" text is possible or even desirable will not be enabled to use writing to transform their lived experiences and the world.

Conclusion

When Jerome Bump suggests that computer-assisted instruction can give marginalized students back their voices, he evokes a kind of nostalgia for that (nonexistent) time in the past when those students had voices and also, presumably, the freedom to use them. Such a perspective neatly elides the historical struggle of marginalized peoples not to regain, but to have for the first time public, political voices that not only can be heard, but also are heeded. This struggle is ongoing.

The voices of marginalized peoples are not ours to give. We can join the struggle for justice and equality by teaching our students to be conscious of the relationship between ideas and the lived social, political, and economic relations out of which ideas emerge. We can work to enable and empower our students to join us in this struggle—to recognize, critique, and dismantle privilege; to resist exploitation; and to struggle to end the exploitation of others. We can try to teach our students not to be complicit in their own or others' oppression. We can encourage students to write for transformation of oppressive social conditions by providing them with opportunities to do so.

Teachers practicing in networked classrooms or utilizing the technology of electronic communications must not be lulled into complacency by the false promise that computers or computer technology will do the work of liberating students. Computer-assisted instruction is liberatory only to the extent that its *practitioners* take up the ethical imperative to labor for social transformation. Further, in using computers and computer technology in our classrooms, we must be vigilant in assuring that we are not, as Eaton might say, merely freeing our students to be exploited. The degree to which the use of computer technology in the classroom is ethical will always be contingent on teachers' and students' commitment to and labor for the abolition of exploitation and oppression.

Works Cited

Barker, T. T., and F. O. Kemp. 1990. "Network Theory: A Postmodern Pedagogy for the Writing Classroom." In *Computers and Community: Teaching Composition in the Twenty-First Century*, ed. C. Handa, 1–27. Portsmouth, NH: Boynton/Cook.

Boiarsky, C. 1990. "Computers in the Classroom: The Instruction, the Mess, the Noise, the Writing." In *Computers and Community: Teaching Composition in the Twenty-First Century*, ed. C. Handa, 47–67. Portsmouth, NH: Boynton/Cook.

Bump, J. 1990. "Radical Changes in Class Discussion Using Networked Computers." *Computers and the Humanities* 24: 49–65.

Coogan, D. 1994. "Towards a Rhetoric of On-line Tutoring." *The Writing Lab Newsletter* 19: 3–5.

Cooper, M. M., and C. L. Selfe. 1990. "Computer Conferences and Learning: Authority, Resistance, and Internally Persuasive Discourse." *College English* 52: 847–69.

Eaton, J. 1966. *Political Economy*. New York: International.

Etzioni, A. 1993. *The Spirit of Community: The Reinvention of American Society.* New York, London: Simon & Schuster.

Faigley, L. 1992. *Fragments of Rationality: Postmodernity and the Subject of Composition.* Pittsburgh: University of Pittsburgh Press.

Freire, P. 1993. *Pedagogy of the Oppressed.* New York: Continuum.

Harold, B. 1972. "Beyond Student-Centered Teaching: The Dialectical Materialist Form of a Literature Course." *College English* 34: 200–14.

Rheingold, H. 1995. "The Virtual Community." *Utne Reader* March–April 68: 60–64.

Selfe, C. L. 1990. "Technology in the English Classroom: Computers Through the Lens of Feminist Theory." In *Computers and Community: Teaching Composition in the Twenty-First Century*, ed. C. Handa, 118–39. Portsmouth, NH: Boynton/Cook.

Selfe, C., and R. J. Selfe, Jr. 1994. "The Politics of the Interface: Power and Its Exercise in Electronic Contact Zones." *College Composition and Communication* 45: 480–504.

5

Positions in Learning and Teaching Literary Criticism

Marguerite H. Helmers

Shortly after passing my doctoral qualifying examination, I dreamed that I entered an echoing and dimly lit lecture hall from a corridor crowded with students. At some distance from me, behind a table draped in gray velvet and raised upon a dais, five of my professors reposed in subtle and contemplative conversation. They were men, tenured and mantled in the red and ermine robes of the British Queen's Council. Knotted, dun-colored wigs bent slightly forward as their low voices rumbled an *ostinato* into the vacant interior of the auditorium. They did not appear to notice that I stood in the shadows at the back of the hall; except for my lone and silent figure, the rows stood empty, although the room was infused with a heavily meaningful atmosphere, the kind of pervasive knowing that dreams foster without words. Feeling that I had intruded, I half-turned to exit and return to the foyer where there was motion and sound, but as I moved backward, the professors judged me competent to step forward. With one motion, they beckoned.

I am at the threshold of action as the dream stops. I awake. In life, at the moment I awake, I am at that same horizon. It is 1991, and I am hesitating expectantly at the limit of becoming a professional. As the paradoxical graduate/ student, I am positioned as judge and adjudicated. Placing the dream there in time, just as I prepared for the doctoral examination, the dream embroiders my anxiety over my qualifications as a Ph.D. The dream makes palpable a particular "stifling anguish of responsibility," to borrow a phrase of Michel Foucault (1973, 247). At the end of graduate study, I was about to move (at the metaphorical level) from the archives to the civic world of a teaching position at a public institution. As I would take on a new identity, I would adopt a new language, new responsibilities, and a new community of professional peers. In life and in the dream world the threshold was fraught with uncertainty, and in the dream the figurative next step is represented literally as the footstep into the hall embedded in mystery, ritual, and tradition. That step and its implied acceptance of the rules that accompany the disciplines is illustrative of an ethical decision, a decision that recognizes the limits of possibility and the space of transgression. Yet, to be ethical requires an active self-authorization as well. Such authority arises in relation to various social expectations and necessitates a development of the intellect that can be associated with asceticism. Asceticism in this sense does not refer to a denial of the world, but a continuous process of testing the perceptions against the disciplines. The ethic, then, is not the rule, but the response to the constraints and entitlements set in motion by rules. Responsibility faces in two directions in English studies: toward the demands and discourses of the profession and toward the needs of the self as a reader and writer.

Michel Foucault, the French philosopher of history upon whose work my discussion of ethics is based, compares asceticism to an art (*techne*) of constituting the self. As Foucault paraphrases this process, "take care of yourself so you can rule the city" (1983, 235). It may seem surprising to turn to Foucault to discuss ethics, when his work has been popularly associated with amoral and nonethical positions. In many respects, though, Foucault's own development as a philosopher recalls the familiar pattern of the *Bildungsroman*, in which the hero undergoes a series of trials while seeking an education, a process of development that we who teach have endured. His early work, dating from the late 1950s, exposes the tyranny of modern institutional regimes: educational, penal, medical. In the 1960s, the Cultural Revolution, and French political and military involvement in Vietnam and Cambodia moved him to become a fervent Maoist, supporting with Jean Paul Sartre populist tribunals that interrogated the state, torture of public officials, and violent revolution. In the 1970s, new French intellectuals declared Marxism dead, and Foucault secreted himself, abandoning close friends to devote himself to his theories of ethics.[1] By 1984, he was dead at the age of fifty-seven. Throughout his work, Foucault's perspective is unmistakably his own; it is replete with existential and Marxist undercurrents: powers, dangers, and struggles of the individual to be free from the restrictions of convention that Foucault refers to as systems of power/knowledge.

In this essay, I consider how the transformation of self occurs in the undergraduate theory classroom. While the term *theory* has become a canopy for a cluster of varied approaches to textual interpretation, I prefer to limit the term to represent poststructuralism, which I am construing to incorporate a wide range of recent critical theories and perspectives on literary interpretation based on the concept of *difference*. In poststructuralist theory, language is defamiliarized, made alien so that readers may learn to see it as a set of conventions. It is made opaque so that readers may question their own desire for language to be transparent.

In the 1980s, the debates over critical theory in the academy and in the public addressed the politics of criticism. These political positions raised questions about what ethnic or gender groups were represented in the literary canon and which writers were at the margins of discourse; how to challenge and alter accepted discourses, such as the discourse of Great Books; and whether the poststructuralist emphasis on difference argued in favor of a dysfunctional "balkanization" of the curriculum. Now the questions have moved beyond politics to ethical considerations, such as what is right to teach and what is good to teach, and toward identifying the consequences of the decision to teach a particular work. These questions stretch academic thought into issues of human rights, human behavior, and censorship. I would like to move our thinking into a slightly different area to reflect on the "human rights" of students, to think about "a feeling for the organism," in Evelyn Fox Keller's words (1993).

The development into an ascetic leaves customary relationships to convention aside. For undergraduate students, the discomfiting nature of this "transformation" is related to the estrangement from an "authentic self." Furthermore, faculty that teach poststructuralism to undergraduates must eventually question the value of the texts they teach, engaging in important moral questions such as whether the construction of an ascetic position authorizes the commission of decentered acts in the name of theory. While this last comment may appear to be an extreme consequence of reading poststructuralist theory, I believe it is nonetheless necessary to consider the affect of disorienting topics upon undergraduate students, noting the loss of voice and the stresses that appear to be the consequence of teaching, learning, and writing.

Archaeology of the Undergraduate Reader

Foucault's project to describe a genealogy of ethics led naturally from his "archaeologies" of history and human experience and the imaginary dream-space of protracted study in the library; yet, his work remained incomplete at his death. While the study of ethics has been historically developed around concerns for the normalizing practices of religion, law, and education, Foucault's late work introduces the conception of a personal ethics that responds to and clarifies systems of disciplinary thought. In leaving his *oeuvre* open, Foucault created a space for discourse on the dialogic. It is this dialogic thinking, influenced by Russian language theorist Mikhail Bakhtin's notions of dialogue and answerability (1986), that forms the basis for my own understanding and use of Foucault's ideas in this essay.

The two writers share a common interest in the genres and rhetoric that constrain and enable speakers. Bakhtin's key term *monoglossia*, the impulse to create a unitary language that he resists with a discourse on *heteroglossia*, finds a point of correspondence with the authoritative speaker (the psychologist, the prison official) that Foucault so distrusts. Both writers emerged from the Marxist tradition, although for Bakhtin, Marxism was the lived experience of Stalinism and for Foucault, it was the studied stance of the twentieth century French intellectual. Bakhtin's writing embodies a nostalgia for the linguistic and cultural differences of tribal Russian provinces where individuals worked, learned, and played within the same circle of agrarian life. Foucault's work, on the other hand, represents urban malaise; his rhetoric points to the fundamental condition of contemporary human existence: its compartmental-ization into institutions with individual discourses and codes of behavior (library, school, home for the aging, shopping mall). While Foucault supported revolution in the Paris riots of May 1968, his later concept of an "aesthetic of existence" is not a revolutionary or heteroglossic entity, because encounters between subjects are, in Foucault's conception, always contests of power, one will attempting to subvert or coerce another.

To avoid this dangerous consequence of power/knowledge, the individual must develop a strong *ethos*. In Bakhtin's work, an *ethos* occurs in response to the standard discourses of a discipline and also in relation to other speakers:

> Thus, all read and integral understanding is actively responsive . . . And the speaker himself is oriented precisely toward such an actively responsive un-derstanding. He does not expect passive understanding that, so to speak, only duplicates his own idea in someone else's mind. Rather, he expects response, agreement, sympathy, objection, execution, and so forth (various speech genres presuppose various integral orientations and speech plans on the part of the speakers or writers). (1986, 69)

At its most enterprising and subtle extreme, the speech genres that con-tribute to the discourse of English have required a sensitivity to paradox and irony and an acquaintance with the research methods, gentlemanly argumen-tative gestures, concessions, and acknowledgments of professional discourse; most of these gestures are hallmarks of the New Critical school of interpreta-tion. Contemporary critical languages, however, are alienating for undergradu-ate students. Whereas undergraduates could at least acquire a documentary knowledge of the prevailing *topos* of the discipline by surveying a full length of shelving pertaining to William Shakespeare and his plays (albeit a servile gesture), critical theory resists such assimilation. There is even more at stake. My own teaching of critical theory leads me to believe that the transformation of students into "disciplined" selves has demanded a sudden and severe isola-tion from their own habits, customs, and traditions: comforts of the past that include gluttonous weekend romance fiction binges and religious devotions to Dickens at Christmas. Too often, as theory enters the profession, the students' tradition is postulated through the gestures of theory itself as an encumbrance, something to objectify through Marxism as "inauthentic," something to cri-tique and renounce. Such a unified disciplinary impulse to objectify the student's untutored past poses a danger to the students' conception of self. If "everything is dangerous," as Foucault comments in "On the Genealogy of Ethics" (1983, 232), an individual's act must be assessed in terms of the strength of its response to technologies of power/knowledge. Learning to read critical theory requires a strengthening of self, the construction of an aesthetic of existence.

Currently, introducing undergraduate students to modern criticism or critical theory acquaints them with the discipline necessary to be a professional in English, because theory represents the prevailing concerns of the whole discipline. For students, this is a radically new terrain lacking familiar place names. There are new canons, new assumptions about human relations and the nature of the self, and conflict and nihilism at the core. Critical theory, having flirted with cultural crisis and having been feared as revolutionary, is now settled into the English major as a nontoxic core requirement, the result of curriculum revisions sponsored by the Modern Language Association and the Fund for the Improvement of Postsecondary Education that began the wider national incentive to rework the English major.[2] As a consequence, my discussion of ethics and theory considers not so much whether teachers have a responsibility to the profession to teach theory (that battle has been fought and won by the theorists), but what it means for students to establish a space within that discourse, an ethical position: an ethics of self. I believe it is imperative that we continue to argue for theory with undergraduate students, drawing attention to the need for their own discipline and foreshadowing for them the disorienting nature of this powerful professional discourse. I believe as well that it is essential to argue among ourselves about the consequences of working with critical theory in the undergraduate classroom—a disarming instance of power/knowledge.

When I reflect on the significance of the dream that inaugurated my entry into the professional world, I realize that it expressed what I could not put into words at the time, that one's academic position and identity depend on an implied difference from others. In the dream of the professors in wigs, those others were left to wander in the hall outside of the theater. Similarly, the teacher of theory is positioned amid a critique that emerged from contemporary culture, for, from the public point of view, literary criticism and critical theory appear to lack the immediate certainty of literary studies. Literature seems to imply in itself a certain self-evident humanistic good, a rationale for reading and teaching that connects great works within a conversation of mankind. This notion of a universal appeal of literature masks the historical relationship between nationalistic and racial concerns and the definition of literature as a second type of religion, for literary study was connected in the early decades of the twentieth century during the time of war with an ideology that stressed the strengthening of (English and American) national and (white) racial pride; to those ends, literatures from disfavored (non-English and non-American) writers were set outside the canon as ancillary reading.[3] Similarly, criticism appears ancillary, once removed from literature, a metatext, or as one student commented, a "hydra." Poststructuralist play with surface techniques of the text is read as irreverent and alienates readers from truth claims and claims of timeless, universal meanings for the human condition. The excursions of theorists into the body and sexual practices seem, at best, puzzling, and, at worst— to the religious fundamentalists in my classes (of whom there are more than a few)—"filthy." Students enter the theory class with popular biases in mind, a repertoire of the already-said that is gathered from a variety of hostile sources that constitute critics, scholars, and intellectuals as faintly ridiculous—absent-minded or "nutty"—and out of touch with reality. (Of course, the professors of theory have long given up on reality, interpreting what is real as a product of language; this is a concept arcane enough to offer confirmation of those who would find fault with the academy.) Thus students are themselves hostile, resistant to the notion of theory because its relationship to an inherent humanistic good and traditional notions of education seems peripheral. When one student of mine encountered difficult reading, she placed the reading squarely in that category of Otherness that represents irreducible difference: "I just laughed," she said, but the laughter was not her inability to comprehend (a giving-in to the carnival of the absurd moment), but a frustrated wail at the institution that demanded her acquaintance with the text.

Ironically, theory is now authorized discourse in the academy, so the necessity for resistance among the professionals has become a memory slipped into a recess like the virtually fictive recollection that we once owned a pair of platform shoes. Reading through the journal entries that summarize the major tenets of deconstruction, we might wonder: Is it possible that members of the discipline once thought theory was but a fad that would be over by Christmas? That it would set us spinning toward the close of the modern era? Such distant notions seem in themselves *fabula* and thus it is that the need to argue for theory in the classroom is forgotten. However, the disorienting rhetoric and transformative power of theory is life-altering for students, representing their own limited experience. Students approach theory courses with hesitancy and hostility. The process of *becoming*—of crafting an aesthetic of existence within the discipline of English—is as alien as cloaking the self in the robes of the QC. The demanding and intensive study appears a fantastic dream.

Evolving from early modernism, contemporary literary criticism can be positioned as a continuation of contemporary artistic movements resulting from crisis and alienation. Theory has been promised as an apocalypse and feared as the apocalypse, "a place where meaning collapses" (Kristeva 1982, 1–2).[4] Julia Kristeva's discussion of abjection describes the abject as that which is not only Other, but also alien or "stray." Signifying that which cannot be assimilated (food, filth, the repressed consciousness), abjection corresponds also to the physical and mental response of the subject. Literary criticism works in much the same way for students: Not only is it difficult to assimilate at the level of language, but it is also representative of a type of "stray" mode of being. The critic is by choice an ascetic, outside and apparently beyond the discourses of daily affairs. The critic is able to discern fragmented and uncertain realities, and the critic also creates such realities through discourse. Thus, while students seek footholds in comforting critical areas such as biography and authorial intent, they are bombarded by discourse that asks them to position their constructed and selfless authentic selves in a pluralistic and contradictory discursive space: "For the space that engrosses the deject, the excluded, in never *one*, nor *homogeneous*, nor *totalizable*, but essentially divisible, foldable, and catastrophic" (1982, 8). The ethical moment of self-forming for students occurs simultaneously as the student apprehends the apocalyptic nature of theory and foresees a position in it. For the student, fashioning an identity can represent crisis and trauma as traditional modes of experience are abandoned. Foucault describes the ethical as a response to what is dangerous. Diana Fuss speaks of contemporary critical theory as a "contaminant," a post-industrial holocaust (1994, 104). She notes her own need as a teacher to draw on an "arsenal" of arguments to bring theory into favor with resistant students (1994, 107). Violence is suggested as essential to the intellectual revolution that will explode conventional systems of thought. The apocalypse is cast as the necessary limit-experience for the transformative trajectory of criticism. But is it the answer?

Cows in the Meadow

Foucault's notion of an ethical subject directs readers' sympathies toward agents who authorize and discipline themselves. This conception of the aesthetics of self-fashioning is articulated in *The Uses of Pleasure* (1985), the "On the Genealogy of Ethics" (1983), and the collection of lectures anthologized as *Technologies of the Self* (1988) as a process by which an individual defines an ethical subject position relative to particular rules and beliefs, the structures of power/knowledge and discourse that restrict action. In becoming ethical, they will develop a "mode of being that will serve as [a] moral goal" (1985, 12). Arnold Davidson points out that Foucault's concern with ethics derives from his analyses of government and creates a unified ethical concept, "the government of the self by the self" (1994, 119). In the context of Foucault's *oeuvre*, there is a dialogic connection between institutional and self-based ethics. For the self to develop its ethical center, a certain level of consciousness and awareness of social demands is necessary; therefore, implicitly, the self is cast as that which grows, develops, changes, and progresses. Philosophy enters this sociopolitical reality as an *askesis*, "an exercise of oneself in the activity of thought" (Davidson 1994, 123). The philosophical turn does not deny the reality of governmental strictures in the world, but became a way of strengthening the self (*ethos*) to act successfully in the world. According to Foucault,

> In the philosophical tradition dominated by Stoicism, askesis means not renunciation but the progressive consideration of self, or mastery over oneself, obtained not through the renunciation of reality but through the acquisition and assimilation of truth. It has as its final aim not preparation for another reality but access to the reality of this world. (in Martin, Gutman, and Hutton 1988, 35)

Yet, the undergraduates I encounter desire authorization from the outside, especially in such a complex, unfamiliar element as the theory course. A problem for students and teachers alike is that disciplines impose technologies of power/knowledge that oppress, and theory initially appears to give nothing back to the reader but cynicism and fear of apocalypse. The student is quickly dismayed: contemporary criticism is host to a language of relativism. Ironically, the invitation to read and learn criticism leads to the discovery that language cannot be trusted absolutely. If language cannot be relied upon to objectively represent reality, why should anyone be persuaded by the language of theory? Logic must govern the development of the very arguments that dissuade us from logocentrism, yet, logocentrism implies a distrust of logical development. As Christopher Norris sardonically notes in his investigation of ethics and theory, the persuasiveness of critical theory implies "inter-articulated statements, judgments, inferences, and truth-claims" that fall "into the forms of rational argumentation," but gives "merely rhetoric" in return through the pervasive "linguistic turn" in which we are all constructed by and restricted by language (1994, 11). Does critical theory engender a greater responsiveness to situations in the real world through the process of understanding that derives from hermeneutical investigation, or does it dismember sacred texts, calling into question traditionally sanctioned accumulated "knowledge" of texts and interpretations? At the point when the constructed world of great literature is under siege more than knowledge is at stake, the student's identity as one-who-knows-English is being challenged, and the teacher's authority as one-who-represents-literature is challenged as well. The stability of the English department is decentered. As a by-product of the theory revolution, students now conclude that they never knew English at all; that their earlier education was a cheat and a fraud; that they must acquire a host of new terms and concepts that are discomfiting and alien to be considered part of the discipline that they came to love through love of stories. The first undergraduate theory course is a dark night of the soul for students.

Even so, theory places a demand on the reader that cannot be denied or ignored; it necessitates self-authorization through an intense period of self-reflection during which the desire to study literature is tested against the shape of the discipline. Therefore, the teacher must conceive of the classroom as an ethical site in which students develop an identity within the discursive space of the discipline. Ideally, ethics is a response in the dialogic sense of the term, a response to texts, to teachers past and present, to discursive realms of power/ knowledge, without recourse to the more dependent and submissive notion of responsibility to the field or to the canon. In arguing for theory in these postreform days when theory is essential to the undergraduate curriculum, teachers must avoid the tendency to invoke criticism as a hegemony. An oppressive system that identifies participants as passive objects of power does not allow each subject to develop what Foucault terms an "aesthetic of existence." One consequence of acquiring a theoretical voice is silence; another is the newly purchased ability to critique familiar situations, such as the classroom practices and reading lists of other members of the English Department. Theory is thus subversive and dangerous, not only to the student studying it, but also to the relationships within the space of the department. The tension evident at the moment of transformation is similar to the development of "the scholarship boy," the template of educational progress that Richard Rodriguez (1982) borrows from Richard Hoggart, in which the student negotiates the environments of home and classroom, necessarily opposed. Home represents pleasure and "intimacy," while the classroom dialogically reflects the degree to which home is alien to the elite and hierarchical language of theory. Rodriguez recalls his own moment of transformation: "Proudly, I announced—to my family's startled silence—that a teacher had said I was losing all trace of a Spanish accent" (1982, 44). That complicated expression of the student's pride, the family's lack of comprehension, and the institutional reification of the desired self expresses the frustration, resistance, anger, and pleasure that can overcome the student of theory. The popular association of literature with entertainment, set forth in the sixteenth century by Sir Philip Sidney (and which I remember as a test question in eighth grade), actively prevents analysis; it is a passive conception of the reader and the reading process, refusing to acknowledge that readers construct texts and interpretations. Nonetheless, reading for passive delight is a prevalent opposition to the recognition that one actively engages a text in the process of signification. Thus, undergraduate students struggle against the vestigial idea that a reader can separate reading "for fun" and reading "to learn something." Ann Rice is assigned the first category, Roland Barthes the second. Repeatedly, my students return to the notion that it is possible to over-intellectualize literature and diminish enjoyment when politics, sociology, representation, and ideology are foregrounded. And they hope I will provide them with the map to their new existence.

When I was assigned a theory course in my third year of professional teaching as an assistant professor, I absorbed the undergraduates' shock waves of hostility and denial. I suffered then from a naive faith in the inherent quality of goodness, the kind of goodness that is like cod-liver oil: A difficult text repays disciplined attention by transforming thought. I saw myself less as a guide who could assist students on their quest for knowledge and, more, as an overseer of the space of theory itself. I provided the texts and topics of discussion but came to learn that the peculiar nature of theory required me to intervene more in the process of learning. In particular, I needed to learn to argue as a teacher for theory (always and already, as a poststructuralist might say) while retaining a sympathetic alliance with my vestigial self, the person who enjoyed a good mystery on a winter day while under cover of an afghan on my grandmother's couch. It is this vestigial self that I can still call up when I turn the cover of *A Book Lover's Journal*, given to me in my first semester of graduate school. Inscribed on the first page is this reminder to grasp firmly my quickly disappearing authentic self, marked "Christmas 1986": "This journal is to be devoted to the record of thoughts on books read for enjoyment." The significance of this comment lies in the date: 1986 marked the fall that I enrolled in my first critical theory course.

My students emerge from public high schools and parish churches and return on weekends and holidays to families and jobs at the Speedway Gas and Go. They arrive from the farm, the trailer parks, and the small towns in central Wisconsin. One is from the aptly named unincorporated town of Rural. Another goes home on weekends to milk the cows at the family dairy; she takes Robert Scholes' *Protocols of Reading* with her; she includes a snapshot of a cow in her reading journal. J. Hillis Miller describes an ethical moment in reading as something that "faces in two directions" (1986, 4). The position of the student who negotiates critical theory with work on the dairy farm is perhaps the most successful position in which to find oneself, a critical Tess of the D'Urbervilles, seduced by poststructuralism. She suggests that she is equally at home in traditional and progressive milieu, while subtly integrating a critique on the texts and authors under study: Derrida, Sedgwick, Scholes—are they the sacred cows of her critical world?

Labyrinth of the Bibliography

Authorial intention, traditional deference, and poststructural dismissal occupy a large share of the discussions in my theory classes. Students often casually punctuate their interpretive commentary with musings about whether their comments are "correct" or if the author meant something to be read in a certain way. Addressing himself to his peers, one student uncertainly noted that although it was difficult to abandon the idea that writing is "inexorably bound" to an author, it was a necessary concession. In such cases, it is clear that the students are hoping for a *deus ex machina* positioned outside the text in order to verify the text's true meaning. Such authority is usually conferred upon the teacher, but the irony is that the teacher is the very person who has already been transformed into rejecting notions of final authority and who thus points them toward crisis and confusion rather than clarification and determinacy. It is no wonder, then, that one of my students cited Magill's *Masterplots* as a critical source. It promises, "You will *master* these *plots*," even headlines: "MASTER PLOTS!" The choice of Magill's is a conservative choice made by an apprentice, someone positioned outside the assumptions of the hermeneutic circle. The student critic cannot break from the tradition of plot quizzes: the plot is objective, factual, *authentic*.

Critical theory affects not only mastery of a subject, but also the conduct of a classroom. In its decentralizing of power, it calls into question not only the notion of knowledge as that-which-can-be-conferred, but also the authority of the teacher as the one who is capable of yielding transformative information. Often this uncertainty leads to the inability to speak, to represent the self through an authoritative written language in which perception, genre, and discourse are integrated with the self. The result is often a traumatic loss of written voice, for the student is overwhelmed by the powerful negotiation of discursive space by the critics. Like reading literature, reading criticism must

become an act of mimesis, of connecting the self with the text. To be successful as a critic, one must not only set innocent reading aside, but also come to
recognize the codes of academic culture that determine what is possible to say
in academic discourse. To follow the trajectory set forth by Foucault, first the
subject must recognize the extent to which consciousness is determined by the
standards, practices, and discourses of social institutions. Second, the subject
must reflect upon the nature of the demands placed upon the self in order to
eventually develop an *ethos* that in some way articulates "originality" in its
mode of disciplinary expression.

Predominantly, however, criticism is alienating for undergraduates, for its
language and philosophical lineage are not part of the primary intellectual
background in English that students bring to an understanding of the disciplines. The response of the profession has been inadequate. Primarily, works
that treat literary theory in the undergraduate classroom discuss the nuts and
bolts of application, supplying syllabi and reading lists.[5] To teach theory and
to learn theory are ethical acts, yet, too often the political responsibility to the
exigencies of the profession masks the real need to be responsive to the self-
development of the students. In other words, professional rhetoric praises the
ways in which students' attitudes, perceptions, political actions, even creativity, will be *transformed* by critical theory. Transformation then becomes a disciplinary requirement of the field. Wagnerian overtones allude to a blissful
enlightenment that matches no classroom into which I have appeared with
Derrida or Brantlinger under my arm. In the political regime of graduate
school applications and MLA interviews, teaching theory becomes a hegemony. Obviously, critics within English can instantiate that the study of theory
occurs at an historical moment in the discipline when the traditional Western
canon is fragmented into a series of canons that include Western and non-
Western literatures. Together with this deprivileging of particular texts arises
a reconception of the nature of the readers' (the ascetics') role from a preserver
of knowledge and a seeker of truth to a decoder of texts. The question, "Why
teach theory?" has disappeared as a question that has any exigency. The answer to those who have been following along for the last ten or twenty years
is self-evident: A text is a text is a text; literature is text, and criticism is text.
The question reveals the existence of an outside, those who are perhaps unini-
tiated: that generous stretch of populace known as the public, our students, and
even our colleagues. When Diana Fuss notes that theory is an essential practice for "weighting, estimating, deliberating" (1994, 111), a "process" capable
of "transforming thought itself" (1994, 103), she overlooks the fact that *theory
itself* (understood here as a collection of philosophic assumptions about ontol-
ogy, epistemology, and hermeneutics) achieves nothing without the corre-
sponding reflection upon the texts by the reader.

James Miller's biography *The Passion of Michel Foucault* (1993) provides
a partial rendering of the relationship between an ethics of reading and an ethics of self. Philosophy becomes in Foucault's work a limit-experience so se-

ductive that at a particular moment in Foucault's life and a particular moment in history (the time of Vietnam and Cambodia), his relationship to questions of morality and ethics became estranged from public notions of right. Limit-experiences define what is societally acceptable, but Miller notes that when the limit is marked, it creates "the space of a possible transgression." For example, the prohibition against suicide marks boundaries between life and death, but also the threshold of acceptability and transgression, thus enhancing the fascination with death as "an essential risk" (1993, 115). In this milieu, what is "imaginary now resides between the book and the lamp" where the "phenomena of the library" connect the ascetic with a fantastic and "imaginative space." According to Foucault, "To dream it is no longer necessary to close our eyes—only to read. The true image springs from knowledge: that of words spoken in the past, of exact recensions, of masses of detailed information, of infinitesimal fragments of monuments, of reproductions of reproductions" (Miller 1993, 109). Readers may, as Miller points out, notice the connection between Foucault's personification of the library and the dream work of Maurice Blanchot and the surrealists. Blanchot read the dream as an artistic experience, "a premonition of the other," in which the other discovers an aspect of self "from which he cannot turn away, but near which he cannot linger" (Miller 1993, 83). If the imaginary life of the ascetic is located in the library, then the library is reconceived as a space that resists finitude or complete knowledge. Returning to the world of the classroom, I will note that my criticism students dream of a complete bibliography, and this dream has pursued them like a grim specter into despair. The act of reflection upon a text or in the library is necessarily dialogic, but it represents as well a potentially dangerous withdrawal to a labyrinth of textual difficulty. We need to reinstate the question, "Why teach theory?" so that the disturbingly violent and amoral aspects of theory are acknowledged and debated with undergraduates. Obviously, the complications with this wound are greatest at the point of entry: The debate over the ethics and morality of the text must arise at the same time that the (hostile and resisting) undergraduates are being invited into the pleasures of the critical text. Every experience of textual pleasure that arises from reading seductive poststructuralism is equaled by a prolonged moment of pain.

Dead Letter?

Like Foucault's own connection of the inner terrain of the imagination with the labyrinth of the bibliography, the progress of my students describes an ironic process of transformation, for in studying critical theory, they frequently become overarticulated by the very texts they turn to for enlightenment. Transformation by the library of critical texts is a painful series of tests: a test of will, a test of self, a test of reading, a test of tradition in which each moment of reflection was replaced by a self-doubt. Inevitably, at least one of these students moved from student to ascetic; however, she struggled for over a year to write an essay that would be responsive to the debates over poststructuralist theory that she saw emerging in various fields.[6] She suffered into silence, never really recovering a written voice, and had a difficult time resisting the persistent reflex to read another book before commenting on anything in writing. Her intense period of study took on a certain dreamlike quality in itself, an attempt to create a work in Blanchot's sense. Taking as her premise that *apocalyptic* and *poststructuralism* are synonymous, after seven months of deliberation Sharon's first paragraph stabilized into the following introductory sequence:

> Recently a group of scholars gathered to discuss the state of critical theory in the American Academy of Religion. Toward the end of her remarks, one of the panel speakers remarked that if historians needed to check their historical positivism, then contemporary theorists should likewise improve their history. The rather defensive remark reveals the tension in the field brought about due to the crossing of boundaries in different fields of study. (Welch 1996, 1)

Sharon assumes that disciplinary boundaries are somehow essential. From a student's point of view, the "location" of a discipline is important to the entire structure of the institution: advisors, majors, employers, graduate admissions committees. In other words, the institution is a master plot. Thus, "crossing boundaries," although fertile for the imagination, is powerfully discomfiting, representing the limit and the transgression. The tension that she locates in the field is also her own tension in trying to write an essay from multiple perspectives that cross disciplines. Yet, she crowds her text with the bodies of the persons writing in the field (in eight pages there are eleven distinct authors mentioned), writing her essay upon the template of a series of other writers. For a time, she loses her face, echoing Foucault: "Do not ask me who I am, and do not tell me to remain the same. More than one person, like me no doubt, writes in order to have no face" (1972, 17). The essay can be read as a way of convincing herself that blurred boundaries are necessary, which teachers recognize as a debate that has already passed into that closet with the platform shoes. Her identification of the "different" disciplines in the same sentence that asserts the disciplines are blurred maintains that desire for distinction even as the text argues in favor of the erasure of boundaries. Notwithstanding, she is in a powerful position because she can recognize conventional disciplinary boundaries as a rhetoric and acknowledge alternatives. In Sharon's case, the self is positioned *inside* the hermeneutic circle because she can now see the way disciplines are organized. To return to the paradigm of disciplinary ethics suggested by the work of Foucault, it is Sharon's sustained reflection on the organization of disciplines that allows her some freedom from the constraints of those disciplines.

In the midst of this process, Sharon forwarded to me an electronic mail message entitled "Postmodernist Drinking Game."[7] She must have sensed that it expressed not only the Scylla and Charybdis of deconstruction, but also the Gog and Magog of her own indeterminate identity, her positioning in the zone of transformation between authenticity and alterity. Even its message, "Have another drink," calling up as it does college binges and fetal alcohol syndrome, serves as a reminder to avoid a similar irresponsible binge reflex in academics, "Read another book." The message is an integral text in Sharon's own developing ethic. It is a cynical commentary on becoming disciplined, but it is also a message from Sharon, emerging from the No Man's Land of her own critical self-fashioning:

> *Rule One.* If "anyone," at any "time," for any "reason," believes in, supports, or likes a person, place, or idea, it's only because they haven't uncovered the fundamental contradictions underlying it and you are allowed to laugh at them because they are Less Jaded than you.
>
> *Qualification One.* If "everyone" disbelieves in, attacks, or dislikes a person, place, or idea, it's only because they haven't uncovered the fundamental contradictions underlying that disbelief, and you may support that person, place, or idea, and you are allowed to laugh at the other players because they are Less Perceptive than you.
>
> *Corollary.* Have a drink.

The resurgence of ethical issues in the humanities marks the time of change in our society, the end of the century, the point of horizon, the limit, the potential termination. Contemporary culture expresses *angst* at the fragmentation of hegemonic societal institutions that range from the governmental to the everyday: the fragmentation of the church into various Protestant religions, including the religion of self-help; the decentering through school choice of the twentieth-century educational system that separated sacred and secular; the dismembering of the nuclear family; the popularity of homeopathic medicines; the choice from a palette of one hundred stations of which evening television program to watch. The humanities have been faulted for decentering truth claims, for challenging society with a mirror of its own insecurity and then claiming that mirrors do not reflect, but revise. The reinvention of ethics in English expresses the need to reestablish order and understanding to prevent an "apocalypse," but within the discipline there are individuals who are seduced by disciplinary language and who falter at the abyss. And it is to their experience I suggest the discipline focus its attention.

During my last semester as a Ph.D. student, I remarked to my husband as I read Foucault that Foucault seemed "dangerous" somehow, a comment I was at a loss to explain at the time. Today, I am disciplined enough to explain that idea. I believe that I felt that while Foucault's erudition is seductive, one is seduced into the world of madness and dissolution. His writings follow his own troubled philosophical forays into terrorism. Having met Foucault in 1971 at the height of Foucault's antisocial political involvement, Noam Chomsky remembered him as "totally amoral" (Miller 1993, 201). And so my concern extends to students who are fascinated with limit-experiences, enigmas, Foucault and his intimations of death, to those who greet me with tears in their eyes and tell me that if reading means reading Foucault, then they want to give up. Forget graduate school. Forget the Ph.D. and the life in the university.

Poststructuralism did precipitate a crisis in the disciplines and continues to engender a crisis in self, as I have observed. As a response to the problems involved in acquiring challenging, alien discourse, Foucault's concept of asceticism requires individual action.[8] Mikhail Bakhtin's work suggests another alternative, that of collective response: heteroglossia as a response to monoglossia. The community provides the social, contextual understanding and even empathy, anticipating fault lines and providing support for students when they fall into the *lacunae*, which they inevitably do. The community is local—the collective members of departments and students who must commit to working together in a safe space—but it is also broader, encompassing the entire membership in the discipline, who must not only endorse poststructuralist theory but also continue to argue about it (rather than for it) and to study its effects on readers and classrooms. This is not to argue that poststructuralism is a dysfunctional discourse that always already fragments. Jacques Derrida's interrogations of the Western philosophical tradition ground poststructuralism in an inherently logical pattern. Yet, its very nature is to decenter the reader.

The initiation process of professional academic study opens up ethical questions that suggest that the learning process may involve nihilism, doubt, and destructiveness. For students in English, encounters with critical works and the history of ideas are initially encounters without empathy, for the books demand a mode of reading that gives nothing familiar back to the students, no characters with which to identify, no plots to compare to life, no representations to test against experience. At this point, teachers who have passed through the valley of critical writing must empathize with the students' reading processes and intervene at critical moments when there are stresses, faults, and breakdowns, whether there is silence, guilt, or resistance. It is imperative for all teachers of theory—rhetorical, critical, literary—to consider traditional ethical questions even as we consider more avant-garde notions of ethics as an aesthetics of self. What educational actions do we perform and what consequences do those actions engender? If ethics is about how we *should live*, as a field of inquiry it encompasses utopian visions as well as utilitarian philosophies. What is the best life of the mind?[9] Can we judge that a pedagogical action is right by asking if it increases happiness? Should our pedagogical actions be judged based on their compliance with disciplinary rules? What metaphors describe the processes of reading and assimilating critical discourse? Invitation? Mystification? Seduction? Rape? Is it ethical to hope that students will be transformed in some way by critical theory? Is the psychic stress of learning critical theory greater on undergraduates than on graduate students? It is possible that we do need to reinstitute the critical debate on what came to be known in the 1980s as "the resistance to theory"—in itself a transgression of institutional and disciplinary beliefs. I suggest as well a new consideration of relationships, responsibilities, and responsiveness, that we turn to the stories of undergraduate students who are struggling with theoretical concepts and critical practices. Such inquiry would enable us to better judge our own responsiveness to students struggling and to students without voice; such inquiry would turn us away from any potential impulse to transmit the truths of powerful theoretical knowledge.

Notes

1. This discussion of Foucault's life is based on several sources, most notably James Miller's biography, *The Passion of Michel Foucault* , and the four film series written by Bernard-Henri Levy, *Spirit of Freedom: French Intellectuals in the Twentieth Century*. Levy was one of the "new philosophers" in France who declared the death of Marxism and exposed the naiveté of the support of bloody revolution by the older French philosophers. For additional, and perhaps less colorful, biographical information on the life of Foucault, see Didier Eribon, *Michel Foucault*.

2. My own department has recently altered its English major, drawing ideas from discussions with colleagues across the United States who were sponsored by the MLA and FIPSE programs to revise the core curricula for undergraduates. Almost any issue of the MLA's ADE *Bulletin* provides a discussion of what undergraduate and graduate students should know about English studies. For an excellent discussion of the changing space of practice and theory in English studies, see the collection of articles in Greenblatt and Gunn's *Redrawing the Boundaries*.

3. This discussion is based, in part, on the critique of "the rise of English" offered in several standard works: Terry Eagleton's *Literary Theory: An Introduction*, Chris Baldick's *The Social Mission of English Studies, 1848–1932*, Peter Barry's *Beginning Theory* (a text designed for undergraduate readers), and to a lesser extent the final chapter of Terence Hawkes' *That Shakespearean Rag* and David Richter's *Falling into Theory: Conflicting Views on Reading Literature*.

4. The readings in this section were suggested to me by my student Nicole Krier, who often describes poststructuralist theory as the "place where meaning collapses."

5. Again, the MLA offers a text to ease the transition into a new program of undergraduate study: Dianne Sadoff and William Cain's *Teaching Contemporary Theory to Undergraduates*. This book is a collection of twenty-one essays. Like similar volumes in the "Options for Teaching" series, this book offers practical suggestions for introducing primarily poststructuralist critical theory into an undergraduate course.

6. The name *Sharon Welch* is a pseudonym. Sharon deserves recognition in this text for her lucid discussions of poststructuralism and for making me aware of its integral relationship to apocalyptic imagery and discourse. In addition, several other students have contributed to this essay through their insights and commentary, among them Stephen Beers, John Berner, Phil Krause, and Nicole Krier, whom I mentioned earlier. I would like to thank them for their intellectual assistance and moral support, even if this small space does not do justice to their insights.

7. This text can be found on-line at "Everything Postmodern," http://helios.augustana.edu/~gmb/postmodern/ (November 1996).

8. My student Nicole Krier made this observation, as well as observations noted earlier. She contends that too often in academe, students are left to work out difference alone, in the space between the imagination and the book that Foucault describes and that what is needed is a collective response to and an ethical consideration of the effects of particular readings on students.

9. These questions are based on questions raised in Peter Singer's introduction to the collection entitled *Ethics*.

Works Cited

Bakhtin, M. M. 1986. *Speech Genres and Other Late Essays*, ed. C. Emerson and M. Holquist. Trans. V. W. McGee. Austin: University of Texas Press.

Baldick, C. 1983. *The Social Mission of English Studies, 1848–1932*. Oxford: Oxford University Press.

Barry, P. 1996. *Beginning Theory*. Manchester: Manchester University Press.

Davidson, A. 1994. "Ethics as Ascetics: Foucault, the History of Ethics, and Ancient Thought." In *The Cambridge Companion to Michel Foucault*, ed. G. Gutting, 115–40. Cambridge: Cambridge University Press.

Eagleton, T. 1983. *Literary Theory: An Introduction*. Minneapolis, MN: University of Minneapolis Press.

Eribon, D. 1991. *Michel Foucault*. Trans. B. Wing. Cambridge, MA: Harvard University Press.

Foucault, M. 1972. *The Archaeology of Knowledge: Including the Discourse on Language*. Trans. A. Sheridan. New York: Pantheon.

———. 1973. Madness and Civilization: *A History of Insanity in the Age of Reason*. Trans. R. Howard. New York: Vintage.

———. 1983. "On the Genealogy of Ethics: An Overview of Work in Progress." In *Michel Foucault: Beyond Structuralism and Hermeneutics*, ed. H. Dreyfus and P. Rabinow, 229–52. 2d ed. Chicago: University of Chicago Press.

———. 1985. *The Uses of Pleasure*. Vol. 2 of *The History of Sexuality*. Trans. R. Hurley. New York: Pantheon.

———. 1988. *Technologies of the Self: A Seminar with Michel Foucault*, eds. L. H. Martin, H. Gutman, and P. Hutton. Amherst: University of Massachusetts Press.

Fuss, D. 1994. "Accounting for Theory in the Undergraduate Classroom." In *Teaching Contemporary Theory to Undergraduates*, eds. D. Sadoff and W. E. Cain, 103–13. New York: Modern Language Association.

Greenblatt, S., and G. Gunn, eds. 1992. *Redrawing the Boundaries: The Transformation of English and American Literary Studies*. New York: Modern Language Association.

Hawkes, T. 1986. *That Shakespearean Rag*. Manchester: Manchester University Press.

Keller, E. F. 1993. *A Feeling for the Organism: The Life and Work of Barbara McClintock*. New York: W. H. Freeman.

Kristeva, J. 1982. "Approaching Abjection." In *Powers of Horror: An Essay on Abjection*, 1–31. New York: Columbia University Press.

Levy, B. 1992. *Spirit of Freedom: French Intellectuals in the Twentieth Century.* Princeton, NJ: Films for the Humanities, Inc.

Miller, J. 1993. *The Passion of Michel Foucault.* New York: Bantam.

Miller, J. H. 1986. *The Ethics of Reading: Kant, De Man, Eliot, Trollope, James, and Benjamin.* New York: Columbia University Press.

Norris, C. 1994. *Truth and the Ethics of Criticism.* Manchester: Manchester University Press.

Richter, D. H. 1994. *Falling into Theory: Conflicting Views on Reading Literature.* New York: Bedford Books.

Rodriguez, R. 1982. *Hunger of Memory: The Education of Richard Rodriguez.* New York: Bantam.

Sadoff, D. E., and W. E. Cain, eds. 1994. *Teaching Contemporary Theory to Undergraduates.* Options for Teaching 12. New York: Modern Language Association.

Singer, P. 1994. *Ethics.* Oxford: Oxford University Press.

Welch, S. 1996. "The Politics and Apolitics of Apocalyptic Discourse." Unpublished manuscript. University of Wisconsin, Oshkosh.

6

Blurring the Boundaries of Academic Intimacy and Moral Neutrality
What Is the Responsibility of the WPA?

William E. Smith

Many WPAs use autobiography as a curricular focus in their writing classes and programs, firmly believing that personal experience is an appropriate and necessary element in the process of self-creation. Through self-disclosure and self-revelation, students learn to move in both directions between monologic and dialogic discourse, to connect their personal lives to their academic lives, and to recreate themselves in the world by investigating the circumstances that shaped and continue to shape them (Goldschmidt 1994). But recently, in "The Ethics of Requiring Students to Write About Their Personal Lives," Swartzlander, Pace, and Stamler warn us of the dangers of creating writing assignments that require "inappropriate self-revelation" (1993, B1). And in "Collaboration and the Pedagogy of Disclosure," David Bleich calls for a "pedagogy of disclosure" while pointing out the essential difference between disclosure and confession as taking "place respectively in either completely private or public contexts" (1995, 48). Although these writers raise important issues for us to consider, none fully discusses the ethical dilemmas teachers and writing program administrators face when student self-disclosure reveals real or perceived criminal acts.[1]

The Story of an Ethical Struggle

In the last two weeks of Spring Quarter 1994, a young teacher stopped me in the hallway seconds before I entered class and asked me to glance over a paper that disturbed him. Two sentences grabbed my attention: "We killed him executionary (sic) style. I held his arm while he died." The gist of the paper was this: A first-year student from a large city hopes his younger brother will escape neighbor gangs. The writer recounts his own gang initiation, three years prior, when he held down a fourteen-year-old while his two friends stabbed the boy to death. The writer names his accomplices, dates, and addresses. He ends his essay with a statement of remorse, describing how this incident tortures his sleep. The teacher believes the paper is a confession, wonders what to do, and asks me to help him.

The following excerpts from my journal reveal the difficulty we had reaching a decision, because the paths through ethical dilemmas are seldom clearly marked. Perhaps the approach the teaching assistant and I used to make our decision will offer a template for dealing with individual and programmatic responses to pseudo-confessions, dishonesty, and criminal acts.

Day One. Later that day, the teacher contextualizes the paper for me. He fears the paper is a real confession because the student did not share his work with his peer group, nor did he write on a topic related to class discussions. The teacher feels he should do something about this "confession" but worries he will betray his student in the process. Instead, he proposes a neutral stance: comment on isolated textual and stylistic features and dismiss the incident. But his presence in my office belies his proposed solution. Together we brainstorm scenarios describing the conditions under which we would and would not inform the police of a crime.

- Would we inform authorities if a student confessed he had stolen in the distant past a CD from a local mall, an act of vandalism? No.
- Would we inform the police if a student told us he had raped another student last term? Yes.
- Would we inform the police if a student told us he was the arsonist responsible for more than 100 fires in the Seattle area? Yes.

Our solution becomes clearer, but not easier. We agree a senseless gang-related murder far exceeds the bond of a student-teacher relationship. We discuss how parents must feel, not knowing the facts surrounding their child's death. We agree we should inform the police of a "possible murder" and not reveal the student's identity until we can verify the essay's facts. The teacher decides to comment on the paper as an interested reader and ask the student if the content is factual.

After the teacher leaves, I call a crisis counselor at the University Counseling Center and read the paper to him. The counselor does not think the student a danger to his peers, his teacher, or himself. Neither he nor I am willing to assume the paper voices the truth. We preface nearly every comment with "If this is true, then . . . . " The counselor suggests if the paper is a real confession, then the student might be trying in an indirect manner to turn himself in, to square himself with his conscience. Next, I meet with the Department Chair, explain the situation, and propose a plan. We agree I should call the University attorney to report a "possible" confession and obtain advice on what steps to take should the paper reveal actual events rather than fictional ones.

I call the University lawyer and ask for advice. She reprimands me for not calling the police to arrest the student, regardless of whether the incident actually occurred. She also tells me the teacher-student relationship is not a legally privileged one in Washington, nor in most states. Before she dismisses me, she orders me to call the police and have them arrest the student during his English 101 class tomorrow.

I call a campus police officer, who asks numerous questions, requests I read the paper to him, and suggests possible scenarios for the confession. His scenarios are similar to the ones suggested by the crisis counselor. He recommends doing nothing until after the Memorial Day weekend. Like the counselor, he feels the student is not a threat to anyone. He also wants to conduct an investigation before arresting the student. He plans to fax the information I have given him to the police department in the city where the alleged murder occurred, asking a homicide unit to investigate. The officer asks me for the student's name and the name of the instructor. I refuse to reveal either identity until I have had more time to think, and he has had more time to investigate. I give him names of gang members, addresses, and dates—details from the essay. The police officer thanks me and says my refusal is a reasonable act at this time. The officer suggests that if I feel unethical revealing the content of a student paper, I should use the weekend to talk my feelings over with other professionals.

Day Two. The teacher returns the graded paper to the student, with comments inquiring about the authenticity of the details. He asks the student after class if he wants to talk about the paper or if he needs to talk with someone else about it. The student says "No," and hurries away.

Over the weekend I skim back issues of the NCTE *Council Chronicle*, remembering a reference to the NCTE Code of Ethics Committee. I conduct an ERIC search to see if other WPAs have written of experiences in similar situations. I skim through the NCTE book, *Scenarios for Teaching Writing* (Anson *et al.*, 1993). I skim over our library's holdings of educational documents such as *Legal Notes for Education, Education Law,* and *NOLPE* (the National Organization on Legal Problems in Education), looking for similar recent educational court rulings. Most of the issues raised in the literature deal with professional ethics of the classroom, the role of teachers in labor and contractual disputes, plagiarism, classroom behavior, and censorship. The Code of Ethics in my University Catalogue does not help much either, referring primarily to free speech, establishing a harmonious academic community, and veiled allusions to maintaining students' privacy through their works. I am not even sure what we're looking for, but I still feel a deep indefinable uneasiness about my role in this process.

On Sunday, I become painfully aware of how little I know about our legal system, police procedures, and my own rights as a citizen. I have literally dozens of questions, but do not have the energy or the self-discipline to talk with the university lawyer again.

Day Three. When I return to campus, I call NCTE Headquarters to speak with someone on the Code of Ethics Committee about the ethics of privilege and disclosure. The switchboard operator connects me to the Deputy Director. For nearly thirty minutes he and I discuss the situation. He agrees that this student's confession is on a higher ethical and moral level than the acts of plagiarism and professional conduct the Council usually deals with. He sympathizes, and feels, at least for him, there is no professional or ethical problem in informing the police. He cautions that I protect both the teacher and myself from future retaliation. He also asks me to keep him informed about the situation.

After this conversation, I know I am simply searching for confirmation or approval of what I am going to do anyway. I am covering moral and ethical bases, searching for support for solutions to my own *crise de conscience.* I also fear I am seeking a scapegoat on which to blame my decision rather than seeking a sympathetic ear or another professional's insights. I feel sheepish because I remember a group of teaching assistants who knocked at my door during the start of the Gulf War and asked me for the Composition program's official stance on the war. I responded that I could tell them only how I felt about the war and that our program could not make moral decisions for them, but I would help them locate materials for class use and devote time in the upcoming staff meeting to an open forum on incorporating reactions to the war into their classes.

After class, the teaching assistant again asks his student if he would like to talk to someone about the paper. The student replies that he has told only two other people about his paper, a friend at home and one on campus, and says, "I can handle it." The teacher now worries that the events in the paper are factual because he has given the student two opportunities in four days to deny the content of the paper or to seek professional help.

Day Four. The teacher is very concerned about turning the paper over to the police. He feels he has betrayed his student. For an hour, we discuss ways of accommodating our feelings of civic responsibility with our personal feelings of student betrayal. The teacher concludes that he still wants to inform the student of his role in this process.

We call campus police. The teacher discusses his reservations with the officer, who assures him nothing will happen to his student should the results of the investigation prove groundless. He also tells the young teacher he will not be liable for prosecution if his student flees after their conversation. He suggests that the teacher do only what he feels comfortable doing. Within the hour, having obtained the teacher's permission, I fax a copy of the paper with the student's name on it to the campus police, who agree not to reveal his identity to off-campus police, unless the investigation merits otherwise.

Day Five. After meeting with a campus counselor to discuss his role in this process, the teacher drops by to inform me he will explain everything to his student the next time he sees him.

Day Six. On Friday, a campus officer updates me on the investigation. According to the neighboring city's police department, many of the facts in the essay are verifiable. Both teens mentioned in the essay, now in their early twenties, head powerful rival gangs responsible for hundreds of crimes, ranging from armed robberies to drug smuggling to suspected murder. The police have not yet been able to detain them for more than a week or two at a time. Moreover, the criminal record of the student writer is hardly more than what the previous generation would have deemed "youthful pranks." Even so, they think the student's information might very well be the information they need to arrest the gang leaders. Off-campus police want to interrogate the student before the term ends; campus police recommend that the investigation continue and the student be questioned at his home during the summer rather than on campus during finals. Campus police still honor my request and do not reveal the student's name to other agencies.

Day Seven. It is Monday and the student cuts class again today. He has not been in class since Thursday.

Day Eight. After class, the teacher informs his student that he gave the paper to me, and I turned it over to the campus police. He advises the student to seek professional help. The student becomes agitated, admits he fictionalized the event, basing it on newspaper articles and one popular book on gangs. His anger increases, and he leaves. Thirty minutes later, he returns to his teacher and reports he has called home to tell his mother what he had written and how the Director of Composition had responded. His mother rebukes him, saying, "What did you expect when you wrote what you did. I'm surprised they don't kick you out of school."

Day Nine. The student calls the Department Chair, confusing the positions of Chair and Director of Composition, identifies himself, and vents his anger at the Chair. When he realizes he is talking to the wrong person, he apologizes and hangs up.

The police call to tell me there were no unsolved murders for the entire month in question anywhere near the location mentioned in the student's essay. I feel relieved. The police will, however, continue their investigation for another week or two. The campus police officer reassures me that the student's name has not been released to off-campus authorities or to anyone else on campus. Only I, the teacher, the police officer, and now the Department Chair, know the student's identity.

Day Ten. The student calls me, angrily accuses me of violating his rights, and sputters, "You had no right to send my paper to the police." I listen to him, and when he calms down, explain the difficult position in which he placed us—himself, his teacher, and me—with his paper. I ask him to tell me about the paper. He explains how he wrote it, borrowing details from local legend, newspapers, and a recent popular book on gangs. He wrote the paper as a real experience because he thought his teacher liked that kind of writing. He did not cite sources because he did not use quotes.

I explain my rationale for turning the paper over to the police only after he had acted evasively and cut class, implying to his teacher that the experience was factual. Furthermore, I explain that we thought he was trying to turn himself in, that we read his paper as a confession, a cry for help, and that we even thought he wanted to be arrested. I also mention that we were not sure initially whether his teacher would be an accomplice if he kept quiet and the event was later found to be real.

I suggest some ways he could prevent himself from being taken so seriously in the future, especially when he did not intend it. We discuss the responsibility writers must take for their works, the relationships between writers and audiences. I give him the name of the campus police officer who heads the investigation and summarize the results of the investigation. I suggest that if his story is factual in any personal sense, he call his parents, hire a lawyer, and turn himself in to the campus police. If his essay is fictional, he should inform his parents that over the summer police from his hometown might question him about the details of the paper he wrote. As our talk concludes, the student asks me to call the police for him and to explain that the experience was fictional, and that he had written the paper to impress his teacher. I promised him I would do so. A few minutes later, I recount the gist of our conversation to the campus police.

Fortunately, this story has a happy ending. But the event and my role in it disturbs me greatly. I wonder if I acted too quickly, prompted by the closing of the school year, or if I fell victim to popular buzz words, such as *gang*. Or if my response was an engendered male response calling for immediate action, as if the solution to a complex problem were mine to determine. I wonder why I felt obligated to gather more factual information before I acted, and why in the process I was so prone to shift my initial analysis of the paper from male posturing to horrible fact. I hope my personal belief in the sanctity of life overrode these more expedient pragmatic rationales.

Pseudoprivate Discourse

I also believe that this student's "confession" is not an isolated event, but one representative of a host of emerging discourse patterns that exist in the new spaces created by postmodernism and our changing perspectives on the traditional notions of "private/public." This student's "pseudo-confession" reflects a different configuration of the relationship between speaker and audience and of the kinds of movement possible between monologic and dialogic discourse, a configuration of which WPAs should be aware.

According to Jurgen Habermas, in democratic cultures the public sphere is "a discursive domain where private individuals, without the authority of state office, debate the general conduct of social and political business, holding official bodies accountable at the bar of reason" (Wells 1996, 327).[2] Confession as monologic discourse may open itself to public discussion, but it does so on the locutor's own terms. Unlike apologies, which also occur after an act, confessions serve the private confessor, not the group, excluding dialogic interaction, reflection, reconfiguration, and movement towards a new solution.

The media and information technology are implicated in the creation of this "pseudoprivate" space, which occurs whenever the media portrays the intensely private in a public context. Live talk shows such as *Rikki Lake, Oprah, Jerry Springer, Montel Williams*, and *Sally Jesse Raphael*, nurture this discourse whenever they bring confrontational audiences together in public spaces designed chiefly for entertainment. Often audience members voice in rapid fire succession their private opinions about the actions of an individual or a panel of people willing to air their private, intimate lives simultaneously before a live audience within a specifically defined public space and an unseen passive audience of television viewers. In McLuhanesque terms, the lure of instant celebrity validates this newly configured space. Because much of the discourse is confessional or sensational, the audience can offer only limited feedback, most often pronouncements of censure or praise that cannot affect the actions of the speakers.

Richard Sennett, in *The Fall of Public Man* (1977), provides a further explanation for the popularity of confession when he says we are currently shifting our sympathies from the public to the private person.[3] This shift, predicated on an intimate view of social reality, values "personality" and devalues and distrusts the impersonal by rejecting social conventions now viewed as barriers between people. For Sennett, the individual displaces *res publica*, and the intimate becomes a goal as well as a basis for social and political action. Ironically, people become tyrannized by intimacy: "The expectation is that when relations are close, they are warm; it is an intense kind of sociability which people seek out in attempting to remove the barriers to intimate contact, but this expectation is defeated by the act. The closer people come, the less sociable, the more painful, the more fratricidal their relations" (1977, 338). According to Sennett, the power of self-distancing, of separating oneself from others, of separating the private from the public, through the use of social conventions prevents us from the self-distortion that derives from self-absorption. When we become too focused on the personal, too self-absorbed, we erase the boundaries between ourselves and others and begin to view the "other" as an extension of the self, thereby diminishing the "other" until it becomes meaningless (1977, 325). The public notion of civility implies a necessary distance between speakers and audiences.

This historical shift from the public to the private also reflects a cultural narcissism that redefines the "other" as the self and prevents socialization leading to public action. This historical shift has little to do with the cognitive act of metonymization, which occurs as individuals personalize complex abstract issues for clearer understanding.[4] When we reduce the complexities of U. S. foreign policy in Bosnia to the less complex sign of the same thing, an argument between Bill Clinton and Robert Dole, we do so for personal understanding. We use this cognitive strategy to negotiate a circular journey from public to private and back again to public. At this point, we have numerous options to take: We can vote for either politician, join some kind of voter protest (demonstration or letter-writing campaign), or do nothing. If, according to Geoffrey Harpham (1995), we choose to act, then our action would be a moral one, an act that assumes a personal principle of responsibility.[5] For Harpham, morality, then, is the "'rigor' of ethical thought, where the rubber of a definitive principle meets the road of reality" (1995, 397). By de-emphasizing the role of acting on one's principles, a narcissistic society based on intimacy sees little or no reason to assume responsibility for its actions. Members of an intimate society focus on motivation, feeling, and intent, rather than action, accomplishments, and knowledge. Consequently, students who confess crimes, real or imagined, might actually expect their audiences to do nothing because they themselves would not act.

Perhaps this feeling of intimacy explains why when confronted with acts of dishonesty—such as plagiarism, submitting a roommate's essay as one's own, or confessing to an imaginary crime—students often seem relieved at confessing their motives for their act, but are genuinely surprised and angered at the institution's conventional penalty system and at their having to take responsibility for their actions. Most likely, this emphasis on motivation is the reason why our student was so surprised when I turned his paper over to campus police and why he reacted so violently to my department chair and me.

Perhaps, too, this same feeling of intimacy implicated both the teaching assistant and me, who saw ourselves in the student's dilemma. One explanation for the teacher's initial plan to withhold comment on the essay reflects how widespread and debilitating the values of an intimate society can be, extending from student to teacher to administrator. In retrospect, I believe our numerous meetings and continuous dialogues were an attempt to break out of the passivity of the intimate and create barriers that distanced us from him so that we could act in a responsible manner.

Without the crucial element of distance between ourselves and others in the public sphere, we burden others with ourselves and we de-emphasize the importance of the differences between our "sentiments and impulses" and those of our audiences (Sennett 1977, 265). An intimate society creates the illusion of equality—that speakers and audiences hold the same motivations and values. An intimate society values feelings over actions, which ultimately devalues responsibility and interaction between speakers and audiences. For all purposes, the "pseudoprivate" speakers assume passive audiences that make no demands on them, because, after all, the audience is just an extension and reflection of their feelings and motivations.[6]

The Media's Role in Pseudoprivate Discourse

William Nothstine, in *Critical Questions: Invention, Creativity, and the Criticism of Discourse and the Media*, implicates electronic media in the creation of the pseudoprivate and believes we do not appreciate the pervasiveness of the pseudoprivate in our culture in part because we "continue to think in language that has not kept pace with change" (1994, 241). Since electronic media frees speakers and audiences from the constraints of a specific physical site (a forum, a lecture hall, a home), *private* and *public* now function as metaphors for *location* rather than as predictors of the roles and personas that individuals assume when they enter that space. We still use the terms *private* and *public* as if they point to the concrete, physical space simultaneously occupied by speakers and audiences, as if these words still carry their associative power to clarify and define roles and modes of anticipated behavior in a specific spatial environment. Electronic media blur the boundaries formerly associated with real sites and expressed as popular commonplaces such as "home and office" or "private and public." The new media, which allow people to occupy two sites simultaneously—that is, watching the Macy's Thanksgiving Parade in the comfort of their living rooms while wearing pajamas—deconstructs the traditional concept of "private/public" and dislocates communicative roles from physical space (Nothstine 1994, 242).

This new space, "the pseudoprivate," allows the speaker to operate within a new set of binary oppositions that reflect current mass cultural value systems. Traditional dichotomies, such as "formal/informal," "subjective/objective," and "public/private," give way to hybrid dichotomies that paradoxically contain hybridizations of the old and new. For example, the current emphasis on "intimacy" shifts the meaning of private in the former opposition, yielding new binaries based on the illusion of intimacy. "Private/public" becomes "genuine/public," "authentic/public," "spontaneous/public," or "off-the-record/public." At the same time, the speaker, freed from the limitations of location and its traditional linguistic commonplaces, can now present "the appearance of private action through the public media," thus making the pseudoprivate a rhetorical reality (Nothstine 1994, 242).

Like other discourses, the "pseudoprivate" display has identifiable elements: a revelatory candid, narrative structure and framing cues or phrases that locate the discourse for a knowledgeable audience. For example, the pseudo-private focuses on what appears to be private (authentic or intimate), drawing its power from its revelatory nature; the audience feels as if it is learning something it really should not know (243). And as Bleich and Wells point out, discourse like that of our student's "pseudo-confession" prohibits interchange and debate. This kind of discourse remains immersed in the monologic, failing to engage others in the dialogic or reflection when the self is seen as "other."[7]

Framing cues are "the means by which the dislocation of public and private is accomplished" (Nothstine 1994, 243). In the case presented here, our student's confessional tone situated his essay within the realm of private discourse, even though his essay was to be submitted for public response by his peers and teacher. Later, the student's non-verbal cues, such as walking away, cutting class, and deflecting his teacher's questions, helped convey the "private" illusion of the writing and a distrust of others.

At the end of his discussion of the pseudoprivate, Nothstine concludes, "So long as we cannot rethink the relationship within which our expectations about 'public' and 'private' now stand with respect to contemporary communicative practice, adequate standards for acting and judging in our communicative world will continue to elude us" (1994, 254). Reading future students' discourses will become problematic for the reader who expects the traditional "private/public"-based discourse and instead encounters this hybrid "intimate/ public" or "pseudoprivate" discourse.

Implications for the WPA

It is more than possible that my reaction to the student's pseudo-confession was a serious misreading, that his paper was a site of conflicting ideologies between us. Perhaps he had unconsciously imitated pseudoprivate models of mass culture—talk shows, pseudo-documentaries, personality-focused news programs, and popular intimate celebrity interviews—and both his instructor and I failed to "see" his discourse strategies because we were blinded by traditional models. Or perhaps we overvalued the dialogic to the extent that we failed to see the student's evasions as signals that his paper was indeed a fictional account, not a factual one.

It is also possible that the instructor and I, implicated in an academic culture of intimacy, saw ourselves in the student's dilemma. In Sennett's terms, we initially failed to see that distance from one another is necessary for responsible social action; in short, we subscribed to an "illusion of equality" based on intimacy, an illusion our writing program encourages for both students and staff. One explanation for the instructor's initial plan to offer "safe" comments on the essay suggests a passive response to an ethical situation demanding moral action. In retrospect, I believe our numerous meetings and continuous dialogues were an attempt to clarify the blurred boundaries of "pseudoprivate" discourse and to relocate those social barriers that distanced us from the student so that we could act in a responsible manner.

In all likelihood, our writing program itself became a nutrient for the "pseudoprivate." After all, our writing classes are small and intimate in comparison to large undergraduate lecture classes. We encourage and praise "honest, strong voices," writing in different persona, autobiography, journal writing, expressive writing, collaboration, and reflection—often under the aegis of neutral "risk-free" environments. We struggle with our students to create classrooms where they can discover their own spaces and create new images of themselves. We redraw boundaries, shift loci of power, and strive to make unheard voices resonate in our classrooms. Because we create environments in which students may conflate academic intimacy with moral neutrality, we WPAs—as privileged readers—should not be surprised at our own confusion when we confront a real life dilemma with life-altering solutions or when we encounter students who represent themselves in naive ways. Even if we stress the writer's responsibility in written communication by clarifying the concepts of civic responsibility and stressing the importance of dialogic interaction, we will encounter students like the one described in this essay, who will confess real or imaginary crimes to us and expect us to do nothing about them.

While this case shows how blurring boundaries among realms of discourse can confuse students and their teachers, WPAs can help them understand their roles in public arenas and the responsibilities they assume when they enter those spaces. Unless we train ourselves and our writing faculties to view our own actions and choices against larger historical, social, and cultural frameworks, we will not be able to make difficult ethical decisions that often affect our students' lives. Underlying our ethical choices is a sense of community and a sense of differences that coexist within that community. We can show our students how institutions and ideologies limit their freedom, how they create and are created by forces that shape their identities and roles in their community. Like them, we, too, live in a society of competing discourses, where pragmatics and idealism collide, and where, ultimately, none of us can remain comfortable as a passive, neutral audience.

Acknowledgment

I would like to thank Donna Qualley for her insightful comments on an earlier draft of this chapter.

Notes

1. I use *ethics* and *morals* interchangeably, following R. Johannesen's usage of the terms in "Ethics," in *Encyclopedia of Rhetoric and Composition: Communication from Ancient Times to the Information Age*. Johannesen also defines *ethics* as involving "degrees of right and wrong, of virtue and vice, and of obligation in human conduct" (235). Also see A. Jagar's sub-section "Current Concerns in Feminist Ethics" (367–70), under "Feminist Ethics" in the *Encyclopedia of Rhetoric and Composition*. Jagar critiques Enlightenment moral theory from a variety of feminist perspectives.

2. In "Rogue Cops and Health Care: What Do We Want from Public Writing?" Wells explains the contradictory nature of Habermas' public sphere and points out that

his "public discourse is a complex array of discursive practices . . . historically situated and contested" (327–29).

3. Sennett's book is an in-depth study of the changes in the public domain in Western culture. His last chapter, "The Actor Deprived of His Art," has specific application to this case.

4. For a detailed discussion of metonymization and personalization in ethical decision making, see Chapter Five, "Paradoxes of Personalization: Race Relations in Milwaukee," 155–78 of B. Brummett's *Rhetoric in Popular Culture.*

5. Harpham argues, "Ethics is the arena in which the claims of otherness—the moral law, the human other, cultural norms, the Good in itself—are articulated and negotiated" (394). What concerns me is how students and teachers value and negotiate "the claims of otherness" within private, public, and private/public spaces.

6. For a discussion of "objectification," a rhetorical coping strategy based on a model of Cartesian dualities in which students posit "objective categories like separate spheres (the public realms for men, the private realm for women)" (17), see K. Fitts and A. France, "Advocacy and Resistance in the Writing Class: Working Toward Stasis," in P. A. Sullivan and D. J. Qualley, eds., *Pedagogy in the Age of Politics.*

7. See D. Qualley, *Turns of Thought: Teaching Composition as Reflexive Inquiry,* (1997), Portsmouth, NH: Heineman/Boynton-Cook. In Chapter One, Qualley explains how, in a reflexive frame of mind, a writer often returns to a point where she views her previous self as an "other."

Works Cited

Anson, C., *et al.* 1993. *Scenarios for Teaching Writing: Contexts for Discussion and Reflective Practice.* Urbana, IL: NCTE.

Brummett, B. 1994. *Rhetoric in Popular Culture.* New York: St. Martin's Press.

Bleich, D. 1995. "Collaboration and the Pedagogy of Disclosure." *College English* 57: 43–61.

Fitts, K., and A. France. 1994. "Advocacy and Resistance in the Writing Class: Working Toward Stasis." In *Pedagogy in the Age of Politics,* ed. P. A. Sullivan and D. J. Qualley, 13–24. Urbana, IL: NCTE.

Goldschmidt, M. 1994. "Self-Disclosure or Self-Creation? The Ethics of Using Autobiography in the Composition Classroom." *CEA Critic* 57: 98–110.

Harpham, G. G. "Ethics." 1995. In *Critical Terms for Literary Study,* 2d ed., ed. F. Lentricchia and T. McLaughlin, 387–405. Chicago: University of Chicago Press.

Jagar, A. 1996. "Feminist Ethics." In *Encyclopedia of Rhetoric and Composition: Communication from Ancient Times to the Information Age,* ed. T. Enos, 367–70. New York: Garland.

Johannesen, R. 1996. "Ethics." In *Encyclopedia of Rhetoric and Composition: Communication from Ancient Times to the Information Age,* ed. T. Enos, 235–39. New York: Garland.

Nothstine, W. L. 1994. "Pseudo-Private and the PTL Ministry Scandal." In *Critical Questions: Invention, Creativity, and the Criticism of Discourse and the Media,* ed. W. L. Nothstine, C. Blair, and G. Copeland, 238–57. New York: St. Martin's Press.

Qualley, D. 1997. *Turns of Thought: Teaching Composition as Reflexive Inquiry*. Portsmouth, NH: Heinemann/Boynton-Cook. 1997.

Sennett, R. 1977. *The Fall of Public Man*. New York: Alfred Knopf.

Swartzlander, S., D. Pace, and V. L. Stamler. 1993. "The Ethics of Requiring Students to Write About Their Personal Lives." *Chronicle of Higher Education* 17 February: B1-2.

Wells, S. 1996. "Rogue Cops and Health Care: What Do We Want from Public Writing?" *College Composition and Communication* 47: 325–41.

7

Revising Administrative Models and Questioning the Value of Appointing Graduate Student WPAs

Sheryl I. Fontaine

The Evolution of Graduate Student WPA Positions

With increasing frequency, graduate students in both master's and doctoral programs are offered the opportunity to apply for positions as writing program administrators (WPAs) in their departments. Graduate Student Writing Program Administrator (GSWPA) positions are temporary, training positions, usually understood to be part of students' academic preparation. They may be part of a writing center, writing program, writing-across-the-curriculum (WAC) program, or a combination of these. Often students are hired into the positions after having acquired a few semesters or a few years of experience working as teaching assistants or writing center tutors (Long, Holberg, and Taylor 1996; Pemberton 1993; Thomas 1991).

The increased number and popularity of these positions is, in part, a response to the current academic job market and English Departments' commitment to graduate student preparation. According to recent accounts, odds are high that individuals hired as Rhetoric and Composition specialists, will be, at some time in their career, expected to take on administrative responsibilities in the department. Graduate programs recognize the need for including administration somewhere in their curriculum as a way to make students more employable and better prepared.

The increased use of GSWPAs also occurs at the same time that faculty WPA positions have become more demanding. Both the *MLA Job List* and personal experience indicate how diverse and far-reaching the responsibilities of many WPA positions have become. It is not at all uncommon for an individual WPA to be expected to direct a writing program, supervise a writing center, and coordinate a WAC program (Janangelo 1991). And these administrative responsibilities are often assigned to faculty *in addition* to teaching and do not in any way diminish the necessity for individual administrators to remain professionally active. In an attempt to meet all of their departmental obligations and to provide an apparently valuable experience, many faculty WPAs, myself included, enlist the help of capable graduate students as GSWPAs.

The greatest value attributed to GSWPA positions by those who have been graduate student writing center coordinators or writing program co-directors is that this hands-on experience provides a crystal clear window into the job that will be expected of them as new faculty WPAs and has, indeed, helped ease the transition from student to faculty WPAs (Friend 1996; Long, Holberg, and Taylor 1996; Young 1993). Students report that until they were actually given the responsibility of meeting with dissatisfied students, scheduling classes or tutors' hours, holding faculty development workshops, and so on, they were not fully aware of the challenges of these tasks.

Considering the Practice Through an Ethical Lens

Yet, while there is some apparent value for those students who hold these positions, the practice takes on a less positive hue when we consider it from an ethical perspective, in terms of the values and obligations it promotes. What we find is that these values are in obvious conflict with those most central to those of contemporary composition pedagogy and theory and toward which most of us aspire.

Shifting particular responsibilities and titles from faculty to students can never be a value-free act. In reassigning administrative responsibilities and designations to individuals of lower rank or status, there is, necessarily, a concurrent reassignment of values and obligations. When a task that was once completed by a full-time faculty member is reassigned to a graduate student, the importance of the task has diminished in the minds of those who make the assignment. Furthermore, the obligation that is to be met in the completion of the task must also have changed.

Consider, for example, the administrative task of meeting with students enrolled in writing courses about grade disputes. By reassigning this task to a GSWPA, the importance of meeting with these disgruntled students has been reduced to a certain extent. Students' concerns now warrant attention by individuals with less authority and institutional power than the faculty administrator who once conferred with them. And the obligation that had precipitated such meetings in the first place has also changed—faculty are no longer directly obligated to the disputing students; now, their obligation is mediated through the lower-ranking graduate students. The ultimate impression created by this particular task reassignment is that students' complaints are considered to be less important than they once were.

Negative Values Promoted
by Creating GSWPA Positions

Beyond this general shifting of values that occurs, the practice of delegating administrative work to select graduate students has the strong potential to foster a set of values that is inconsistent with those expressed through the literature of the discipline and through our own professional practices. These conflicting values include disrespect, unnecessary competition, deception, exploitation, and the significance of the individual over the group, the job over the intellectual work.

Current and past GSWPAs report that many graduate students, particularly those who already operate from a sense of self-interest, are unwilling to respect supervision by their peers (Brooks 1993; Friend 1996). For those teaching assistants or tutors who attend staff development functions only because they are required to or whose central motivation for arriving in class or the writing center on time is to increase their chances of being rehired, or who believe that they can learn little if anything from their peers, being accountable to another graduate student is very difficult. As a result, workshops offered by GSWPAs may not be as well attended as those offered by faculty WPAs, policies not as carefully adhered to, or daily procedures as adequately followed.

Christy Friend, a past GSWPA from the University of Texas at Austin, recommends that faculty stay in close contact with the GSWPA, providing some backbone to the policies and requests (1996, 5). While this strategy makes sense and would certainly be reassuring for the GSWPA, it can also add to an already divisive situation. Graduate students can become suspicious of one another, seeing those with administrative appointments as "narcs" who will report untoward behavior to the advising faculty member. In this scenario, the GSWPA works, not from a basis of authority, but from the unearned power that comes from having a pipeline to more powerful faculty members. Though programs may work diligently to dispel this attitude, it is, in fact, very difficult for graduate programs, especially at the master's level, to provide enough time and peer contact for GSWPAs to establish themselves as authorities among their peers and, consequently, to earn their respect.

Keep in mind that the authority graduate students establish with faculty is not comparable to that which they establish with one another. The evaluations faculty make of students when they hire them as GSWPAs are based not only on more available information than students have about one another (seminar papers, conferences, discussions with other faculty, an interview and application, etc.), but also on the particular ethos that exists between faculty and student. Students "perform" for faculty in ways that they do not for their peers. In addition, faculty and student perceptions differ. What a faculty member admires as a student's sense of responsibility and commitment to the profession, fellow graduate students may see as "bootlicking" and pretentiousness.

Even if departments carefully outline the requirements of the GSWPA positions and the ways in which selected students meet these requirements, the competitive nature of the selection process is likely to undermine attempts to diffuse feelings of anger and disrespect. Most probably, someone who did not receive a GSWPA appointment will be expected to work under the supervision of those who did. Unlike jobs students will eventually compete for when they graduate, this one requires that those not selected work *with* those who were selected, but also *for* them.

The negative values that are fostered by GSWPA positions exist beyond student-to-student relationships, infecting student and faculty relations with dishonesty and deception. Faculty who have served as WPAs know quite well the way in which the job spills beyond its neatly defined borders. Information as concrete as Crossley's description of Wendy Bishop's daily administrative activity (Bishop and Crossley 1996) and as broad as the *Guidelines for Writing Program Administrator Positions* (1992) indicates both the amorphous nature and the immensity of administration. Disheartenment resounds in journal articles, conference papers, and professional conversations—the expectations are far too often incommensurate with the time and reward.

In spite of the anger and frustration that many WPAs feel, however, we create GSWPA positions in our image and magnanimously invite graduate students to apply. We find ourselves overworked and underrewarded—exploited by a department and a university that recognizes the need for the work we do, but that cannot seem to recognize its value. In an effort to protect ourselves and to improve others' abilities to do this work that we both love and hate, we pass the exploitation on to our graduate students.

At a recent WPA Summer Conference, a young GSWPA admitted that he was well aware that he was being exploited by his department, being asked to do more work than his stipend paid for. But, the student argued, the value of his experience and the prospect of being fully employed the following year far outweighed any negative value carried by the exploitation. This student may be far too optimistic in his expectations for employment, but even more importantly, his attitude and the situation that created it are extremely damaging for the profession.

By establishing GSWPA positions, we perpetuate the system of exploitation to which we, as WPAs, are not just opposed but have, ourselves, fallen victim. Certainly an element of exploitation exists in our teaching assistantship and writing center tutor programs—graduate students are paid lower wages to do the jobs others do for significantly more pay. But this tradition does not need to be extended beyond the classroom. We should not provide students with another opportunity to become quietly accustomed to and accepting of exploitation. And we should not promote a system for which we already play an unhappy role.

Finally, promoting the use of GSWPA positions also promotes the value of administration as a job rather than as a type of intellectual work. To define the nature of administration, departments often begin with lists similar to those created by *The Portland Resolution: Guidelines for Writing Program Administration* (Hult *et al.* 1992). While such guidelines may be useful for conveying to hiring departments its broad scope, they erroneously confine administration to being a list of discrete "tasks" or "jobs" for the WPA to manage and complete. A sample of these jobs includes "designing or teaching faculty development seminars," "training tutors," "supervising teaching assistants and writing staff," "administering writing placement exams and diagnostics." Accepting this characterization of administration, departments can easily parcel out some jobs to graduate students while keeping faculty responsible for managing the whole. In such a job-based characterization of administration, significance is given to the individual tasks and to the WPA's ability to orchestrate the overall completion of each. What is not valued is the part of administration that does not fit neatly into a list of guidelines or jobs, the intellectual work that requires the WPA to synthesize research and scholarship into a coherent philosophy.

So, rather than judging administration as intellectual work, departments determine its value, and, by extension, the value of the profession, based on the job lists at hand and on the fact that administration can be distributed to and accomplished by graduate students. Administration cannot be valued or rewarded as intellectual work as long as we continue to promote the idea that it can be reduced to a list of items to be checked off, parceled out, and accomplished by preprofessionals.

Revising the Traditional Administrative Hierarchy

Many GSWPAs *are* respected by both peers and faculty, and feelings of disrespect or deception may never ignite. Many graduate students and faculty, like those I have cited in this essay, praise departments that have created GSWPA positions. But these fortunate occurrences do not justify the fact that values inherent in the process of appointing GSWPAs are antithetical to those most promoted by our discipline. Nor should the sincere urgings of others allow us to overlook the obligation we have to our own values. Yet, in arguing against the use of these positions, I would be remiss in turning away from the pedagogical and professional obligation to prepare graduate students for the administrative appointments they are likely to hold. How, then, can we meet this obligation without inadvertently denying another, promoting negative values, and potentially devaluing our work in the eyes of the profession?

Before answering that question, I need to examine the administrative model that exists in most departments and into which most faculty expect to be hired. Most commonly, departments appoint or elect one or two individual faculty to be responsible for all of the "jobs" of writing program administration. As a hierarchical model, then, this administrative design relies on a division of authority, of some faculty voices and votes having privilege over others'. These administrative faculty are often the only Composition and Rhetoric faculty in the department. Consequently, "[t]he WPA is perceived as the seat not only of program authority but disciplinary authority; this authority derives from the position itself" (Gunner 1994, 12). In this way, hierarchical administration cannot be accurately defined as a position of earned authority, but one that "deals in power" with "power games [that] demand aggressive players," and "administrators [who] must "assert that [they] have power (even if [they] don't)" (White 1991, 3). At its core, this model is one that encourages the bullying self-interest of a few.

Options to this model have begun to emerge in the literature. Jeanne Gunner argues that we revise the current hierarchy in administration in an effort to make it more democratic (1994, 14). To accomplish this, Gunner proposes that the position of the WPA be "decentered," such that "no one position or person occupies the center . . . [and] [a]dministrative responsibility is spread out rather than condensed . . . " (1994, 13;14). Recent feminist and "post-masculinist" models of administration seem to be in harmony with Gunner's views in that they do not locate authority or power in any one individual. According to Marcia Dickson, "[a] feminist model . . . is more concerned with doing away with hierarchies rather than perpetuating them" (1993, 148). Hildy Miller explicates the "feminist vision of personal power" further, explaining that "it is based on a different notion of what power is. At base, power is seen as a limitless rather than finite quantity. Therefore, power cannot be subject to a zero-sum game in which we are led to believe that increasing one person's power necessarily diminishes another's" (1996, 52).

At first look, it would appear that GSWPA positions make happen just what Gunner (1994), Dickson (1993), and Miller (1996) describe. Indeed, in their essay about the professional development of graduate students, Long, Holberg, and Taylor cite Gunner's essay. They point to the use of graduate student administrators, extolling its aim of "decentralizing and delegating day-to-day tasks of the program" (1996, 67). This claim is accurate—using GSWPAs, the faculty administrator is no longer the sole keeper of the keys to administrative power. Instead, there is a "collaborative administrative structure" that includes students (1996, 67).

However, in *de*centralizing the position of the WPA, the GSWPA positions have effectively *re*centralized it among more individuals. In designating one or more students as apprentice WPAs with whom to share the responsibility of administration, faculty perpetuate the traditional academic hierarchy in which particular individuals hold administrative titles and power. Now, instead of one master WPA and many apprentices, there are two tiers of master WPAs supervising the work of fewer apprentices. Collaboration occurs, but only among a few select individuals. In the end, a hierarchy still exists—along with all of the negative values it engenders.

By distributing administration among some graduate students, we have succeeded only in extending the existing model, placing some new players onto the same hierarchical game board. If we are truly to revise the traditional hierarchical model of administration, we must identify and change those features that make it most troublesome—that prevent it from being democratic and collaborative, that promote the kinds of antithetical values I have described.

The first feature to change in this revision is the name designations themselves. Given the power of naming to affect human perception (Armstrong and Fontaine 1989), it is no surprise that so much power emerges from administrative titles alone. The very act of naming individual students "Co-Director" or "Assistant Director," beknighting another "Co-supervisor" or "Coordinator," necessarily empowers some students while excluding others from the administrative realm, drawing clearly defined limits around its parameters. A truly democratic model begins by our rejecting the titles that divide one group of graduate students from another. The nature of administration must be separated from the titles that limit it.

Recall the other set of names that appear in discussions about administration, the task-names that commonly represent it. Administration is, consequently, reduced to being a "zero-sum game" of tasks whose value is measured by their completion and the status of the individual who completes them. In arguing for the GSWPA position, Long, Holberg, and Taylor may inadvertently perpetuate this view: ". . . with these tasks distributed among the members of a collaborative administrative structure, the WPA can act as a *more dynamic force* in program development. *Freed* from the constraints of day-to-day program operation, the WPA can focus on overarching issues . . ." (1996, 74) (emphasis added). As an administrator, I applaud this goal of "freeing up" the WPA. However, consider the evaluation that is implicit in such a description—that graduate students are shackled to the less important day-to-day tasks; the WPA is then "free" to be more dynamic and to focus on more important concerns. But if administration is separated from traditional administrative titles and names, how shall it be defined and labeled?

In the recently published article, "Evaluating the Intellectual Work of Writing Program Administrators: A Draft," the authors provide a way for us to think about administration not as discrete jobs or tasks, but as intellectual work that "does not either derive from or produce simplistic products or services. Rather, it draws upon historical and contemporary knowledge, and it contributes to the formation of new knowledge and improved decision making" (WPA Executive Committee 1996, 98). If administration is to be valued within the academic world, it cannot be defined in terms of "products and services." Yet, when we characterize administration in terms of tasks that can be handed off to preprofessionals, we are, indeed, defining it in these very terms.

In the revision that I am proposing of the traditional hierarchical model, administration must be characterized in terms of both the knowledge it draws upon and the "new knowledge and improved decision making" that it contributes to the discipline. Administration will be understood only as intellectual work if it takes its place in the academy alongside the other intellectual work that we and our students do. Such work

> generates new knowledge based on research, theory, and sound pedagogical practice . . . requires disciplinary knowledge . . . requires highly developed analytical or problem solving skills derived from specific expertise, training, or research derived from scholarly knowledge . . . generates or implements knowledge in ways that can be recognized and evaluated by peers . . . and is recognized as the contribution of the individual's insight, research, and disciplinary knowledge. (WPA Executive Committee 1996, 102)

Administration will not be experienced or understood as intellectual work if it remains isolated from general academic instruction for most Composition and Rhetoric graduate students. Indeed, since all students have available the "disciplinary knowledge" that the intellectual work of administration draws upon, they should all have the opportunity to use it for the problem solving and knowledge making that has, heretofore, been reserved only for designated GSWPAs.

Promoting Positive Values
While Preparing Students for the Future

Because this revised model does not rely on common titles or task lists, but on the active making of knowledge and decisions, it could take many forms. It might, for example, appear as an opportunity for individuals to make decisions about themselves that would, in a hierarchical model, have been the responsibility of an individual faculty or student WPA. In a writing center, tutors could have a number of "unscheduled hours," time for which they are responsible but that has no designated assignment. They would then generate a list of optional ways they might fulfill this responsibility in relation to the "overarching" theory of the center. Staff meetings, graduate seminars on teaching or response, journal articles available in the graduate student lounge, and past experiences with tutoring, would all provide individual tutors with the knowledge-base from which they could analyze the problem of how to responsibly fulfill their time commitment in a way that is based not on someone else's rules or their own self-interest, but on the overall philosophy and direction of their particular writing center. So, rather than designating one or two tutors as "co-supervisors" who assign tutors their duties, all tutors will learn to think about such problems, to think "administratively," and to see these choices as intellectual problems for which the solutions are based on disciplinary knowledge and experience.

Another example of how the revised administrative model might work would be in the form of the particular requirements for the standard pedagogy course that most teaching assistants take. Rather than writing the customary seminar paper for their instructor, students would be asked to apply what they study about the teaching of composition, composition theory, and composition research to writing real program documents (program evaluations, program histories, student handbooks, course descriptions, TA guidelines, etc.) or to planning and making real pieces or collections of writing (journal articles, collections of freshman composition or developmental writing students' essays, newsletters, interviews with students or instructors in the program, etc.). In addition to satisfying the course requirements, students would have contributed to the writing program's administrative archive. Furthermore, in the course of completing this requirement, students also will have learned about how to implement "[administrative] knowledge in ways that can be recognized and evaluated by peers" (WPA Executive Committee 1996, 102), a valuable lesson for any future faculty member who must produce such scholarly "implementations" of knowledge in order to be promoted.

In the end, all students, not just a few select GSWPAs, will have the opportunity to use administration to "become active institutional agents" (Long, Holberg, and Taylor 1996, 72). Administration will be integrated throughout the academic experience, throughout students' learning about scholarship in the discipline. Because hierarchy and status continue to be important in most academic activity, the faculty administrator (who, one hopes, has tenure) will necessarily continue to function as a program representative outside of the department and can use her faculty vantage point to the benefit of all students. However, in this revised administrative structure, the faculty WPA functions most like a facilitator, identifying and creating opportunities for students to use the disciplinary knowledge and experience they are acquiring to analyze and act on problems of curriculum, faculty development, evaluation, and so forth. And, as a result, whether or not they become WPAs, graduate students will carry with them the understanding that administration is, in actuality, an equal part of the intellectual work we all do as scholars, work that fosters the respect of others, of oneself, and of the discipline.

Acknowledgments

Initial research for this essay was funded by a grant from the National Council of Writing Program Administrators.

The author dedicates this essay to the memory of Kathy Brooks, whose professional diligence and critical questioning provided the spark for these reflections.

Works Cited

Armstrong, C., and S. I. Fontaine. 1989. "The Power of Naming: Names that Create and Define the Discipline." *WPA: Writing Program Administration* 13.1–2: 5–14.

Bishop, W., and G. L. Crossley. 1996. "How to Tell a Story of Stopping: The Complexities of Narrating a WPA's Experience." *WPA: Writing Program Administration.* 19.3: 70–79.

Brooks, K. 1993. Letter to the author.

Dickson, M. 1993. "Directing Without Power: Adventures in Constructing a Model of Feminist Writing Program Administration." In *Writing Ourselves into the Story: Unheard Voices from Composition Studies*, ed. S. I. Fontaine and S. Hunter, 140–53. Carbondale: Southern Illinois University Press.

Friend, C. 1996. "Playing with Fire: Authority, Risk, and the Role of Graduate Student Administrators in an Undergraduate Writing Program." Conference on College Composition and Communication, Milwaukee, WI.

Gunner, J. 1994. "Decentering the WPA." *WPA: Writing Program Administration*. 18.1–2: 8–15.

Hult, C., D. Joliffe, K. Kelly, D. Mead, and C. I. Schuster. 1992. "The Portland Resolution: Guidelines for Writing Program Administrator Positions." *WPA: Writing Program Administration*. 16.1–2: 88–94.

Janangelo, J. 1991. "Somewhere Between Disparity and Despair: Writing Program Administrators, Image Problems, and the MLA Job Information List." *WPA: Writing Program Administration* 15.1–2: 60–66.

Long, M. C., J. H. Holberg, and M. M. Taylor. 1996. "Beyond Apprenticeship: Graduate Students, Professional Development Programs and the Future(s) of English Studies." *WPA: Writing Program Administration* 20.1–2: 66–78.

Miller, H. 1996. "Postmasculinist Directions in Writing Program Administration." *WPA: Writing Program Administration* 20.1–2: 49–61.

Pemberton, M. 1993. "Tales Too Terrible to Tell: Unstated Truths and Underpreparation in Graduate Composition Programs." In *Writing Ourselves into the Story: Unheard Voices from Composition Studies*, ed. S. I. Fontaine and S. Hunter, 154–73. Carbondale: Southern Illinois University Press.

Thomas, T. 1991. "The Graduate Student as Apprentice WPA: Experiencing the Future." *WPA: Writing Program Administration* 14.3: 41–51.

White, E. 1991. "Use It or Lose It: Power and the WPA." *WPA: Writing Program Administration* 15.1–2: 3–12.

WPA Executive Committee. 1996. "Evaluating the Intellectual Work of Writing Program Administrators: A Draft." *WPA: Writing Program Administration* 20.1–2: 92–103.

Young, B. 1993. Letter to the author.

8

Teaching Through the Looking-Glass
The Ethics of Preparing Students for Timed-Writing Exit Examinations

Olivia G. Castellano
Cherryl Armstrong Smith

Now, if you'll attend, Kitty, and not talk so much, I'll tell you all my ideas about Looking-glass House. First, there's the room you can see through the glass—that's just the same as our drawing-room, only the things go the other way.

Lewis Carroll

Whereas good normal validity means that the assessment gives a good picture of what we are trying to look at, good "mirror validity" would mean that the assessment gives a good picture of how we actually look at pictures . . . .

Peter Elbow

Like Alice, we find ourselves in a strange world, in our case, trying to teach writing meaningfully while peering through the murky looking-glass of holistic scoring and one-time impromptu proficiency testing. But, unlike Alice, we cannot change our surroundings by dreaming. Our opposition to the type of writing assessment required by our university puts us in a powerful, ethical dilemma. The desire to help students liberate their own fantasies and dreams by becoming better writers propels us to teach a course required of students who have failed the examination at least twice. Helping students explore the larger range of expression possible in their voices has led us to develop teaching strategies that capitalize on what we call a "looking-glass" paradigm for preparing students to write exit examinations.

In agreeing to teach this course—English 109, Writing for Proficiency—we place ourselves in a matrix of ethical dilemmas stemming from two central concerns. First, agreeing to teach the course makes us complicitous with an examination to which we are philosophically opposed, an examination that we feel we have a professional responsibility to oppose. Second, teaching a course whose sole purpose is to help students pass this test compromises our role as writing teachers to an extraordinary degree; inevitably, we end up helping students to write formulaically and superficially and to approach writing as pure performance rather than as meaning making.

Our pedagogical problems are exacerbated by several other realities. First, a disproportionate percentage of the students who fail the examination are from minority groups. The Office of Educational Equity and Student Retention on our campus provides the following figures for the 1994–1995 academic year: The overall pass rate is fifty-five percent, and for white students, sixty-five percent, while for African-American students, it is forty percent; for Hispanics, fifty-four percent; and Asians, forty-two percent. Among students whose second language is English, the pass rate remains consistently low at thirty-eight percent. Second, while in the early years there was an interest in field testing, the assessment instrument on our campus no longer appears to be undergoing the necessary scrutiny of periodic field testing. Examination questions are simply reworded and recycled from previous years. Third, the examination itself does nothing to improve student writing. An informal survey of colleagues from a wide cross-section of disciplines indicates that faculty are mystified by the examination, many feel they know little about how it is administered, and some question the need for such an examination (Castellano 1996a). Finally, there is an enormous disparity between the exit testing on our campus and current research in assessment theory.

The ethics of overtly opposing the examination—we have voiced our objections to the examination locally as well as at national conferences (Castellano 1996b; Smith 1995)—yet participating in it by teaching the course disturbs us. We might refuse to teach the course in protest to the examination, but there are always many full-time faculty members to teach it, because it is a good alternative to the requirement of teaching freshman composition: Papers are shorter; students who pass the writing proficiency exit examination (WPE) in mid-semester can drop the course, reducing class size; and substantive revision, of the kind a student might be expected to do in a composition course not tied to an exit examination, is not necessary. These issues are significant at a university where most professors teach four courses per semester. And, even if professors refuse to teach the course, there are many part-time faculty members available and eager to teach it as they struggle to find enough courses to make a living. So, our protest does not seem to affect, at all, the examination's secure existence.

Still, refusing to teach the course may be a more personally satisfying option. We tend to feel better about our moral consistency when we take this alternative. However, we have been persuaded to continue teaching the course, in part, because we understand our students' apprehension of the examination. Their gratitude to some extent offsets our feelings of guilt for our complicity with the examination. Caught in our own dilemma as outsiders representing an opposing view of writing assessment, we understand our students' sense of alienation and their strong resistance to the whole machinery of the examination.

The Looking-Glass Paradigm

The instant that student writers step through the looking-glass of one-time impromptu examination writing and holistic assessment, the process of writing becomes truncated, turned backward, inside out. To prepare for such examinations, students must be guided to understand the nature of this rhetorical truncation. Notwithstanding other variables—such as control of sentence structure, ability to edit and proofread effectively, the soundness of ideas and appropriateness of examples—success in this type of examination depends on students' awareness of ways in which such tests go against the usual composing practices of competent writers.

We introduce the looking-glass paradigm by distinguishing between what we call real and unreal writing. We make clear to our students that to pass our campus WPE, they must learn how to subvert the process of creating *real* writing. That is, real writing results when writers care about what they write; have some voice in deciding what to write about; can brainstorm, discover, and revise what they want to say; and can work in an untimed environment.

But, the timed writing called for by the WPE violates all of these conditions. Students get topics disconnected from any course work or prior thinking they may have done, test questions that, without opportunity for collaboration or discussion, they may not be able to understand fully, much less care about. Students have no voice in determining these topics; they have virtually no time to brainstorm, discover, and revise their ideas. The two-and-a-half-hour session allowed for writing (four hours for ESL students) is not sufficient time for addressing the question any way but superficially. Furthermore, this time constraint places student writers in a particularly stressful situation. It is difficult to remain calm when their entire academic career depends on passing the examination.

Helping students achieve a complete understanding of the looking-glass paradigm may be overly ambitious, but this goal helps us deliver a genuine writing course despite the examination's threatening shadow, looming over our students throughout the semester. And, it keeps us from giving up as we continue to teach against ourselves, despite our philosophical and pedagogical beliefs that traditional, one-time impromptu examinations as state university graduation requirements are unfair, counterproductive, and invalid.

Underlying Problems

In 1976, a legislative mandate required the California State University (CSU) system to develop a graduation literacy requirement (GWAR) whereby students at each of the nineteen campuses would demonstrate that they had achieved competence as writers before being allowed to graduate with a BA degree or enter an MA program. Since about 1977, California State University, Sacramento (CSUS), where we both teach, has met this requirement, not by providing instruction in writing beyond freshman composition, but by instituting a two-and-a-half-hour, impromptu essay examination to be taken in the junior year. With some modifications, the examination remains essentially the same as it was in 1977 despite much opposition, locally, from many camps—students, faculty, and administrators.

Edward M. White, a principal proponent of essay testing in the 1970s, confirms that such examinations are currently "under attack from all sides as formulaic, unresponsive to the nature of writing, and destructive to the curriculum" (1995, 30). And Peter Elbow writes, " . . . not only do most writing assessments give us an unsatisfactory picture of the student's skill, the picture they give us is of the student using a skill that most of us would not really call *writing*" (1991, xiv). In 1992, a National Council of Teachers of English (NCTE) Sense of the House Motion (no. 3) resolved to "oppose the practice of claiming to measure a student's overall ability at writing by means of a single score on a single piece of writing produced at one sitting, and . . . to work to eliminate this practice." The CCC Commission on Assessment, in 1995 provided guidelines for the testing of writing that examinations like the one at our campus do not meet.

To be sure, CSUS is not alone in conducting such tests. Sandra Murphy *et al.* found that, nationally, over seventy percent of colleges and universities that assess writing were using some form of impromptu essay, either for placement or exit (White 1995, 30). In the CSU, nearly all campuses (there are now twenty-one) use an impromptu essay examination to satisfy the Graduate Writing Assessment Requirement (GWAR). On approximately half of the campuses, the exit test is used in combination with a course option. At the San Marcos campus, there is a writing requirement attached to courses in place of exit testing. And at the Chico campus, a test is used as a placement instrument for upper division writing courses rather than as an exit condition (CSU *Report* 1994). There has been much discussion about assessment at CSU faculty conferences, and some modifications have begun to take place. But the timed test dominates, despite scholarship examining the limitations of impromptu essays scored holistically and proposing more valid measures.

We think in particular of Huot's essay, "Toward a New Theory of Writing Assessment" (1996), which deconstructs traditional writing assessment, revealing how it overlooks validity for the sake of reliability. Such assessments "are based upon classical test theory, with roots in a positivist epistemology that assumes 'that there exists a reality out there, driven by immutable natural laws'" (1996, 549). Huot views these practices as invalid because they "attempt to fix objectively a student's ability to write" (1996, 552). His clearly outlined theory is, for the two of us, liberating because it precisely identifies what is deeply problematic in the form of assessment that we confront. None of the criteria of Huot's model is met by the assessment on our campus. At our university, we are a long way from even beginning to consider the crucial implications of Huot's theory or the alternative models he outlines, which are being used and have been used successfully at various universities. The fourth principle of his model succinctly highlights what is under erasure in our campus' assessment procedures: "All writing assignments, scoring criteria, writing environments, and reading procedures should adhere to recognizable and supportable rhetorical principles integral to the thoughtful expression and reflective interpretation of texts" (1996, 562).

From its inception, this examination has had at its core confusion between *proficiency testing*—that is, the complexity of actually analyzing a student's writing ability—and *scoring*, or the means of sorting and ranking writing samples. Since holistic scoring of writing samples had in the seventies begun to replace machine scoring of multiple-choice tests used for placement, holistic scoring was touted as if it could account for writing ability rather than merely rank-order pieces of student writing (Smith 1991, 287–88). Such misunderstandings have not only not been resolved in the almost twenty-year history of the examination, they have, in fact, grown deeper. Adjustments to the examination have never focused on the incongruity between impromptu testing and the writing process that demands revision, on the inherent contradiction between how writing is taught (in usual writing courses) on our own campus and how it is tested. The question of how one might authentically assess writing has never been meaningfully addressed. The focus then and now has been on how an examination might be read and scored rather than on what competencies of writing we might be looking for in determining whether our students are "proficient" enough to graduate.

Power Relationships

When the statewide literacy requirement went into effect, it stirred much controversy on our campus. A group of concerned faculty members, including Olivia, worked unsuccessfully to oppose the use of an examination in favor of satisfactory completion of a composition course as fulfillment of the literacy

requirement. Some in this group were directors of special admission and retention programs or faculty from various disciplines who worked primarily
with underrepresented students. But, proponents of the examination prevailed.
The examination, to be administered by the English Department, would be
read holistically and offered several times each year, and students could keep
taking the examination until they passed it. We have had students arrive in our
classes after having failed the examination as many as eight times.

The one concession made by the examination supporters was that while
native speakers would get two and a half hours to complete the examination,
ESL students would get four hours. The way that ESL writers were singled out
is particularly telling, because attention was placed not on evaluating their writing ability, but on how best to fit them into the scoring procedures designed for
native speakers. Opponents of the examination argued that this native speaker/
ESL distinction was too simplistic. It failed to consider that U. S.-born, bilingual writers, whose writing does not have the sentence-level and diction patterns of ESL writers, may show other complex rhetorical and syntactical
influences from their native language. Similarly, it completely overlooked
speakers of dialects such as Black English Vernacular (BEV) and Chicano English, whose rhetorical and linguistic performance is influenced by cultural traditions and language differences (Dillard 1972; Baugh 1988; Wald 1988).

The traditional holistic criteria of the WPE still have not addressed these
concerns. Like all scoring rubrics we have seen, the rubric for the WPE values
content as more significant than usage. And yet, the sentence level is the major distinguishing factor separating passing from failing essays. In holistic
scoring of impromptu essays "readers are unduly influenced by such surface
features as length, handwriting, mechanical mistakes, and unevenness"
(Haswell and Wyche-Smith 1994, 228). To pass, an essay must be perceived
as fitting a standard format (a deductive argument with supporting examples)
and demonstrating a predominance of standard usage. These are the major
expectations of the examination readers. With no time for revision, this goal is
naturally harder to achieve for nonstandard speakers. To help address the special circumstance of Spanish/English bilinguals and speakers of Chicano English and BEV, soon after the test was institutionalized, Olivia developed a
section of English 109 for bilingual and bidialectal speakers.

Many students who enroll in that course and in Cherryl's regular English
109 classes are the first in their immediate families to go to college. Many enter the university through special admissions programs like the Educational
Opportunity Program and the College Assistance Migrant Program. Virtually
all arrive in our classes with great apprehension about the WPE, knowing that
it can delay their graduation date until they are able to pass the examination.
We have had students in our classes who, except for the examination, have
completed all course requirements. The WPE is for them the final gatekeeper
to their hard-earned Bachelor's degree.

This apprehension intensifies as students become aware that modifications are occurring in the WPE program. Since Spring 1997, a revised WPE preparation class has been in place to be taken by students who have failed the WPE twice. Whereas the old course was ungraded, now students must complete the course with a C- or higher, prepare a portfolio of essays written in response to exit examination questions, and must pass the examination at the end of the semester to satisfy the GWAR. If a student fails the examination, instructors can submit the portfolio. But instructors can submit only those portfolios of students the instructor feels have made significant progress. And the portfolio must then be deemed "proficient" by a "portfolio assessment committee," of which the instructors themselves are not members. Students whose portfolios are rejected by the committee must repeat the course, even if the instructor has given them a passing grade. In fact, some instructors report having been warned not to submit "weak" portfolios that could be rejected and thereby hurt the instructor's credibility with the committee.

Furthermore, the contents of the portfolio belie the term *portfolio*. That is, students still write to an examination prompt, and faculty are necessarily guiding the students' writing by essentially the holistic scoring rubric set in place in 1977. The portfolios are simply a collection of exit examinations (though some may be composed outside of class) to be scored holistically by a committee that does not include the instructors submitting portfolios. We must emphasize that the particularities of the changes are not at issue. In fact, they stem from a good-faith effort to improve upon the existing testing program. Yet, until the power relationships fostered by this kind of examination are scrutinized and allowed to be reconfigured, nothing substantive will have changed. A community, of the kind Huot describes, involving all the stakeholders will not flourish. As Huot points out: "Changing the foundation which directs the way student writing is assessed involves altering the power relations between students and teachers and teachers and administrators. It can also change what we will come to value as literacy in and outside of school" (1996, 564). But when the power relationships are not changed, as is the case here, we would argue that such examinations play a role in undermining faculty morale, lowering students' expectations of themselves as writers, and trivializing both the discipline of composition and the complexity of the art of writing at the university.

"The responsibility of deciding what we shall measure and how is profound, and even cantankerous colleagues sometimes find themselves listening to each other, wavering on long-held views, agreeing to agree" (White 1995, 39–40). But our colleagues are not cantankerous, so much as feeling left totally outside the decision-making parameters of this test. Vis-a-vis the test, they feel powerless, confused, and resentful. And, they share this resentment with their students, who arrive in our Writing for Proficiency classes in the double-edged state of panic and outrage.

Teaching Despite the Examination

Allowing students space to voice their outrage becomes our point of departure in the course. We begin by explaining our ethical dilemma in opposing exit testing yet participating in the process by agreeing to teach the course. We make clear that we are not allowing the examination to sabotage our responsibility to help them. Revealing to students our own conflict cuts through some of the armor of their resistance, making it easier to introduce the looking-glass paradigm that directs our course pedagogy.

What one first encounters on the other side of the looking-glass is that the examination readers have certain expectations of a passing essay. We delineate these expectations, teaching how alternative discourses are often displaced by traditional, academic forms. Next, one faces the WPE questions; we demonstrate how these questions all have a hidden agenda because they presuppose a particular type of expository essay. Although the examination question and instructions suggest that no particular form is required, indeed often suggest that students are to "examine" an issue or "discuss" a problem, the expected finished product is always a thesis-driven, five-to-seven-paragraph essay of assertions followed by supporting examples. While it is possible for a quite sophisticated writer to pass the examination by using a less rigid format, the overwhelming majority of passing essays we have seen in our classes and in the scoring sessions—no matter what prompt is used—tend to follow either the classic five-paragraph design or something very similar.

These questions pose a myriad of problems. In the first years of the assessment, the questions called for a fairly personal essay, with questions like "Discuss an event that significantly changed your life" and "Discuss a person, book, or film that significantly touched your life." For approximately the past ten years, the questions have shown a more sociological emphasis. Representative questions include "Discuss how a business or product affects people's lives" and "Discuss what advertising reveals about American society."

We make clear that while a certain amount of narration was acceptable in the early, personal questions, the sociological ones leave little room for personal narrative. Also, with the sociologically focused topics, the complexity of analysis expected in a passing essay varies greatly. The simple cause-effect analysis called for by the aforementioned "business" topic may be easier to execute than the more argumentative demands of the "advertising" topic. Furthermore, the cause-effect analysis called for by some questions requires even more in-depth critical analysis, hypothetical examples, and creative solutions as in this topic: "By the year 2000, no one ethnicity will constitute a majority in California. Write an essay in which you examine the possible effects this will have on one aspect of our society." On the other hand, the compare/contrast accompanied by cause-effect analysis required by the next question is even more ambitious: "Describe what you believe have been the positive and/or negative effects of the Women's Movement."

Thus, we help our students see that the examination questions are inconsistent in complexity. Each question is embedded in a larger context of rhetorical expectations for examination readers and student writers and will vary in terms of the emotional, intellectual, and psychological reactions it elicits in our students. We are reminded of the student who wished aloud during the last week of class before the examination in one English 109 class: "I hope I luck out and get one of the easy ones." Even more telling is the student who complained after she had failed the WPE: "My friend in another class passed the test. But I'm the one who helps her write papers for her classes. I get her A's and B's but can't pass my own WPE!"

In some ways, our greatest difficulty in the class comes when we try to explain how the examination is graded. We begin by showing that, because the test was appropriated from timed-writing placement tests, it is scored on a six-point scale (with 6 being highest, and 1 being lowest), but, it is really a pass/fail examination. The student must receive an "8" to pass. In our experience both as examination readers and teachers of the course, the majority of passing essays are given a combined score above "8." Many of our students who pass with an "8" feel that they must be poor writers because they "barely passed."

One unusual feature of the holistic assessment on our campus is that a score of "3" by one reader and a score of "4" by the second reader is treated as a "split score," and it is sent to a Review Board to be reread. This is done because an "8" is needed to pass. The Review Board reader determines whether the essay is really a "3" or "4" paper, that is, whether the paper should fail or pass. But "resolving" a split score in this way is a misnomer, because even the most reliable holistic scoring norms raters to score within one point of each other, not to agree to the same score. If a first reader gives a paper a "5" and the second gives it a "3," the usual holistic scoring would ask for a third reading. But a "3" and a "4" is an accurate scoring and no further reading is needed. In this fashion, we demystify the examination for our students, helping them to understand why it is impossible to tell why one paper passes and another one does not. We make use of this peculiarity in the scoring to highlight for students the disparity between numerical labeling of timed writing and genuine evaluation of their abilities as writers.

Given that this scoring is arbitrary and the examination questions place students in a rhetorical trap from which they cannot extricate themselves, they respond readily to the distinction between *real* and *unreal* writing, as we help them understand that the latter leaves no room for creativity or flexibility. The examination requires that students know how to manipulate a particular diction and formulaic structure. Here, we teach them several different patterns of organization, including the traditional five-paragraph formulaic structure, simply because it is fast and easy to perform in the time allotted. We emphasize that the five-paragraph structure is not popular in *real* writing because it tends to lock the writer into a simplistic structure, which often leads to superficial content. It is not the format they would want to use in real writing, because in the "real writing process," content generates its own structures.

However, in the time allotted, the five-paragraph structure can lead to a passing paper. We show how this structure can lead to a manageable draft in the allotted time and will easily generate the type of essay the criteria define as a passing "8" essay. It is an essay that contains a clear introduction, a set of well-organized body paragraphs in which assertions are qualified and supported by examples, and a conclusion that brings together the writer's main argument. Clearly, if they had more than two and a half hours, they would be able to generate a more dynamic, perhaps inductive arrangement of ideas and would be able to present them in a more creative way.

To help them see the difference between *real* and *unreal* writing, we have students rewrite their in-class, formulaic essays in a different, more dynamic, less predictable, and more creative structure. They are able to see for themselves the differences. One typical WPE-type of question that allows for this comparison is an older one that asks students to "discuss a problem in society that you feel strongly about and that you believe should be solved." In class, applying the five-paragraph structure, students usually generate predictable but proficient essays that often follow this rhetorical pattern: "There are three reasons why I believe child abuse is a problem in my community." When allowed to take the topic home and apply a more creative approach, they break out of the rhetorical trap and can generate powerful essays, citing actual incidents of abuse from print and television news coverage. But, while their diction becomes more precise, their descriptions more vivid, and their proofreading more careful, they make "larger" errors in argumentation. Usually, they are able to revise these when we return their first drafts. While they are proud of their "at home" essays, most echo one girl's comment when we told her how beautifully she had written and how sophisticated her argument: "Yes, I'm proud of myself. But it took me two weeks to write this. I could never have done this type of essay in the WPE!"

In addition to having them analyze the differences between "in-class" and "out-of-class" essays on the same topic, we ask our students to compare the differences in the process of composing. They all admit that in in-class essays, their nervousness creates a blank in their thinking because they are not able to read up on the topic or discuss it with anyone. To show how they could never really "write themselves" or write honestly in the WPE, we give them creative journal assignments, which allow them to experiment with language and tap into the real world where they live emotionally, physically, and spiritually. Some of these assignments result in the students' first-time-ever pieces of what they call "creative writing." One exercise they particularly like is: "You are on a boat that has been swept out to sea. You have but days left. Write a letter to your loved ones." Besides the expected farewell love letters, we get letters to the small pueblo in Mexico that the student will never see free of oppression or the small inner city neighborhood where police sirens are the only sounds on Friday and Saturday nights.

When asked what they like most about these assignments, they point out that they are able to "write from the heart," that there is no expected structure, that they have time at home to write and rewrite until they "find the right words" and until a "perfect structure for this piece" emerges. The students respond with great enthusiasm. Most have never really had a chance to write for enjoyment; writing has been, for the most part, a hated chore. To reinforce the difference between real and unreal writing, all we need to do at this point is ask, "Could you have written this way in the WPE?" One student answered, "Are you kidding? I'm too busy being nervous to think about my hometown."

Our teaching task is daunting, our ethical position exasperating. And given the ubiquitous presence of examinations like this in colleges throughout the United States, it is a dilemma the profession itself must continue to address. Our own strategy is to embrace our dilemma wholeheartedly for the sake of these students. As composition teachers, we are saboteurs of culture, breakers of barriers between the academy and the precarious, challenging world where our students live. This does not resolve our dilemma. Daily, we are confronted with the reality that this examination will not go away, that its criteria are ambiguous and unfair, and that the power relations involving the examination are not likely to change soon.

But given the needs of our students and the fact that our proficiency classes are their last chance to address those needs, we believe that our expertise is best spent in the classroom helping them rather than in trying, as we still continue to do, to change an unchanging institution. Greater satisfaction comes from seeing student writers successfully negotiate the demands of both sides of the looking-glass.

Works Cited

Baugh, J. 1988. "Chicano English: The Anguish of Definition." In *Form and Function in Chicano English*, ed. J. Ornstein-Galicia, 3–13. Malabar, FL: Krieger.

California State University. 1994. *Remedial/Graduate Writing Assessment Requirement Report*.

Carroll, L. 1971. *Through the Looking-Glass and What Alice Found There in Alice in Wonderland*. New York: Norton.

Castellano, O. 1996a. "Faculty Attitudes Toward the Writing Proficiency Test." Unpublished manuscript.

———. 1996b. "Who Are the Students in Our Classes and How Did They Get There? Bilingual/Bidialectal Perspectives on Academic English." Paper presented at the Conference of College Composition and Communication, Milwaukee, WI.

College Composition and Communication. 1995. *Report of CCC Commission on Assessment*. Urbana, IL: NCTE.

Dillard, J. 1972. *Black English: Its History and Usage in the United States*. New York: Random House.

Elbow, P. 1991. "Forward." In *Portfolios: Process and Product*, ed. P. Belanoff and M. Dickson, ix–xvi. Portsmouth, NH: Boynton/Cook Heinemann.

Haswell, R., and S. Wyche-Smith. 1994. "Adventuring into Writing Assessment." *College Composition and Communication* 45.2: 220–36.

Huot, B. 1996. "Toward a New Theory of Writing Assessment." *College Composition and Communication* 47.4: 549–65.

National Council of Teachers of English. 1992. *Sense of the House Motion #3.*

Smith. C. 1991. "Writing Without Testing." In *Portfolios: Process and Product*, ed. P. Belanoff and M. Dickson, 279–91. Portsmouth, NH: Boynton/Cook Heinemann.

_____. 1995. "Teaching to Writing Tests That Conflict with Teaching Writing." Paper presented at National Council of Teachers of English Annual Convention, San Diego, CA.

Wald, B. 1988. "The Status of Chicano English as a Dialect of American English." In *Form and Function in Chicano English*, ed. J. Ornstein-Galicia, 14–31. Malabar, FL: Krieger.

White, E. 1995. "An Apologia for the Timed Impromptu Essay Test." *College Composition and Communication* 46.1: 30–45.

9

Secrets and Ethics in Ethnographic Writing Research

Devan Cook

On manuscript approval day, I carry three big covered boxes up the stairs to the administration building: three copies of my dissertation. The morning is hot, the boxes heavy, and I walk slowly, thankful that they are "in" on time. This seems to indicate, somehow, that I have finished, that the project is over, that all questions have been settled, all lingering doubts and what-ifs quelled. But (as is true of so many other things concerning ethnography) appearances are deceiving, and nothing could be further from the truth. The boxes contain three copies of a piece of ethnographic writing research captured and mounted (like an insect) at the point at which the academy has examined it and been satisfied.

In the spring and summer of 1995, I began an ethnomethodological writing research project investigating the writing lives of working students. I began the project for a variety of reasons: I had been a working student and felt that their concerns are often slighted in the academy; I had students in my writing classes whose work lives caused them problems that they were strangely loath to discuss; and I was interested, as a writing teacher who conceives literacy as a life rather than simply an academic skill, in learning more about the relationship of workplace to academic writing.

I interviewed twenty-two working undergraduate students at four different institutions with different teachers and different pedagogical principles and practices. The students were employed as nurse's aides, fry cooks, staple pullers, gofers, golf pros, auto parts salesmen, substitute teachers, accountants, administrative assistants, editors, and secretaries. In an attempt to keep the focus on students (and also, I must admit, to simplify data collection), I emphasized students' stories about their lives and avoided the classroom and their teachers as much as possible. The processes of ethnographic writing research resulted in my dissertation, titled "Literacies at Work: The Writing Lives of Working Students."

It all sounds straightforward, fair, open, and above-board: How could ethical considerations and problems have kept popping up from beneath the research's floorboards? The making of meaning is a value-laden enterprise, as rhetors from the Sophists to the present day have insisted. In addition, anyone who has been involved with ethnomethodological research recognizes the seeming ethical simplicity of my project as an artful illusion, a ruse or disguise. I had worked hard to honor my own teaching and writing values in designing the project, but I had already learned, from previous experience with microethnographies, that naturalistic research methods tend to raise difficult ethical questions, to foreground gray areas or ambiguities precisely because of their situated nature. The processes of ethnographic writing research, then, ask us as researchers to confront our values in situation, on-site, fully embedded in action and context. The decisions we are forced to make are often difficult ones. Certainly this happened to me, and I expect it will again. But often I learned more from those events than I did from times when I had little to interrogate and therefore examine thoughtfully.

Now that my boxes are turned in, I can further explore some of the situations I encountered and found especially perilous: hidden emotions and hidden agenda, which reinforced each other in the project's progress. In doing so, I will briefly discuss ethnography, identifying some ethical considerations in its processes, and then tell a few stories that will, I hope, illustrate some dilemmas I found in trying to "do" ethnography in a way that satisfied—and expanded—my own understanding of research value and values. (See Mortensen and Kirsch 1996 for discussions of other kinds of ethical issues in ethnographic studies.)

Why Ethnographic Research?

The purpose of ethnographic research, as Harry Wolcott writes in "On Ethnographic Intent," "is to describe and interpret cultural behavior" (1987, 43). Norman K. Denzin and Yvonna Lincoln foreground the situated, contextual nature of ethnography when they wrote that "qualitative researchers study things in their natural settings, attempting to make sense of . . . phenomena in terms of the meanings people bring to them" (1994, 2). And such "local" description and interpretation of cultural behaviors, whether undertaken as a means of inquiry in anthropology, women's studies, postcolonial literature, or composition (or any of the other disciplines that rely on ethnographic methodologies to gather knowledge), is framed by a generally agreed upon set of standard practices.

An ethnographic researcher does fieldwork—that is, she enters a setting. Whether the setting is totally novel to her, culturally or even geographically removed from her day-to-day experience, or as familiar as her own classroom, the setting is the research's "field." Once in the field, the ethnographic researcher becomes a participant-observer, both fully involved in what occurs in the field and fully observant of it. The involvement provides "insider" knowledge, or at least as much insider knowledge as it is possible for an outsider to have. The ethnographer's description of the participants, including herself, make up the body, the stuff, of ethnography, what Wolcott calls the description and interpretation of culture. These observations are collected textually in several modes. Fieldnotes, a written compendium that commonly contains much of the primary data, may be partly a narrative of events, part diary, part research journal, part record of reactions, and part script.

Providing information about contexts, then, is exactly what ethnography does best by means of what Clifford Geertz (1988) calls "thick description": amassing data, trying to observe and collect artifacts concerning everything in the lives of the population studied. Because ethnographies are ecological and weblike rather than linear, the method is well suited for discovering, uncovering, and unpacking cultural practices that, because they seem ordinary and everyday, we may be unlikely to examine thoroughly. Ethnography proved well-suited for studying my interests—the tangle of connections between school, work, writing, researcher, and respondents. Ethnography's phenomenological basis made it ideal for my study, in which individual discourses shaped and were shaped by participants' lives in multiple contexts and communities—including those of the researcher.

The researcher's discourses are thus also subject to investigation as a constant and ongoing part of ethnography's processes. In fact, Stephen North proposes that naturalistic researchers are "looking to unseat their own taken-for-granted notions of what is—what it means, how it comes to mean . . ." (1987, 279). Thus, the ethnographer, by examining her own meaning-making processes, involves herself in research that is, at least in theory, a kind of collaboration, one in which secrecy or concealment—from others or herself—need have no place. In the planning stages, overcome at times with the idealism from which I am prone to suffer, I ignored Wolcott's suggestion that no one, including the researcher, ever knows or understands it all, and James Clifford's caveat that "[e]thnography is actively situated between powerful systems of meaning" (1984, 2).

In many ways, then, ethnomethodological research possesses its own internal ethical authority and balance, grounded in intensive data collection, scrupulous honesty and thoroughness, and unceasing self-reflexivity and questioning on the part of the researcher. The researcher, in this ideal ethnographic world, tells the truth and examines her own perspectives and subject positions while maintaining a dialogue with student participants throughout the process. While this is going on, the unexpected often happens, but it is to be accepted, included, and learned from. Ethnography can seem spectacularly out of control; the ethically grounded checks and balances the methodology prescribes are part of its control mechanism, its gyroscope.

But in Clifford's warning, the word I should have noted most carefully is *powerful*. If researcher and respondents were entirely disinterested, without motives, emotions, or needs, the dialogue between cultures, which many writers describe as ethnography's purpose (Denzin and Lincoln 1994; Geertz 1988; North 1987; Wolcott 1987), could proceed to the mutual benefit of all concerned, unhindered by the inscriptions of power upon that discourse. But as Wendy Bishop observes, "Anyone who has entered a writing culture learns that her point of entry is interested" (1994, 272). And (paradoxically and ironically) the only thing a researcher can do to further the desired dialogue is be as honest and forthcoming about her interestedness and the conflicts it causes in her discussion of the situation as possible. I found that no matter how truthful I intended to be and how closely I interrogated my motives, it was easy to tell myself that partial rather than full disclosure of my situation was not concealing anything important, certainly nothing that could influence the course or findings of the research. Sidestepping ethnography's ethical balances proved tempting. Although in principle I remained loyal to untiring, almost global data collection and honest about my own agenda when talking with participants and in writing, in practice it was easy to tell myself that I was doing these things wholeheartedly and completely, when, in fact, I was not.

Thus, while at times doing the project made me look more closely at myself—or at the congeries of experiences and discourses that constitute my "self" at any given moment, my set of narrative filters through which the stories of these working students were processed—than at students, my own self-interest remained in the forefront of my concerns. I entered the setting, I gathered data, and then I went home to the university and wrote about what I found, mainly for my own benefit as well as for the benefit of other academics. Certainly it would be possible to say that in the long run, what I learned will benefit future writing students. It would even be possible to claim—in fact, I did claim in the letter I passed out to students in which I explained my project and asked for their (strictly voluntary) assistance—that talking about their writing lives increased students' awareness of their own processes and helped them to achieve greater writerly agency and authority as a result. But what that letter did not claim, and what I continued to downplay in my conversations with students, was that I knew I would reap much more good than they from our interactions.

As the study progressed and my uneasiness grew, I began to ask myself a fine old question, *"Cui bono?"* ("For whose benefit?"). It seemed to hold a useful lens for viewing a variety of ethical questions my study raised. In researching and writing, I struggled with my own strong feelings about people in the study; forced myself to listen to the data rather than to my beloved "big picture," which the data did not flawlessly accommodate; tried to work through issues raised by being a white researcher at an historically Black school; and, finally, attempted to address the ethical concerns of the committee at my university, which supervised research on human subjects, while remaining faithful to my own ideas about doing ethical ethnography. On each occasion, I was tempted to ignore the necessity of including my own situatedness and contexts in the dialogue between students' cultures and mine. Asking myself why I chose my attitudes and ideas—whether I was their primary beneficiary—clarified my researcher values.

Choices Resulting from Strong Feelings

The processes of ethnographic writing research are frequently uncomfortable, and discomfort, for me, can lead to temptation. As I drove forty miles to spend a hot afternoon waiting to be stood up by working students whom I could not even blame for standing me up, because I knew they had thirty minutes between work and class in which they might prefer to grab a hamburger, I envied my office mate, who only had to walk five minutes over to the library in order to conduct all of her research. I envied her so often that I continually fought a desire to fictionalize my respondents—to make them up. That I did not do so had more to do with the generosity and articulateness—the "good stories"— of students who talked with me than it had to do with me as a researcher. At times, I wonder what I would have done if I were better at writing fiction.

Not only is a researcher tempted to fabricate, but often I was so excited about someone who gave a "good" interview—who told interesting stories with quotable lines (or lines and stories that could be related to composition theorists that I like best and think are right)—that I was also tempted to reward these students, to give them more time, more attention, more feedback, even more smiles. And more space in the written record later on. I did not tell students who spoke with me that what they said in their interviews might or might not become a detailed part of the written report: Many of them assumed that the transcripts of their tapes, or selections from them, would be included, and I said nothing to change their minds or to suggest that their stories would be more likely for inclusion if they illustrated one of my ideas—the connection between opportunities for meaning-making writing at work and at school, for instance— or if they said things in a colorful way. Otherwise, our talks were likely to become part of the background data—methodological information chronicling the research process, or a list of names or pseudonyms of students whose stories are similar to the ones I discuss in more detail: Here is another female returning student who has worked as a nurse's aide for twenty years, for example, or another traditional student who works as a go-fer and writes in snatches.

In fact, I habitually rewarded students about whom I felt strongly. I did not realize how obvious this was until my defense, when we were discussing a student, Sam, whom I admitted to liking in the chapter where he appears. Someone on my committee commented, "Well, it's obvious that you like him." Sam was articulate, opinionated, thoughtful, and comfortable with talking about his writing; he also was never late for interviews and willingly spoke with me over the phone. At the beginning of my research, when I was being stood up over and over and beginning to suspect that my results would focus more on the fail-ure of the project I had originally designed than about the writing lives of work-ing students, Sam encouraged me by calling to say that he remembered I had visited his class, and he wondered when his interviews would be scheduled.

In many ways a writing researcher's dream respondent, Sam nevertheless spurred my thinking by raising some interesting issues. During one interview, he asked me about an argumentative essay he had been assigned to write which he did not believe was convincing; in essence, he asked me to step outside my role as an interviewing observer and respond to the essay as a reader and teacher. My gratitude for Sam's help led me to forget about being a researcher to spend thirty minutes reading and talking about his essay.

In talking to Sam, I wore my researcher heart on my sleeve. My interactions with him were not unique in my study; I was also very fond of some female returning students whose life stories seemed to parallel my own, reentering the academy at mid-life while working blue-collar jobs and living in the rural South, and of several young men who seemed especially clear and focused about who they were, what they were doing, and the roles that writing played in their lives. Their talk and ideas are covered in fairly extensive detail in my dissertation, even though they are not the only people who expressed similar perspectives. I began to learn how my leanings and biases could reward some research respondents and to question exactly which (or whose) experiences held primacy when I chose to emphasize students whose uplifting narratives helped me write readable, involving prose or with whom I identified on a purely personal level. While I discussed my selectivity as I wrote, I also did not feel compelled to rewrite for more inclusiveness and a perhaps more am-biguous, less easily told story.

Other identifications I felt tempted me neither to fabricate nor to reward, but to advance certain "readings" of what students said while ignoring other, equally plausible readings. Often, I found the identifications to be emotional, rooted in my personal history, and in every instance, I needed another reader to point them out to me—it was as if I were wearing blinders. Unfortunately, the critical self-reflexivity that ethnography's internal ethical compass requires does not automatically kick in. During my defense, for example, I was taken to task by several committee members over my discussion of two women stu-dents. One professor said, "You're just being hard on this student because she's your younger self," which was unquestionably true and so obvious that I was stunned by my not seeing or even suspecting it. Another argued (about the other woman student), "You're saying this because you're horrified at some of her attitudes toward other women with whom she works" (I was). Both pro-fessors were better able to read and name my emotions than I was: Despite my commitment to honesty, involvement, and self-criticism and questioning, I had not been aware of how emotionally loaded my readings of interactions with these two women were. Here I had an agenda—a desire to address how little writing many women do on the job and how that lack relates to their school writing—snarled in an emotional knot. Blinded by emotional identification, I interpreted their data in a fairly problematic way and did not sufficiently emphasize alternate readings of the same data, readings that pointed out that overall, both women were successful school and work writers—an important point.

Strong feelings, then, can tempt a researcher to fabricate, to reward, and to see only what she wants or needs to see. But bidding farewell to a favorite theory or strategy that almost works for organizing data is not easy. Ethnography asks us to respect our data; writing a dissertation—a process loaded with expectations and needs—asks us to produce an organized, informed piece of writing. I found that meeting the requirements of both situations provided a special kind of temptation. Liking, ways of reading, and writerly and scholarly expediency can bend one another—and a researcher's purposes—in odd ways; for me, their hidden or unacknowledged pressures were sometimes impossible to resist.

Being in Love with My "Grand Design"

Wendy Bishop writes that "Anyone who has entered a writing culture learns that her point of entry is interested. . . . Therefore, we are also predisposed to see already-familiar patterns . . . " (1994, 272). But being in love with a classificatory strategy (more of those troublesome emotions) can lead to concealment and to eliding or ignoring data. This is poor scholarship, but it is tempting to see only what one wants to see.

Brett and Chris, two students whom I liked a lot because they were interesting personalities and independent thinkers and writers, almost fell out of the dissertation report because their perspectives on writing did not fit my overall scheme, which separated employed writing students into outsiders and insiders. While this language is problematic, it is familiar in Composition and often provides a powerful metaphoric description of the contexts of working students' lives.

Many such students—often returning and/or blue-collar students—see themselves as outsiders in the academy who would like to become insiders; they believe that education is the key that will open the door to better jobs and better lives. Because introductory writing classes are almost universally required, students see successful completion of these courses as hoops they must jump through in order to achieve their goals. A good showing in a writing class will help them become (or achieve self-identity as) insiders: people who belong in and have been empowered by their schooling in general and their writing classes in particular. Other working students already seem to possess this understanding; they may have much to learn about writing, but they are confident that they can, and they have some idea of how to go about doing so. These students are insider-writers who write well and happily before going into their writing classes and even better and more happily afterward.

I had planned to talk about these two groups of students in separate chapters and to discuss their outsider-insider identifications as community issues.

My thinking was inspired mainly by Robert Brooke's *Writing and Sense of Self* (1991) and Deborah Brandt's *Literacy as Involvement* (1990), both of which I greatly admire. They echo what I believe about my own writing life—that involvement in and identification with a community of writers is essential—and their ideas frame and buttress my teaching. They are, in fact, my favorite composition theorists. In addition, the stories of most of the students with whom I spoke fit very nicely into my classificatory scheme.

A positive aura surrounded this theoretical framework: theories I liked, students I liked, students I liked whose stories dovetailed nicely with the theories—except, of course, for those of Brett and Chris. It bothered me that they did not seem to belong anywhere in my scheme, although writing played a large part in both of their lives and in the ways they approached the world. In one way, they could both be called insider-writers. But honesty compelled me to admit that although both Brett and Chris wrote to, for, and with other writers, neither of them cared whether he was an insider or an outsider at work or at school. For my scheme to work, it had to actually represent something that mattered to students.

For most students who work while taking writing classes, or rather, among the students I interviewed, writing is a means to a goal: The classifications I used are based on student desire. Brett and Chris had no desire for success, conventionally defined, in either place. Brett was interested in exploring his mind and his thinking through writing. He wrote in a variety of modes: While he saw himself as a writer at school and in his father's office, his spectacular, almost Olympian lack of interest in advancement placed him neither inside nor outside. Yet he wrote more and talked more critically about writing than anyone else in the study; I could not leave him out. If he did not fit into my scheme, something was wrong with the scheme.

Chris's interview reinforced my growing distrust of trying to lead the data rather than being guided by them. Chris had a chronic and potentially life-threatening disease. He needed to remain on his mother's health insurance to receive his treatment and therapy; he had to attend college and remain in student status to be covered by his mother's health insurance; and he had to work in order to stay in school. College enrollment, then, greatly enhanced his chances of survival. Writing classes were required by his college; considering his health, Chris had little choice in any of this. He was interested in stasis rather than progress—he wanted to stay healthy and working through the bizarre equations of health care; writing classes helped him to do that. Like Brett, he had his own purposes for writing and his own uses for writing classes; as with Brett, I could not honestly say that as a writer Chris was outside or inside anything.

Brett and Chris reminded me that writing students are infinitely varied and do not deserve simplification, generalization, or abstraction. They have their own purposes, goals, and agendas that have nothing to do with my research. If the culture of working student writers was to be described and interpreted by my project, as ethnography inherently and ethically required, then Brett and Chris would have to be included. I finally gave the two of them their own chapter; I liked them that much, after all. In it I talked about how my grand classificatory scheme was actually a limited, but still useful, strategy, and reminded myself and my readers that ethnography is situated and local. That knowledge was highlighted further by another quandary I found as a white researcher when I began to interview students at an historically Black university.

White Researcher, Black School

A white academic like me, who is researching a Black school, must confront several now almost classic worries about ethnography: that it is a colonizing research methodology; that it casts the study's participants in the role of Object or Other; and that it is inherently, unavoidably, essentially ethnocentric (Geertz 1988). Doing ethical ethnography means facing those questions, but for me they were complicated by other, equally ethical considerations that depended largely on my own history and positioning. Ethnography, because it depends on a researcher's perceptions, also depends upon her—and her awareness and honesty—as the primary research instrument.

Sherryl Kleinman, a sociologist who practices and writes about ethnographic research, began her career with a study of seminarians. During this research project, she was aware of her identity as a woman and as a nonobservant Jew among Christian ministers-in-training. Her religion intrigued the seminarians, and she was able to use their interest as a means of entry. Sensitive to gender issues, she attended women's caucus meetings, was pleased with the number of women students, and observed how these women were preparing for the ministry. But she failed to notice, somehow, that Black students sat apart from others in the cafeteria and had their own caucus, which she never visited. Writing up her research, she excluded considerations of race. She comments,

> Fieldworkers enter the field as more than researchers. Our identities and life experiences shape the political and ideological stances we take in our research . . . I was not conscious of my race as an important identity. (1993, 10)

In trying to protect her "liberal self-image" (1993, 12), she left out a large part of the story.

Although I was "conscious of my race as an important identity," it was not until I began interviewing students at an historically Black university in the area that I began to see the parameters of its importance for me. Unfortunately, I did not find Sherryl Kleinman until after my fieldwork was complete. When I designed the project, I intended to avoid this university altogether and to focus on students at several other local postsecondary institutions where African-American students are approximately half of the student body. Having visited the campus beforehand, I knew how uncomfortable I felt there. My most closely related experience is seeing something I had not previously known or recognized about my body in a department store mirror—a conventional example that trivializes the confrontation I felt. I was not confronting other people: It was my own attitudes, my perception of my space and place in the world that were at issue. Was I really, secretly, a racist? I had also taught a writing class with mostly African-American students, and it was not a happy experience, for me or for them; we seemed not to understand each other's perspectives or ways of expressing them. I, therefore, doubted my ability to research and write about African-American working students with honesty or involvement.

Then, a professor I knew who had some connections with the historically Black university urged me to reconsider; many students enrolled there were employed. And I thought, "I'm being lazy. Worse, I'm being biased." I made arrangements to visit the campus and speak to a class about my research, asking for volunteers who would like to talk with me about their working and writing lives. Four women indicated their willingness, and I took phone numbers and arranged to call them soon to arrange interview times and places. When I called, two of them were at work and one at school: I left messages. When no one followed up, I decided not to make a second call, believing that scheduling an interview in light of their commitments to job, family, and school was more than they wanted to take on at the time. This was a strategy I followed with working and writing students at other institutions as well; if someone were at work at 9 p.m., after having spent the day in school, I accepted their reluctance to be interviewed as a purely practical decision. At other schools, however, I was more likely to hang on and find someone who was willing to talk to me, even if three out of four people I called could or would not. I did not feel so much like a colonizer, putting African-Americans under the microscope of white academic research and appropriating their discourses for my own ends. Whether rightly or wrongly, I felt that my original plan to steer clear of this university had been a wise one for me and that in the interests of protecting themselves and their privacy, students with whom I had attempted to speak had delivered a clear message.

In the first writing I did about the project, my failure to pursue interviews with students at the university is recorded in a footnote. I was still trying to keep it hidden, under the line separating "text" from "gloss" or "marginalia." My reluctance to push contact with these students felt complicated: No other aspect of my research, perhaps, would have involved so much soul-searching and self-definition had I pursued it. But I did not. Kleinman and Copp suggest, "If we incorporated the idea that emotions encompass the research process, we would begin to use all our feelings, even the ones we now consider inappropriate, as tools for analysis" (1993, 52). As shameful as I feel this whole confession is, it is true that the research design and progress were undoubtedly influenced by what it contains. I was more comfortable interviewing African-American students where the tower was ivory.

Human Subjects Research Committee

The power of the academy—the ivory tower—raises another set of issues concerning ethical authority in ethnography. Who is empowered to define an ethically conducted piece of research? Where does ethical authority in ethnographic research ultimately reside: with the researcher, the professional community, or the institution? Maurice Punch's *The Politics and Ethics of Fieldwork* (1986) discusses his struggles with this question in great and illuminating detail; having read and admired his book, I should have been forewarned. At my university, the Human Subjects Research Committee had different ideas about the processes of ethical research than I did, and I discovered I needed the Committee's approval in order for my dissertation to be accepted. I had distributed a letter to all students and teachers who had been remotely connected with my study, explaining exactly what would be asked of them and what they might be likely to expect from participating in it. They would sign a permission slip and use my questions as a starting-off point to talk to me about their working and writing lives. I would record and transcribe our conversations and discuss what they had to say under a pseudonym, if they wished. I would also be careful to obscure other facts about their lives so that no one reading my work could discover who they were. The letter told students that talking about their writing lives might give them more understanding of and control over their processes of writing, but this was not guaranteed. The fact that these interviews were part of my dissertation research was made clear.

The permission slip repeated that the research was part of my dissertation process. When they signed it, students gave permission to be interviewed and allowed me to use what they had to say in my writing. They had a choice about whether to select a pseudonym or appear under their own names, and they left me with a phone number or an address where they could be contacted later on.

Any student who expressed an interest in the research and any teacher whose students were involved in it received a copy of this letter. If I actually met with a student for an interview, the first order of business was to discuss and sign the permission slip, place the tape recorder in an obvious position, ostentatiously switch it on, and begin talking. Much time in my first interactions with students, then, was devoted to what I considered a groundwork for honest and ethical research, making sure that students knew the uses to which their data might be put and foregrounding the willingness of their consent. I was well satisfied with my approach and tactics here and did not think either was problematic.

Because I felt that the privacy of students involved in the study was protected by the research design, I did not take my proposal to the Human Subjects Research Committee before I began. After data collection was complete and the resulting piece of writing began to be more about me as a researcher and less about the students with whom I spoke, I concluded that what I had was both research guide and ethnographic study, something not likely to be worth the Committee's attention, because I was its main subject and I had given my informed, if anguished, consent to the process.

But the person who approves dissertation manuscripts, noticing transcript selections in an appendix, mandated the Committee's involvement. Without it, I could not be approved for graduation. When I picked up the packet of forms I needed to complete, I noticed discrepancies between the Committee's and my ideas of what constituted ethical research practices. While the Committee and I shared a commitment to protecting the privacy and confidentiality of research participants, we disagreed about how to do this.

For example, in filling out their forms, I affirmed that students would be discussed only with pseudonyms (which was simply untrue—more about this later), that interview tapes would be kept in a locked cabinet, that I would check with all respondents before publishing anything about them and get their approval, and that I would destroy all research materials after two years. I duly complied, explaining that I kept the tapes at home and never left my door unlocked, but wondered how I would contact a set of respondents who move around as much as students do. Because I had, in fact, already attempted to contact them all when I completed my dissertation and failed to find about a third, who had, I hoped, moved on to greener pastures, I was unsure—and still am—about what I would do to fulfill that portion of my promise to the Committee should I publish portions of my dissertation.

The pseudonym issue is murkier, muddied further by the fact that I lied because it was expedient to do so. Although it is common practice in writing research to assign pseudonyms, I remain of two minds on the issue. None of the real names that appear in my study are uncommon or likely to stand out, and the contexts and settings of student lives are also obscured, so that identifying actual respondents would be difficult indeed. I like allowing students to pick their own pseudonyms, as the permission letter allowed them to do, and I was impressed by how few of them (less than twenty-five percent) actually did so. In a way, asking them to decide about a pseudonym seemed to me a more respecting and therefore more ethical choice: They had an opportunity to really think about how they wanted to position themselves in what they told me and to be more fully invested and involved in the research process itself.

I am also aware, however, that people change, and that it can be a disconcerting surprise to find one's name in print. Nor would I like to be sued. At the moment, arbitrarily assigning pseudonyms seems more appropriative of student discourses yet perhaps safer for students and researchers alike. Still, I expect to continue my practice of discussing the pseudonym issue with research respondents and to allow them to decide the name under which they would like to appear in writing. To me, this choice seems slightly more ethical than the other because it allows students to retain self-image and agency.

But even this approach has flaws. I am still not sure about the whole ethics of naming and pseudonyming, change my mind frequently as I shuffle through the manuscript boxes, and suspect that names and pseudo-names are best assigned on a case-by-case basis, further proof of ethnography's contextualized and situated nature. Sometimes students pick odd pseudonyms, such as the names of famous baseball players. Or they select a nickname that makes them sound, in writing, like a much different person than the one in the interview, so that their choice is inappropriate for their research persona that we constructed together and that I am editing. When this happened in the course of my dissertation research, I chose a less-colorful pseudonym for the student. In this essay, the three students discussed have pseudonyms. Research respondents are not units of knowledge; they are people.

Conclusion

My first extensive piece of ethnographic research and writing taught me that maintaining ethical perspectives throughout the processes of ethnographic research is both possible and necessary. Because each ethnographic research project is different—because participants and cultures are different and waver and change in the interactions that ethnographic encounters cause—locating those perspectives is always a challenge. At the same time, doing ethical ethnography raises questions about where ethical boundaries might lie, places where what's generally accepted as ethical research procedure does not apply or does not agree: Where does research follow-up end? Should respondents be asked to respond to chapters written about them? If they do not like the chapter, should it be included? Or would the inclusion of their response (as an endnote or appendix) be enough? Or does the researcher own the data (and the student's stories) once a permission form is signed? In other words, is it more ethical to be more observant of a student's or a researcher's readings of data, remembering that both parties may be far from disinterested in this question? What might happen to a researcher's academic career if all of a researcher's respondents changed their minds and pulled out at the last minute?

The foregoing examples indicate how one tiny aspect of ethnographic writing research can quickly devolve into a series of ethical questions over which a researcher can gnash her teeth for weeks or months. There are temptations to fabricate, temptations to reward, temptations to misread. There are even temptations to play shell games—games of chance—with writing up the research, hoping to substitute a closely related and more satisfying discussion for the ones that the data actually call for. There are issues of difference—race, class, and gender—that finally ask a researcher to address not only "Who are you?" but also "Who am I?" And there are varying interpretations of what ethical practice might be, and decisions to make between ethics and expediency or between idealistic ethics and practical ethics. (It is easy to see, is it not, where I am trying to convince myself that what I have done has an ethical rationale.) Conflated with all of this is what I think of as "the ethnographic dilemma": its selectivity and incompleteness, its commitment not to *the* truth, but to *a* truth or truths. Not coincidentally, these are also the attributes that make ethnographic methodologies so useful in researching diverse and variable contexts for writing: in a classroom, at work, and in other areas of students' lives.

In Composition studies these days, ethnographic research is perceived as positive, and it is expected to result in what Thomas Newkirk refers to as "transformative narratives," "ones in which the individual experiences some sort of conflict and undergoes a qualitative change in the resolution of that conflict" (1992, 134). The successful researcher conquers all adversities, maybe even before lunch. Nevertheless, as Van Maanen, Manning, and Miller comment,

> This curious policing of socially correct feeling within the fieldwork community can lead to a rather bizarre slanting of research reports wherein the fieldworker is represented as wallowing in an almost unmitigated delight while engaged in the research process. (1993, vii)

And such "slanting" means that hard, important questions are sometimes not asked, are glossed over, or are omitted from the final piece of writing. The research experience is happy, the researcher is getting a Ph.D., and the research respondents are being treated and represented ethically: I would like to believe that the interests and purposes of all those involved in ethnographic writing research would dovetail in just this way. Perhaps it does happen sometimes, but for me, the effort to maintain some semblance of the aforementioned fiction led to concealed purposes, conflated emotions and values, and a more-than-necessary partiality and secrecy in the research process. As Alice Brand writes, "We have authorized such cognitive terms as attitudes, beliefs, and values to stand proxy for emotion . . ." (1990, 290). By calling desires and feelings something else, I found them easier to ignore.

The problem is that cognition is not the whole story. For me to achieve my goal and earn a Ph.D., it was important that my project be completed successfully, and in order to do so, I often confused emotion, goals, and values. I put the best "spin" on decisions I made that were motivated mostly by expediency: my decision to discuss certain students more thoroughly than others, the readings I made of some students' interview tapes, my decision to stop research at an historically Black university, and my dealings with the Human Subjects Research Committee, which amounted to my agreeing to their requirements with my fingers crossed behind my back.

In ethnography, expediency—and slanting—need to be talked about. A discussion of ethnographic ethics very similar to this one was also part of my dissertation: Ethnography's validity and ethical authority proceed from its insistence on examining the subject positions of the researcher. But I find that here I have been more honest than I was there; after all, the stakes are different, and my diploma hangs framed on my wall.

Scrupulous observation and honest writing are essential in conducting naturalistic research, but a researcher should remain aware of her own interestedness, her locations, the cultures where only she is rewarded. Encounters in ethnographic writing research have much in common with what Mary Louise Pratt calls "contact zones," "social spaces where cultures meet, clash, and grapple with each other . . ." (1993, 444). And Margery Wolf reminds us that "separating Subject from Other is not so simple as one might expect, even though acts and actors are much the same in each. At times, the Subject becomes the Other and neither is Me" (1992, 12). Admitting my role as Subject was especially difficult.

In my research, I usually tried to be honest about where I thought I was. But because I was blinded by some particular slant of light or need, often other readers located my selves-at-the-time more easily than I did. The processes of ethnographic research also provided feedback. Through them, I learned to examine my emotions and to question the temptations they bring my way; to participate, observe, and listen rather than to always talk and guide; to honestly discuss my own identifications and attitudes and to constantly question my interactions with students whose race, class, gender, and background are different from my own; and to understand that both students and I must constantly negotiate among our values, perspectives, and needs, which may or may not coincide. That fine old question, "*Cui bono?*", ethically benefits ethnography.

Works Cited

Bishop, W. 1994. "The Perils, Pleasures, and Processes of Ethnographic Writing Research." In *Taking Stock: The Writing Process Movement in the '90s*, ed. L. Tobin and T. Newkirk, 261–79. Portsmouth, NH: Boynton/Cook Heinemann.

Brand, A. 1990. "Writing and Feelings: Checking Our Vital Signs." *Rhetoric Review* 8: 290–307.

Brandt, D. 1990. *Literacy as Involvement: The Acts of Writers, Readers, and Texts*. Carbondale: Southern Illinois University Press.

Brooke, R. 1991. *Writing and Sense of Self: Identity Negotiations in Writing Workshops*. Urbana, IL: NCTE.

Clifford, J. 1984. Introduction: "Partial Truths." In *Writing Culture: The Poetics and Politics of Ethnography*, ed. J. Clifford and G. Marcus, 1–26. Berkeley: University of California Press.

Denzin, N., and Y. Lincoln. 1994. Introduction: "Entering the Field of Qualitative Research." In *Handbook of Qualitative Research*, ed. N. Denzin and Y. Lincoln, 1–17. Thousand Oaks, CA: Sage.

Geertz, C. 1988. *Works and Lives: The Anthropologist as Author.* Stanford, CA: Stanford University Press.

Kleinman, S., and M. Copp. 1993. *Emotions and Fieldwork*. Newbury Park, CA: Sage.

Mortensen, P., and G. E. Kirsch, eds. 1996. *Ethics and Representation in Qualitative Studies of Literacy*. Urbana, IL: NCTE.

Newkirk, T. 1992. "The Narrative Roots of the Case Study." In *Methods and Methodology in Composition Research*, ed. G. Kirsch and P. Sullivan, 130–52. Carbondale: Southern Illinois University Press.

North, S. 1987. *The Making of Knowledge in Composition: Portrait of an Emerging Field*. Portsmouth, NH: Boynton/Cook.

Pratt, M. 1993. "Arts of the Contact Zone." In *Ways of Reading: An Anthology for Writers*, 3d ed., ed. D. Bartholomae and A. Petrosky, 442–55. Boston: Bedford Books of St. Martin's.

Punch, M. 1986. *The Politics and Ethics of Fieldwork*. Beverly Hills, CA: Sage.

Van Maanen, J., P. Manning, and M. Miller. 1993. Editors' Introduction. In *Emotions and Fieldwork*, ed. S. Kleinman and M. Copp, vii–viii. Newbury Park, CA: Sage.

Wolcott, H. 1987. "On Ethnographic Intent." In *Interpretive Ethnography of Education: At Home and Abroad*, ed. G. Spindler and L. Spindler, 37–57. Hillsdale, NJ: Erlbaum.

Wolf, M. 1992. *A Thrice-Told Tale*. Stanford, CA: Stanford University Press.

10

The English Doctoral Metacurriculum
An Issue of Ethics
Richard Fulkerson

Ethical Dimensions of Doctoral Curricula

In what follows, I make two assumptions about English doctoral programs. To me, they seem beyond question, but I want to be explicit. First, earning a doctorate in English is getting a job credential; it is only rarely disinterested study of knowledge for knowledge's sake. Specifically, if you earn a doctorate in English, you are preparing for the job of being an English professor. You might be able to succeed as a consultant, or a government researcher, or a technical writer in business, but that is not what you are preparing for; it is not what you want. Nor are you planning to earn a living as a literary critic.

In "No Openings at This Time: Job Market Collapse and Graduate Education," Erik Curren, who was President of the MLA Graduate Student Caucus, put it this way: "For all its benefits, graduate school was not an end in itself but, rather, an apprenticeship with the promise of eventual full-time academic employment . . . the promise of a job at the end of graduate school is on the order of a contractual agreement for most graduate students" (1994, 57).

The idea that the humanities doctorate is essentially an apprenticeship for the *profession*, not of being a scholar, but of being a college teacher, runs throughout our thinking, our brochures, and our programmatic decisions. As Michael Berube noted wryly during a small group discussion at the 1996 Wyoming conference, the difference between a traditional apprenticeship to a guild and the current one of the English doctoral student is that historically apprentices have been guaranteed membership in the guild once all of their requirements are met.

My second assumption is that being in the business of preparing apprentices for a profession creates ethical obligations on those doing the preparing. I do not go as far as Curren or Berube, both of whom imply that completing an apprenticeship ought to guarantee a job. But surely there is at least the implied ethical obligation to the candidate: If I set myself up as able to prepare you, and you in turn fulfill my requirements, then when you leave, you are at least fully capable of performing the job in question. In addition, if I put my stamp of approval on you as adequately skilled to enter the profession, I have accepted a similar ethical obligation toward those who may be interested in hiring you. They have a right to believe, upon my say-so, that you have been adequately prepared to do the job they want done.

To fail in these obligations is to violate two of our most basic ethical tenets. It is, first, a failure to keep one's word, a failure to fulfill the conditions of an implicit contract with both the candidate and the hiring department about the candidate's abilities. It is reneging on a promise. And second, it potentially harms innocent people who have relied on your assurances: the doctoral student, the department that hires her, and the students she teaches. In a legal context, to guarantee the quality of a product to a consumer and then to deliver one that fails to live up to that guarantee constitutes fraud.

English doctoral programs are the *de facto* credentialing agencies for the profession of college English teacher. To certify a candidate who then cannot do the job is just as unethical as it would be to certify a surgeon or lawyer who had put in the years in a program but could not in fact remove an appendix or draw up a will. Both the candidates and those they might later work for have been ill-served.

A Proposal

This, then, is my point: Because doctoral programs in English have an ethical obligation to their clientele to prepare candidates for the realities of the profession for which we are the accrediting agents, I propose, doctoral students should be required to study a sequence of courses, and to participate in extracurricular experiences, that will prepare them for the *profession*, over and above the courses that prepare them to understand the substance of their academic discipline. This required sequence I call a "professional metacurriculum." And I maintain it should be required even if the candidates object (we would not let law students or medical students choose whether to take courses central to their professional identities).[1]

In the last few years, as more graduate programs have begun to institute for-credit courses to prepare their own teaching assistants plus non-credit mentoring relations of various kinds, and as graduate study of composition has expanded (Brown, Meyer, and Enos 1994), some departments have been forced into taking significant steps in this direction, especially where Composition is concerned. I applaud such programs, but I know of no doctoral program that has created a parallel set of experiences concerning the teaching of literature. And even the most advanced internship programs in Composition seem, to me, to fall short in that they fail to address issues beyond departmental scope, such as the role of the professor in the university, and of the university in our culture.

The Mismatch Between Doctoral Preparation and the Job Market

Everyone in English knows that the job market for English doctoral graduates is terrible. The yearly total of positions advertised in the MLA *Job Information Lists* has been declining steadily from their recent highest point (2025 openings in 1988–1989). The 1993–1994 figure, 1056, was the lowest recorded since the MLA began its list in 1975–1976 ("1995–96 *Job Information List* Figures" 1996, 1).

Figures on degrees awarded are hard to get with much accuracy, and it is harder still to know exactly when a "new" Ph.D. was seeking a job. But the most helpful number is that during 1993–1994, 987 degrees were conferred in English and American literature (Huber 1995). In general, the number of degrees granted has been on the rise. [2]

The consequences are that for 1993-1994, the most recent year this information is available, of those new Ph.D.s whose employment status could be tracked, only 46.5 percent had gotten tenure track positions in higher education. And 10.5 percent were known to be unemployed (Huber 1995, 46). These figures do not differ significantly from those for previous years.

One assumes that some of those who found tenure-track positions will be looking for better ones and that many of the remaining fifty-five percent or so will be searching like crazy for *some* tenure-track appointment. Thus, in any year, the pressure from job hunters is actually greater than the number of new doctorates would suggest.

So, the overall job prospects for a new Ph.D. in English, even one from a prestigious school, are grim. Michael Berube, for instance, points out that at the University of Illinois, in 1993–1994, twenty new Ph.D.s in English graduated, and seven of them found tenure-track jobs, which he calls "not a bad record in the profession's worst year since the MLA began compiling job statistics" (1990, 26).

Where are the available jobs? Well, in the United States, there are only 493 four-year colleges with over 5000 students. There are 828 with fewer than 1000 students, and 843 with enrollments between 1000 and 5000 ("Almanac Issue" 1996, 14). According to a survey by Richard Sherry of Asbury College, from 1993 to 1998, these four-year colleges with between 1000 and 5000 students are projected to have over 3000 job openings for English professors (1993, 7). Accurate figures on future hiring are difficult to obtain, but these are apparently reasonable approximations. And whereas it used to be the case that smaller schools and community colleges were satisfied to hire permanent faculty with master's degrees, such is rarely if ever the case now.

Even researchers who optimistically predict a dramatic upswing in the need for new Ph.D.s beginning around 1997 agree that many of the positions will be in "comprehensive and liberal arts institutions without graduate programs . . . where the emphasis is on undergraduate teaching and on teaching for students in nonhumanities curricula" (Ziolkowski 1990, 15). "Few graduate students will secure jobs in research universities. If they get academic positions at all, they will be in state universities, liberal-arts colleges, or community colleges," says Jerry Gaff, vice-president of the Association of American Colleges and Universities (in Cage 1996, A20). In other words, that is where a lot of graduates from Penn State, from the University of Texas, from Yale are going to find tenure-track positions—*if they are fortunate.*

Others—again, if they are fortunate—will teach in community colleges. I have been unable to locate any figures about how many new Ph.D.s find employment in community colleges, which typically do not advertise in the MLA job list, but there are 1400 of them in the nation ("Almanac Issue" 1996, 14). About half of the graduates of the doctoral program at Texas A&M-Commerce take such jobs and remain in them. But our program is not typical. On the other hand, most of the community colleges in our region (which includes the Dallas County Community College District) want their new full-time faculty to have doctorates.

As a consequence, the graduates of major research universities (along with their mentors) need to alter their career assumptions. They are less and less likely to find positions in the sort of institutions from which they earned their doctorates, and more and more likely to find them in smaller schools and community colleges with more open admission policies and fewer, if any, specialized classes to teach, not to mention heavier teaching loads.

I do not recite this grim paradox as yet one more lament about the terrible status of the job market. That is not news. Nor do I intend to address the important issue of whether doctorate-granting departments have an ethical responsibility to reduce their enrollments, an issue raised pointedly in the *Chronicle of Higher Education* by Nelson and Berube (1994).[3]

Instead, I want to stress that most new Ph.D.s who succeed in finding teaching positions will not now, and probably not ever, work in the sort of institution in which they did their graduate work—and for which their graduate work best prepared them. Graduates from high-powered research programs are often likely to spend their careers at much smaller institutions, institutions with different teaching loads, different leave policies and support services, different institutional cultures, and different missions.

You can make this situation concrete simply by looking at the English faculty of a regional college. I recently received a brochure from one in Texas. It has an enrollment of about 12,000 and gives a master's degree in English. The brochure notes that its department members "represent eighteen of the nation's top universities." As I examine the list of twenty-three graduate faculty, I see professors with doctorates from the Universities of North Carolina, Southern California, Michigan, and Connecticut, plus Indiana University, Purdue, and Rice. The situation is the same in my own smaller department of fifteen, where professors have degrees from Southern California, Louisiana State, Pittsburgh, Harvard, Johns Hopkins, Vanderbilt, Indiana, and Ohio State. For most of us, little in our doctoral training prepared us for the sort of work we actually do. For doctoral programs not to prepare their candidates for the real careers most of them face constitutes, as I argued earlier, an ethical, as well as a practical, failure.

Of course, whether this is a crisis depends partly on your perspective. From the viewpoint of the new Ph.D. or her adviser, the situation is potentially tragic. From the viewpoint of departments with the opportunity to hire, it is at least a buyer's market with a wealth of really bright applicants available, whether or not they have been fully prepared for what lies ahead. A department can afford to be choosy and to ask for extensive documentation of abilities from prospective hires. For instance, Marta Caminero-Santangelo (1994) discusses a department that requires all applicants to write fairly elaborate essays answering three questions about their specific teaching interests, how these interests would fit with the department's revised curriculum, and how scholarship and criticism contribute to the applicant's teaching. (More on this later.)

My own department has recently begun to require that each on-campus candidate teach a real class of our students, not just give the more traditional presentation to the faculty. Walking into a group of students you do not know, and teaching effectively, while a group of faculty and search committee members watch from the back of the room, is a pretty stiff challenge. In fact, sometimes we think it is unfair, but we are quite happy with the results of our last eight hires done under this system. In several instances, however, it has revealed truly serious problems with otherwise excellent candidates. And that is what I mean by a mismatch between market and preparation. Consequently, I suggest that those who prepare doctoral students can no longer see the job as that of replicating themselves in their graduates.[4]

The English doctorate in the United States was essentially built on the much-admired German philological model, a model in which it was quite acceptable for a professor to be a "dismal failure" as a teacher (Graff and Warner 1989, 7) so long as *he* contributed to the "advancement of knowledge." Said James Morgan Hart, later to be president of the MLA, "The [German] professor has but one aim in life: scholarly renown" (1989, 21). Teaching was a by-product of *his* scholarship, and the tasks we now refer to vaguely and collectively as "service" were not part of the job.

Although that model has not gone unchallenged, the central values of the German/Johns Hopkins model still dominate most English graduate programs. They include minimal teaching, small classes of mostly graduate students, a high degree of specialization, sabbaticals and leaves of absence, rewards for publication, and a devaluation of undergraduate teaching, especially of lower-division courses for non-majors. One result, as articulated by Seth Katz, is that "graduate programs typically do students a disservice by making it seem as if the profession is just about doing research in one's field" (1995, 62). Katz, himself a graduate of a prestigious program, made this remark after landing a tenure-track position, but he had been "on the market" for four years. In his article, he catalogues at some length what his doctoral work failed to teach him that he needed to know about the profession, including the need to be familiar with both pedagogical and professional issues (1995, 63).

Certainly the Germanic ideal was the model of "success" that prevailed in my graduate work at a Big Ten university a quarter of a century ago. While I was well-prepared "academically," what I did not know about the profession, about education, about departmental and university politics would literally fill several books.

Students who have spent six or more years living in an environment in which scholarship is everything get a warped sense of what most of higher education actually involves. As Sherry says, "Jobseekers have very inaccurate expectations of the small college job market" (1993, 4). And Nona Fienberg, Coordinator of the English and Journalism Department at Keene State College, in an article subtitled "Hiring at a Nonelite College," notes, "We see job candidates who fully expect that their careers will be played on the same chessboard that they have been making moves on for their undergraduate and graduate careers" (1995, 12). She tells of interviewing one candidate who was articulate about her dissertation topic, female American multicultural autobiographies, but could not answer a simple question about the possible connection of her work to a literature classroom. Fienberg concludes that her department has decided it must include the word *teaching* four times in a job ad to make the point about their school's professional identity (1995, 12).

Another illustration, in "The Ethics of Hiring," doctoral candidate Marta Caminero-Santangelo (1994) complains bitterly about being exploited by a department she wanted to apply to. The problem? That department required all applicants to include in their applications written answers to three specific questions about some relationships among a new curriculum, the applicant's research, teaching, theory, and making writing assignments. To Caminero-Santangelo, this is exploiting the candidates because "applicants, then, had to guess at the search committee's hidden agenda and to spend a significant amount of time and effort on a single application letter" (1994, 63). She calls this the "most blatant abuse of a buyer's market situation that I have encountered" (1994, 62). I would say it is no abuse to ask an applicant to spend "a significant amount of time" preparing an application (the committee will, after all, spend a significant amount of time reading it).[5] Moreover, by asking the questions it did, the department was really sending a clearer message than usual about what its values were.

If job candidates seem unprepared for the pedagogical demands of many of the available jobs, it is a good bet they are even less ready for the "service" component of being a professor at one of the "nonelite" colleges. In the first few years of my current job, I was asked to perform the following tasks:

- Chair the departmental first-year composition committee;
- Evaluate the effectiveness of classroom teaching by both teaching assistants in my own department, and professors nominated for a teaching award from across the university;
- Chair a committee to revise the university's mission statement as part of an accreditation self-study;
- Justify to a university-wide committee the intellectual integrity and general educational value of one of my undergraduate courses;
- Serve on search committees within my own department, including one for a new head;
- Help determine who would receive grant money across the university, from art to math to chemistry to education;
- Do Saturday morning enrichment workshops in critical thinking for gifted students in Dallas middle schools;
- Chair a university-wide committee to create a *Faculty Handbook*.

Had I been at a different nonelite college or university, I might have been involved in tenure appeals of professors not in my field, in collective bargaining, in determining insurance and retirement packages, in creating industry/university coalitions, and in writing programmatic grant proposals.

These activities have two features in common; they are perfectly ordinary parts of a professor's work at a small- to medium-size American college or university, and none of them is part of the training one gets during doctoral study to be "a professor."

In our world, it is not professionally adequate for a new holder of a doctorate in English to be a scholar in a specialty. A century ago, Hart could wax eloquent about the wonders of the Germanic system of higher education, then being brought into the United States through the port of Johns Hopkins University. But we live in a different context. Of course, a few of the yearly 1000 doctoral graduates in English will still find research positions with light teaching loads, frequent sabbaticals, and the leisure time to think and write, but we all know such positions are getting rare and are now more likely to go to someone who has been out of graduate school a few years and used the time to build an impressive *vitae*. As we create such a backlog of scholars who are not where they want to be, more and more of our new graduates will not be able to get the sorts of jobs they used to assume were their due. Of course it is unethical for the leaders in a doctoral program not to inform candidates about such a situation at the beginning of their work (lying by omission about a topic of direct relevance to the candidate's future), but it is equally unethical for their training not to fit them to do well the sorts of jobs that may be available—the ones with the heavier and more diverse teaching loads.

Some Paradoxes of Preparing "for the Profession"

In a bad job market, students are doing everything they can to make themselves competitive for the few prestige positions available. They (and more importantly their departments) are in large measure, however, ignoring the professional (not scholarly) preparation that would make them more flexible and more broadly aware of a professor's total role, and thus good candidates for a wider range of teaching positions.

Let me illustrate with two anecdotes. First, a few years ago I heard then president of MLA, Patricia Spacks, remark over cocktails that at her school (University of Virginia), graduate students were complaining about having to take graduate seminars at all. She later explained the point in print. The current depressed job market has increased the emphasis on specialization, publication, and research, so that ever younger graduate students are taught that in order to get teaching positions, they must already have published several articles and given convention presentations (1994, 3). (Unlike the Germanic scholar, whose motto was "Think much, publish little.") Spacks notes that her students in a teaching colloquium said that "their classes on the whole were pretty much a waste of time. Classes don't help students publish articles" (1994, 3). And she concludes, rightly I think, that "graduate students have been pushed already in directions that may not contribute to good teaching and that may arguably interfere in the long run with the best kind of writing" (1994, 3).

Second, James Knapp tells the story of the University of Pittsburgh's attempt to "professionalize" its graduate English program. The Pitt department had long had the traditional single graduate course in "how to teach composition," but in the mid-eighties they added a second required seminar "designed to provide our students with a more historically informed and self-reflective understanding of what teaching English might involve" (1995, 7). Knapp says he "would like to be able to report that this seminar is one successful step in our departmental efforts to prepare students for the jobs they will one day take" (1995, 8). However, the course was abolished a few years later because "large numbers of graduate students were bitterly opposed to the requirement . . . most argued that the course prevented students from getting started on what was generally referred to as 'their work'" (1995, 8).

Many of the schools at which these candidates will actually find work reject the Germanic/Johns Hopkins model: These schools value teaching and service over research (Sherry 1993, 6; Katz 1995, 63). Teaching *is* "their work," whether the graduate students realize it. And in a further departure from the Germanic model, such "teaching" now includes nurturing and mentoring (even outside the classroom) students of all ages and social backgrounds, students with families and jobs, students with financial and social problems, students that yesterday's Germanic university did not bring to the campus.

This is a real catch-22 for graduate training. As Director of Graduate Studies, I certainly do not want to go on record as opposing research and scholarship. My own institution now has pretensions to scholarship, pretensions that did not exist when I was hired in 1970. So, on hiring committees we must look at the likelihood of scholarly productivity from a candidate, knowing that without it the best faculty member in the world will not earn tenure or promotion, at a university that nevertheless declares that teaching is its primary mission. (One of my younger colleagues has a sign on her office wall saying, "It's the publications, stupid!") But if new doctoral graduates have, in fact, concentrated on publication and in consequence slighted other aspects of the profession, they will do poorly in our interviews and will not be hired either. Moreover, I am constantly aware of this catch-22 when I emphasize to graduate students who are genuinely interested in teaching that they need to be giving conference papers and trying to publish in order to create those all-important *vitae* lines.

Some Attempts to Professionalize Graduate Programs

In response to the awful job market, a number of graduate programs are making moves to "professionalize" their graduating doctoral students, although it is not clear that *professionalizing* means the same thing in different programs. Too often, it merely means more scholarship, published sooner. To Gary Olson at the University of South Florida, it means working on publishing and on becoming active at conferences such as CCCC. Olson teaches a required course for doctoral students in Writing for Publication, and he notes that his last ten doctoral students have all converted their dissertations into books (Parham 1995, 6). There is a similar course at the University of Texas at Austin.

New Mexico State University has a course in "Professional Issues," in which students examine the job market, the MLA *Job Information Lists*, and the *curricula vitae* of students who have succeeded in the job hunt. Later, weekly meetings are held to practice interviews, to prepare *vitaes*, and so on (Parham 1995, 6). The same is done at Ohio State University, where practice interviews are videotaped and then critiqued by professors. Arizona State University has eliminated the doctoral written examination and substituted a graduate portfolio. In the portfolio must be three papers judged "publishable" by a faculty committee.

Clearly, in these cases, the attempt to professionalize means more and earlier scholarly publication. Steve Watt of Indiana University identifies what he calls "an ideology of grinding scholar production" and says, "One result of this ideology is the driving of students into print and onto conference programs long before they are ready" (1995, 31). But at the University of Iowa, a section on pedagogy has recently been added to the doctoral examination (Parham 1995, 7; see also Heller 1994).[6]

These represent two, virtually opposite, responses to the job crisis. The first set, much the more common, emphasizes scholarship and savvy—in other words, selling the traditional package even harder and with "higher quality" students, making the race to get one of the prestige jobs yet more frantic. It is not uncommon to hear some variation of the remark that brand new English Ph.D.s now have better credentials than those needed for tenure a decade or so ago. Or the flip side, from someone on a hiring committee to another member as they go through the several hundred applications for an opening: "Do you realize that we wouldn't stand a chance of getting this job?"

But the Iowa approach suggests that maybe, just maybe, one sensible approach to the current market is to take further steps to assure that the prospective doctoral student is both a good and an informed teacher. And there is evidence out there that for many of the smaller schools, and certainly the community colleges, teaching really is important, and may even come first. It may be no accident that in a terrible job market, doctoral graduates from the University of Iowa are being employed at near record rates (Heller 1994, A16).[7]

The Doctoral Metacurriculum

I have more in mind than one or two courses in how to teach freshman composition or modest elaboration of doctoral examination areas. I envision an extended sequence of for-credit work that all English doctoral students need in addition to their field-specific studies. When Katz says, "Graduate programs do well at teaching students to appreciate the intellectual rewards of academic research. Typically, though, graduate programs do not train students to be professional academics" (1995, 66), he has identified a serious problem, a serious failure on the part of the programs. While we cannot solve the problems of the job market in any direct way that I can see, we can modify the doctoral curriculum to make it a genuinely appropriate apprenticeship experience not just for scholarship, but for the full life of being a professor. I refer to such modifications as a "metacurriculum" because the types of courses I am proposing are either non-disciplinary or only tangentially "within" the field and because they involve a substantial amount of reflection about "the English curriculum."

Let me try to clarify the difference between the graduate curriculum in English and this "metacurriculum." We frequently distinguish (loosely) between theory and practice; thus our students may well take one or more courses in "Theory" plus several courses in literature or composition in which the "theory" is applied—let us say a course in "The Construction of Gender in Contemporary African-American Female Writers." In my terms, these are both within the regular English curriculum. If, however, you taught a seminar in how to use theory to design a curriculum, conduct classes in literature or composition, assess students, or explain the importance of these courses to people outside the discipline, that seminar would be part of the metacurriculum. In other words, I propose turning the theory/practice binary into a triad of theory/practice/profession (with all three in constant interanimation).

Obviously, the distinction between curricular courses and metacurricular courses is not a clean one. In some universities, courses in how to teach composition are considered metacurricular (often without carrying credit). In other universities, those same courses are (now) part of a comp/rhet concentration. In my department, we have a sequence of comp/rhet courses, but we distinguish them from courses on professional and pedagogical issues. Thus "Classical Rhetoric" and "Stylistics" are "curricular" courses, but "Theory and Practice of Argumentation" is a metacurricular course required of all students; it deals explicitly with issues of whether, why, and how argumentative writing should be and/or can be taught to college freshmen. A three-hour colloquium on teaching literature is a metacurricular requirement for literature majors, whereas "Literary Theory" is a "curricular" offering.

Here is another way to highlight the differences. I presume that we have come far enough now that virtually all new Ph.D.s in English would be familiar with Boynton/Cook and Southern Illinois University Press as leading publishers of composition scholarship, just as they would know works from Oxford University Press, Chicago, and others, in literary studies. But how many new Ph.D.s in English are familiar with the listings for Jossey-Bass, a company that plays for the profession of college teaching approximately the same role that Boynton/Cook does for Composition studies? And surely all new Ph.D.s know the leading scholarly journals in both literature and composition, but how many are familiar with journals such as *The Teaching Professor*, or the *Journal of General Education*, or *Academe*, or *Perspectives* (the journal of the Association for General and Liberal Studies)? (Or even *The ADE Bulletin*?) For that matter, how many new English doctorates even know there are organizations such as the Association for General and Liberal Studies, whose concerns are directly relevant to what many English professors will spend their careers doing? Reading journals such as these is as important to being a professional in higher education as is reading the journals in composition or literature.

I am not interested in arguing for any specific set of courses. Proposing a precise configuration of the metacurriculum would be premature. But I do not believe this is essentially a local issue; this is one that the profession needs to settle on through dialectic. I merely intend to offer some representative possibilities.

Naturally, I have a particular fondness for the doctoral program that I oversee, which by state mandate has stressed different versions of the metacurriculum since 1968. As that program has evolved, it has allowed concentrations in either literature or composition, but for either concentration, in a sixty-hour program, at least eighteen hours must be metacurricular courses.

Let me be a bit more specific, however. What sorts of topics should English doctoral students address in this metacurriculum? As a general outline, I suggest they need metacurricular study in five overlapping areas: pedagogy itself, the philosophy of education, the sociology of the profession, the politics of the profession, and educational and professional history.[8] (And running throughout these studies should be attention to the ethical issues professors face, presented in context.)[9]

Pedagogy

I think it obvious why pedagogy is crucial, now more than ever. It is a major part of any professor's job. From the point of view of the public who in one way or another pays all our salaries, it is our central task. It is not a natural activity, and it does not derive naturally from being a superior scholar. With the broadening socioeconomic and multicultural makeup of the American college population, it becomes all the more important that college professors engage in what George Hillocks has addressed as "reflective practice." And with the controversies over canonicity, interpretive theory, and general education requirements, it is more than ever important that professors of English be skilled in addressing a wide variety of audiences and issues. In my department, there is a sort of standing ironic myth that when the Director of General Education (who was an English professor) would come to visit a colloquium in teaching literature, none of our graduate students could provide an articulate answer to the question, "Why should American college students take courses in literature?"[10]

So, the main emphasis within the metacurriculum is teaching itself—and I do not mean simply a survival course in one university's incarnation of undergraduate composition, nor do I mean courses in various theories of literature. Knowing the theories does *not* mean knowing how to teach a course in "British Literature after 1800" to thirty-five sophomores who are not English majors. I agree with James Slevin when he says of modern graduate students, "Teaching is rarely discussed and even more rarely presented as a vital part of their preparation for their careers" (1992, 2). I mean coursework that would include learning theory in general, classroom management alternatives, resources about teaching (such as the journals I mentioned), alternative approaches to *teaching* composition and literature, ethical issues in the classroom, and the place(s) of composition and literature in American general education. We know that one of the scandals of the large research university is that classroom effectiveness is of only minimal significance in overall faculty "success." But that is not the case at the many smaller four-year schools, where effective teaching is valued (Sherry 1993, 6), and where small departments often provide the flexibility for young teachers to try out new and unusual approaches to courses, if they just know how to go about it. Where, in our current doctoral programs, does a graduate student learn how to design a new course and/or write a convincing proposal for its inclusion in the department or college curriculum?[11]

The Philosophy of Education

When I was an undergraduate mathematics major, earning a certificate to teach in the public schools of Illinois, a course in Philosophy of Education was a requirement for the certificate. I found the study invaluable in raising the large question of what education in a democracy is for, and then asking what curricular, ethical, and financial implications follow from alternate views of its role. It constantly surprises and distresses me when I run into university professors who have not asked these questions, who indeed take them as non-questions because they are tacitly settled—even though, just as we differ over literary theory, when the issues actually surface (such as in response to a challenge to our curriculum), it turns out that we disagree about educational purpose.

My department does not offer any course in Philosophy of Education, although, naturally, issues relevant to it come up in our teaching colloquiums, in our Classical Rhetoric seminar, in relation to our Basic Writing requirement (mandated by the state), and in a new course in disciplinary history. But I frequently recommend that students actually enroll in a serious course in Educational Philosophy taught by the head of our Department of Secondary and Higher Education. It deals explicitly with seven competing philosophies of education, ranging from Platonic Idealism, to Neo-Thomism, to Deweyan experimentalism (Morris and Pai 1976).

The Sociology of the Profession

I suggest that graduate students actually study what I am calling The Sociology of the Profession because it seems to me that a university faculty forms a culture, with the English department being a component. Newly hired young faculty with doctorates need to be aware of how that culture operates, what its imperatives are, how social class levels and governing structures operate. Yet, as Janet Gezari of Connecticut College puts it,

> What no one is preparing graduate students for is life as a faculty member. This life, which may be more compelling at colleges than at universities, requires graduate students to identify themselves not just with their disciplines but with other faculty. I think the widespread lack of understanding of the values of academic life and of the struggles by faculty that have made academic communities different from other communities of workers has put those values and those communities in jeopardy. The teaching mission is, in my view, sustained by the academic world we create as its setting. (in Slevin 1992, 1)

Understanding the sociology of the professoriat would extend, I think, to matters of governance, all the way from how a college or university is financed, through the faculty senate, and departmental committees. At a minimum, during doctoral work, graduate students should be real members of at least departmental committees, and perhaps college or university ones as well. My department does have graduate students on all department committees (although they are non-voting members on most), and that includes the three committees involved in recommending to the head annual faculty evaluations (for teaching, scholarship, and service). And at my university, two graduate students each year are elected to serve on the Graduate Council. That is a good start, I guess, but it means only two out of almost 2000 (including master's and doctoral students) from across the university have the experience. It would not hurt if graduate students were given explicit guidance about how to chair a committee, how to call meetings, how to run a meeting, how to write up minutes, and how to write a committee report. I cannot imagine that doctoral students need an entire course in such matters, but it seems reasonable to me that a significant portion of some course about the profession could be devoted to them.

Again, this is more complicated than I am making it seem, because the professoriat is not just one culture; to an extent, every university and every department is its own culture, and the new immigrant scholar coming to live there needs as much general knowledge about academic cultures as possible in order to understand how to examine and live in the culture of the department that hires her. Fienberg contrasts the cultures of large research departments with those at "nonelite" colleges, and says, "All academics need to learn about the diversity of academic cultures," but that she regularly has job applicants "who have learned exclusively and narrowly the monolithic discourse of the research institution" (1995, 13).

The Politics of the Profession

Distinguishing the Politics of the Profession from the sociology may be impossible and unnecessary, but in English today, we put so much emphasis on the political (power) dimensions of cultural study that I want to make explicit that this is also something new doctoral students need to know, for their own good. When I graduated from Ohio State University in 1970, I had the arrogance of recent study, and fully expected to be hired by a major research university. When no such job appeared and I ended up at a compass-point university in the South, I lost my expectations but not my arrogance. I will not go into the details, but having at least landed a tenure-track position (at a university that did not expect publication), I almost managed not to earn tenure because I did not understand that young assistant professors, even from elite programs, were in fact on the bottom rung of a fairly long ladder of power relations. In addition, I did not understand the importance of getting to know the other folks involved, especially those with the power—*networking*, we would call it today. Six of us were hired in the department that year, all young, all male, all with new doctorates from elite universities. Only two of us wound up with tenure.

I admit that when it comes to studying the sociology and politics of the profession, I do not know exactly how this is to be done within the formal curriculum. It is clear that in some graduate programs students learn a good deal of this information through informal grapevines (often less than accurate, at least in my department), through mentoring relationships, and sometimes in such venues as workshops about interviewing for jobs. I do not think that is enough, but I am not prepared to offer any specific approach to designing such a course, except to say that it should include readings from *The ADE Bulletin* and *The Chronicle of Higher Education*, plus perhaps books like *The Academic's Handbook* (DeNeef and Goodwin 1995), and perhaps Solomon and Solomon's *Up the University* (1993).

Educational and Professional History

Finally, it has only recently become clear to me that a new professor in English is immensely better off if he is aware of the peculiar history that has led to the role of higher education in the United States today, and, specifically, to the often less than harmonious jointure of literature in English with composition/rhetoric in one administrative unit. Having developed such a course in my own department and taught it twice, I can be more specific about it than about most of my other topic areas.

The new seminar is called "Professing English in America." According to our catalogue, English 678

> Examines the historical and contemporary situation of the profession of teaching college English. Topics to be discussed may include the relationship of scholarship and teaching, literature and composition, departments and their publics, curriculum and assessment, and professional ethics and academic freedom.

When I wrote that passage, I evidently wanted to cover all the bases; that description would certainly allow me to teach the sociology and politics of the profession, but I have chosen to stress the history—along with whatever conclusions about sociology and politics that strategy may allow. The course is an elective that counts toward either a composition or a literature concentration. I am persuaded that such a course ought to be required of all doctoral students, as it is at SUNY-Albany, but I was unwilling to add a further requirement to every doctoral student's degree program—at least until the course had been tried out. I probably do not need to add that my department had no staff member with sufficient expertise to teach the course. Because I was the one pushing it, it fell to me to teach it. I am afraid that my graduate students and I both suffered from my ignorance and my obvious bias toward composition over literature. And it is abundantly clear that I learned more from the course than my students could have, even though their own research projects seem to have opened up important new avenues for them. Five students took the course each of the two times it has been offered.

While I frequently felt myself floundering, my students handled it with aplomb. As a group, we read five major books dealing with the history of the discipline: James Berlin's two monographs *Writing Instruction in Nineteenth-Century American Colleges* (1984) and *Rhetoric and Reality: Writing Instruction in American Colleges, 1900–1985* (1987); Kitzhaber's famous dissertation *Rhetoric in American Colleges, 1850–1900* (1953); Graff's *Professing Literature* (1987); and Graff and Warner's *The Origins of Literary Studies in America*

(1989). That was for the first offering of the course. Since that time, several important new books have become available: *The Elephants Teach* (1996) by D. G. Myers, and John Brereton's collection (1995) of original documents about composition. We also read, as a class, a number of theoretical and historical articles, and each student read other articles plus one book in order to produce abstracts for class presentation. In general, my students, in anonymous post-semester evaluations, praised the class. One from the first section wrote,

> This is a very useful course. It helps incredibly to know where you came from, professionally. I am not sure if this is a class to take at the beginning of a program or at the end. At the end you have a lot of accumulated knowledge to call on while reading, but early on you need to know that everything is not etched in stone somewhere. It's all been made up in the last 100–200 years. It also makes me feel secure in my confusion knowing that everyone and the whole field has been confused—so it's not my fault.

The other student holistic comments were similar.

The second time the course was offered, one student, an experienced teacher in a community college, wrote, "I found the course to be extremely valuable. I don't know how I got along for so long without knowing this material." Another from that section said, "I found the course very effective/useful/valuable. When I started the course I was without a clue, but now have a general sense of the history, movements, and the current status of this profession."

A Different Approach to Professionalization

Recognizing the problem of a frequent mismatch between professional realities and doctoral preparation, the Association of American Colleges and Universities, in cooperation with the Pew Charitable Trusts and the Council of Graduate Schools, has recently experimented with an extended metacurricular project called Preparing Future Faculty. Originally (1990–1991), the project paired graduate students in history, classics, religious studies, political science, psychology, and English from three large research universities, with teaching faculty in those disciplines from nearby liberal arts colleges. In 1994 an expanded version of the project became operative, involving seventeen doctoral institutions, five of which received grants of $170,000 to create special programs for preparing future professors, programs that involved expanded alliances with nearby community colleges and undergraduate four-year schools (Cage 1996, A19). Reading James Slevin's report (1992) on the initial project is both enlightening and discouraging. The project was judged a success, but it seems so idealistic as scarcely to hold out much hope for the rest of us. Most institutions of higher education are not going to have large foundation grants to enable extensive travel and planned interaction of doctoral students at research universities with faculty members at undergraduate or community colleges. And, ironically, faculty members in the graduate programs often balk at the program, either because "they view it as a 'distraction' from a student's graduate course work and research" (Cage 1996, A19), or because "it exposes graduate students to the realities of the job market (both its range and its uncertainty) and demonstrates the extent to which the preparation they are receiving is inappropriate to what they are likely to be doing, if they are in the profession at all" (Schwalm 1995).

While Preparing Future Faculty and other similar programs should certainly be encouraged, and the rest of us can benefit from what is learned as a result of them, most schools with doctoral programs in English need to find more practicable ways of their own to institute some version of what I have been calling the doctoral metacurriculum.

Ethical Issues Once More

If a doctoral program required some version of the professional metacurriculum I am proposing, then we could be relatively sure that several of our ethical obligations would be better satisfied than they are at present. As I see it, we owe two obligations to our students and one to the departments that will hire them. First, we owe it to students to be frank with them, early and often, about the shortage of available jobs. As I see the metacurriculum, that topic would come up regularly in a variety of contexts. We would no longer be engaging in a deceptive conspiracy of silence right up until the job search begins.

Second, we owe it to our students to prepare them effectively for the diverse sorts of available jobs. Whether they learned about the market in a course on professional history or one on The Culture of American Colleges, students studying this professional metacurriculum would understand from early in their careers not only that jobs are scarce, but also that the market is diverse. All doctoral students would have examined the variety of American colleges, their alternative missions, values, and curricula. None of them should be surprised to find departments with heavy teaching loads, or departments that emphasize interdisciplinary general education for undergraduate non-majors, or departments that value teaching over scholarship.

Moreover, by adopting some version of this metacurriculum, we also would be acting more ethically toward those interested in hiring our graduates. Our students would have taught under our close mentoring; they would have been observed teaching, and been required to study, reflect on, and write about classroom practices and professional issues. Thus, when they go on the market, and we professors write letters attesting to their virtues, we could, honestly, assure our peers who consider hiring them that they do indeed possess the professional abilities those departments value, not just the scholarly and interpretive skills currently stressed in the prestige departments, following the Johns Hopkins model.

Now, going through such a program is no guarantee that the newly created Ph.D. will find a slot in the guild, because the program does nothing to alter the disparity between supply and demand. However, the candidates would have known that from the start, and thus we would at least not be guilty of duplicitous advertising. Moreover, I am willing to go out on a limb and make a prediction that many readers may doubt: I predict that in competing for the available openings, the graduate of a doctoral program with a metacurriculum is likely to be the more desirable and the more flexible candidate. Thus, as a result of the metacurricular experiences, both the new hire and the hiring department will be better satisfied with the result, and this will remain true even if the job market itself turns around within a decade. This is one of those rare cases in which the idealistic and ethical turns out also to be the practical.

Notes

1. It seems to me important that the activities I am advocating be part of the required curriculum for which real course credit is given, along with real grades. To relegate such matters to extracurricular non-credit venues is to send a clear message that they are of only marginal importance.

2. The job market figures are actually more complex than this. There was a temporary upswing of announced openings in 1994–1995, but it did not continue. The number of advertised English positions for the last three years is as follows:

* 1993–1994: 1056

* 1994–1995: 1142

* 1995–1996: 1078

The number of openings is meaningless without knowing how many new degrees the approximately 150 ("The MLA's 1991–92 Survey" 1994, 1) doctorate-granting English departments in the United States confer each year. That number of programs contrasts with the sixty programs in 1958, 124 in 1972, 132 in 1988 (Bowen and Rudenstine 1992, 27).

To provide historical perspective, the number of English doctorates granted rose steadily in the 1960s, hitting its peak of about 1400 in 1973 (Bowen and Rudenstine 1992, 388). Degrees awarded dropped after that. The Winter 1993 *ADE Bulletin*, tells us that an average of 666 new doctorates in English were given yearly for academic years 1985–1989 (Huber 1993, 56). Currently, the number of yearly doctoral graduates in English is just under 1000, a figure that has been mostly steady, with a slight increase for the last several years (Huber 1995). Note, however, that while the MLA figure for 1993–1994 is 943 according to Huber, the *Chronicle of Higher Education* gives 1,344 for that same year (1996, 22).

In one sense, then, the relevant figures for 1993–1994 do not look too bad—1056 openings and something under 1000 new English Ph.D.s. At least three factors make those figures misleading. First, the openings include a significant number of senior positions as well as positions for new Ph.D.s. From 1982 to 1995, of the tenure-track positions announced in the October *Job Information List*, only about one-third were junior positions ("Latest *Job Information List* Figures" 1996, 2). Second, the count of openings is for all positions announced, whether they are tenure-track, temporary, adjunct, and so forth (and whether they actually turn into filled positions or not). Third, we know that there is a backlog of Ph.D.s from previous years who did not find employment, or at least not permanent employment.

So, for those 1056 openings (including senior and temporary as well as tenure-track), there are not merely 1000 interested applicants. This explains why only forty-six percent of new doctoral graduates find tenure-track positions, while twenty percent had some sort of non-tenure job in higher education, and 10.5 percent had found employment outside of education (Huber 1995, 46).

One more complicating factor in the data is the number of jobs teaching English in community colleges in the United States. Most of them are not advertised in the MLA *Job Information List*. It is my impression that a good many of the permanent, full-time community college positions now go to candidates with doctorates, but on the other hand, many of the community college openings are for part-time, temporary staff. I have found no published data dealing with this segment of the job market.

3. Actually, I have my doubts about the logic or ethics of dealing with the supply/demand imbalance by restricting entry into graduate programs. From long experience, I have realized that our usual criteria for admitting a student into a program—a GRE score, a writing sample, letters of recommendation—are anything but solid predictors of success, especially success in the classroom. So, demanding, let us say, even higher admission scores, and thus cutting down the size of an entering class of graduate students, may well be unfair to students who would later shine, and thus eventually lead to a less effective group of graduates for hiring institutions to interview.

4. I write as if I believe the traditional scholarly doctorate was satisfactory in the past but is no longer so. Actually, I believe a doctorate emphasizing teaching has always been preferable and ethical. The job crisis has merely highlighted a situation that was not so dramatic when many universities would still hire people with master's degrees, perhaps even with public school teaching experience and credentials, to staff tenure-track positions.

5. I am here, of course, assuming that the department doing the search is also behaving in an ethical manner: that they have been honest about the likelihood of an opening, that they have described it as clearly as possible, that they are following EEO guidelines, that there is no "understood" internal candidate who will get the job, that all credentials will be read with care and evaluated, and so on.

6. Ironically, in my own department, which prides itself on preparing effective teachers and professionals and actually awards only an Ed.D. in The College Teaching of English, when we revised our doctoral examinations, we eliminated the pedagogical sections that had been in place for the previous twenty-five years.

7. I also find it revealing that ninety-five percent of the graduates of the Texas A&M–Commerce (formerly East Texas State University) English doctoral program have positions teaching in community colleges and four-year schools, nearly all of them either tenured or on tenure tracks. This, despite the albatross initials "Ed.D." after their names. I credit the extensive professional internship we require, along with careful mentoring.

8. James Slevin has made a somewhat similar proposal in which he calls for four courses: "The English Curriculum and Its Contexts," "Scholarship and Its Contexts," "Teaching and Its Contexts," and "The Graduate Program and Its Contexts" (1989; 1991a; 1991b).

9. I propose that ethical issues are not likely to be best dealt with in a separate course, but within the contexts that would raise them. And while I am not prepared to discuss methodology of such teaching here, I am impressed with what has come to be called the case method. See Merserth 1991; Hutchings 1993; Anson *et al.* 1993.

10. With double irony, the question on our campus grows directly out of a revision of our general education curriculum about fifteen years ago. All courses proposed as general education requirements or options had to be justified within an appropriate sub-area of knowledge to the university-wide committee, also chaired by an English professor. The department was unable to articulate a satisfactory defense of the study of literature from a general education perspective, and thus lost the requirement that all students take two semesters of sophomore literature courses. The general education committee agreed, however, that students need to study the arts. Because we could not defend literature as uniquely more valuable than other arts, students may now choose among literature, drama, visual arts, music, or esthetics.

11. Actually, courses about teaching have been called for as part of the English Ph.D. quite regularly since at least 1958. George Ridge and Edward Foster criticized programs for lacking such a component in "Doctoral Studies in English" in *The CEA Critic* for February 1958. Warner Rice made a similar point in *College English* for May of 1959 ("The Preparation of Teachers in Colleges and Universities") and again in 1963. In 1958, William Riley Parker, former Executive Secretary of the MLA and Editor of *PMLA*, called for rethinking "the entire graduate program in terms of present and foreseeable realities, beginning with recognition of the fact that, whatever its original purposes, a chief and urgent business of graduate schools is now the training of college teachers" (192).

In April of 1963, James Miller, the editor of *College English*, called for a revision of doctoral programs, asking for "a little more work in psychology and methodology" and for the option of dissertations about teaching (556). In 1968, the famous Allen report, *The Ph. D. in English and American Literature*, commissioned by the MLA, made forty-four specific recommendations about doctoral study. Numbers 38, 39, and 40 concern the need for doctoral students to be carefully prepared for their roles as teachers (116-18).

Perhaps the most direct of the older reports suggesting some version of a metacurriculum is Kenneth Eble's *Preparing College Teachers of English* (1972). After seconding Allen's recommendations, Eble proposes specific coursework in teaching, saying, "Making the preparation of the teacher a genuine part of the student's graduate program is the major step to be taken" (19). (More recently James Slevin has published extensively advocating this viewpoint. See note 8.) And see Richard Dunn, a department chair, who argues, "All graduate students should have the opportunity to teach and to consider the pedagogical issues of a discipline whose teaching, now more than ever, must reflect the dynamics of changing definitions of English Studies" (1990, 47).

Works Cited

"1995–96 *Job Information List* Figures." 1996. *MLA Newsletter* 28 (2): 1.

Allen, D. C. 1968. *The Ph. D. in English and American Literature*. New York: Holt.

"Almanac Issue." 1996. *Chronicle of Higher Education*, 2 Sept.

Anson, C., *et al.* 1993. *Scenarios for Teaching Writing: Contexts for Discussion and Reflective Practice.* Urbana, IL: NCTE.

Berlin, J. 1984. *Writing Instruction in Nineteenth-Century American Colleges.* Carbondale, IL: Southern Illinois University Press.

———. 1987. *Rhetoric and Reality: Writing Instruction in American Colleges, 1900– 1985.* Carbondale, IL: Southern Illinois University Press.

Berube, M. 1990. "Standard Deviation: Skyrocketing Job Requirements Inflame Political Tensions." *Academe*, Nov.–Dec., 26–29.

Bowen, W. G., and N. L. Rudenstine. 1992. *In Pursuit of the PhD.* Princeton, NJ: Princeton University Press.

Brereton, J., ed. 1995. *The Origins of Composition Studies in the American College: A Documentary History.* Pittsburgh: University of Pittsburgh Press.

Brown, S. C., P. R. Meyer, and T. Enos. 1994. "Doctoral Programs in Rhetoric and Composition: A Catalog of the Profession." *Rhetoric Review* 12 (2): 240–51.

Cage, M. C. 1996. "Learning to Teach: New Programs Prepare Graduate Students for Careers Creating and Leading Courses." *Chronicle of Higher Education*, 9 Feb., A19–A20.

Caminero-Santangelo, M. 1994. "The Ethics of Hiring." *Profession* 94. New York: MLA. 62–63.

Curren, E. D. 1994. "No Openings at This Time: Job Market Collapse and Graduate Education." *Profession* 94. New York: MLA. 57–61.

DeNeef, A. L., and C. D. Goodwin, eds. 1995. *The Academic's Handbook.* 2d ed. Durham, NC: Duke University Press.

Dunn, R. J. 1990. "Teaching Assistance, Not Teaching Assistants." *ADE Bulletin* 97 (Winter): 47–50.

Eble, K. E. 1972. "Preparing College Teachers of English." *College English* 33: 385–406.

Fienberg, N. 1995. "'The Most of It': Hiring at a Nonelite College." *ADE Bulletin* 112 (Winter): 11–13.

"Final Count for *Job Information List* Ads, 1993–94." 1994. *MLA Newsletter* 26 (2): 14.

Graff, G. 1987. *Professing Literature: An Institutional History.* Chicago: University of Chicago Press.

Graff, G., and M. Warner. 1989. "Introduction." *The Origins of Literary Studies in America: A Documentary Anthology.* New York: Routledge. 1–14.

Hart, J. M. 1989. "From *German Universities: A Narrative of Personal Experience.*" In *The Origins of Literary Studies in America: A Documentary Anthology*, ed. G. Graff and M. Warner, 17–24. New York: Routledge.

Heller, S. 1994. "In an Awful Job Market, U. of Iowa Is Adept at Placing English Graduates on Tenure Track." *Chronicle of Higher Education,* 27 July, A16.

Hillocks, G. 1995. *Teaching Writing as Reflective Practice.* New York: Teachers College Press.

Huber, B. J. 1993. "Recent and Anticipated Growth in English Doctoral Programs: Findings from the MLA's 1990 Survey." *ADE Bulletin* 106 (Winter): 45–60.

————. 1995. "The MLA's 1993–94 Survey of Ph.D. Placement: The Latest English Findings and Trends Through Time." *ADE Bulletin* 112 (Winter): 40–51.

Hutchings, P. 1993. *Using Cases to Improve College Teaching: A Guide to More Reflective Practice.* Washington, D.C.: American Association for Higher Education.

Katz, S. R. 1995. "Graduate Programs and Job Training." *Profession* 95. New York: MLA. 62– 67.

Knapp, J. F. 1995. "Graduate Education and the Preparation of New Faculty Members." *ADE Bulletin* 112 (Winter): 7–10.

Kitzhaber, A. [1953] 1990. *Rhetoric in American Colleges, 1850–1900.* Dallas: Southern Methodist University Press.

"Latest *Job Information List* Figures Available." 1996. *MLA Newsletter* 28 (1): 1–2.

Merseth, K. K. 1991. *The Case for Cases in Teacher Education.* Washington, D.C.: American Association of Colleges for Teacher Education.

Miller, J. E. 1963. "Notes from an Editor." *College English* 24: 554–56.

"The MLA's 1991–92 Survey of Ph.D. Placement: Major Findings." 1994. *MLA Newsletter* 26 (2): 1–2.

Morris, V. C., and Y. Pai. 1976. *Philosophy and the American School.* 2d ed. Boston: Houghton Mifflin.

Myers, D. G. 1996. *The Elephants Teach: Creative Writing Since 1880.* Englewood Cliffs, NJ: Prentice-Hall.

Nelson, C., and M. Berube. 1994. "Graduate Education Is Losing Its Moral Base." *Chronicle of Higher Education,* 23 March, B1–B2.

Parham, K. 1995. "Academics Take a Hard Look at the Current Job Market." *The Council Chronicle,* June, 6–7.

Parker, W. R. 1958. "Afterthoughts on a Profession: Graduate Training in the Humanities Today." *College English* 19: 191–99.

Rice, W. G. 1959. "The Preparation of Teachers in Colleges and Universities." *College English* 20: 413–14.

————. 1963. "The Preparation of College Teachers of English." *College English* 24: 635–38.

Ridge, G. R., and E. Foster. 1958. "Doctoral Studies in English." *The CEA Critic* 20 (February): 1, 8–9.

Schwalm, D. 1995. WPA E-Mail Discussion List. 19 Dec.

Sherry, R. J. 1993. "The Small College Job Market." *The ADGSE Bulletin* 1 (Fall): 4–9.

Slevin, J. F. 1989. "Conceptual Frameworks and Curricular Arrangements: A Response." In *The Future of Doctoral Studies in English,* ed. A. Lunsford, H. Moglen, and J. Slevin, 30–39. New York: MLA.

————. 1991a. "Depoliticizing and Politicizing Composition Studies." In *The Politics of Writing Instruction: Postsecondary,* ed. R. Bullock and J. Trimbur, 1–21. Portsmouth, NH: Boynton/Cook.

————. 1991b. "The Politics of the Profession." In *An Introduction to Composition Studies,* eds. E. Lindemann and G. Tate, 135–59. New York: Oxford.

_____ . 1992. *The Next Generation: Preparing Graduate Students for the Professional Responsibilities of College Teachers*. Washington, D.C.: Association of American Colleges.

Solomon, R., and J. Solomon. 1993. *Up the University: Re-Creating Higher Education in America*. Reading, MA: Addison-Wesley.

Spacks, P. M. 1994. "The Academic Marketplace: Who Pays Its Costs." *MLA Newsletter* 26 (2): 3.

Watt, S. 1995. "The Human Costs of Graduate Education; Or, The Need to Get Practical." *Academe*, Nov.–Dec., 30–35.

Ziolkowski, T. 1990. "The Shape of the Ph.D.: Present, Past and Future." *ADE Bulletin* 97 (Winter): 12–17.

11

Missionary Projects and Anthropological Accounts
Ethics and Conflict in Writing Across the Curriculum

Linda S. Bergmann

The Underlying Compromises

Writing Across the Curriculum (WAC), which in the past twenty years has been instituted at nearly half of the colleges and universities in the United States,[1] is founded on a series of compromises and coalitions that, as writers like David Russell (1994; 1991) and Daniel Mahala (1991) have observed, do not stand up to theoretical scrutiny and may well break down in periods of institutional change. WAC may perhaps be best imagined as a loose, baggy sort of "movement" rather than a single theory or approach (Walvoord 1996, 58–61), a movement that fosters a number of diverse ideas and practices, and that draws from both sides of the expressivist/constructivist split in Composition studies.[2] My point in this paper is not to denounce the concept of WAC, to cast doubt on the considerable accomplishments it claims, or to repudiate "programs that work," like those documented by Toby Fulwiler and Art Young (1990). Instead, I will consider how WACs accomplishments are based on collaboration between disciplines and on accommodation between theories of pedagogy and knowledge, and I will pick at the uneasy compromises that underlie these claims to success. I expect not so much to propose a course of action as to highlight the implications—ethical, as well as intellectual—of these broad compromises between the idea of writing as individual expression and the claims of disciplinarity.[3]

There are, of course, many compromise positions between the expressivist and the constructivist positions, and it may well be that the extreme positions exist more in theory than in practice. I will, however, exaggerate the differences between these positions in order to highlight the compromises among theoretical positions about the nature of writing and how it is learned that have obtained since the early days of WAC. During the 1970s and early 1980s, while WAC was spreading from university to university (Russell 1994, 11–12), Rhetoric and Composition was developing as a field of theory and of research, distinct from other areas of English studies, and its practitioners were distinguishing themselves professionally by establishing and expanding graduate programs in Rhetoric and Composition and by rethinking and restructuring undergraduate composition programs. Early WAC proponents, like Toby Fulwiler and Art Young, were part of this effort, drawing on the work of James Britton and other expressivists (Russell 1991, 278; McLeod 1992, 4) to formulate projects that adapted journal writing and other expressive forms being developed in composition programs to disciplinary writing in math, engineering, science, and other fields in which transactional, product-oriented writing was much more the norm, if any writing took place at all. They tried to introduce expressivist activities into disciplinary courses by arguing or implying that such activities would ultimately make students better writers of professional discourse (Fulwiler 1986a, 24). Naturally, even as WAC programs were drawing on many of the same ideas as composition research and involving overlapping groups of teachers, researchers, students, and friends, they also tended to focus on points of contact with other disciplines and professions— on potential theoretical and practical agreements between English studies and the disciplines in which WAC was trying to set up programs—rather than focusing on disciplinary differences in theory and practice. This focus on agreement reinforces the idea that it is possible both to extend Composition practices to other disciplines and to help initiate future practitioners of other professions into their own discourses (McCulley 1986, 44–46; Bergmann 1996). David Russell notes, however, that while these goals can overlap, they can also conflict (1991, 294). I would suggest that the inconsistency between goals is exacerbated as WAC programs move into "second" and "third" ph. ses (McLeod 1994, 79–80), taking on more of the trappings of an "institutional church" than of a "movement" or a "mission" into the educational wilderness.

I use the religious metaphor designedly, as I did in the title of this paper; it has been noted by a number of writers, including Russell (1991, 295), Robert Jones and Joseph Comprone (1993, 64), and Barbara Walvoord (1992, 15). The early discourse of WAC has a religious fervor and reads like missionary writing: Projects were often described as cultural outposts in a wilderness of "other" disciplines, sites from which dedicated WAC coordinators evangelized the creed of expressive writing, the writing process, writing to learn, journal keeping, and so on, to listeners who were often doubtful or incredulous, but who, as Toby Fulwiler noted, could be lured to try a few of Composition's (more civilized) discursive and pedagogical practices, and with each success, to try more.[4] The WAC workshop, with its technique of "fogging" the participants with myriad possible applications of WAC, bears a certain resemblance to the enthusiastic community building of the camp meeting or revival.

Although I clearly remember the excitement generated by workshop leaders like Elaine Maimon in the early and mid-1980s, and although I appreciate the efficacy of the missionary approach in consolidating the theoretical compromises that made WAC possible, I admit to some discomfort about finding myself in the camp of the missionaries, and writing this essay is a way of exploring that discomfort. Never having had the certainty of the true believer in any aspect of my life, I am not particularly comfortable in the role of missionary; nor am I absolutely confident of the superiority of the values and practices of my own discipline to those of the disciplines I am trying to convert. This is perhaps because at heart I am an academic, not a writer, to use the distinction that underlies Peter Elbow's argument that "we take a larger view of human discourse" (1991, 137) than adjustment to the expectations of the academy—whatever they are—in teaching first-year composition. I do not with ease write my own experience or teach my students to do so. For me, writing is work, not fun. I have found learning the discourse of my profession difficult (because most of the important rules, as Elbow implies, are unwritten and unspoken), but I have also found disciplinary writing to be, if not liberatory, at least crucial to my development as a human being. Thus, I cannot honestly be a missionary for expressivism except perhaps as a means to a disciplinary end.

I also find the role of missionary uncomfortable because of my work with the rhetoric of nineteenth-century exploration narratives. These narratives reveal the cultural arrogance of earlier missionary projects and disclose the role of missions in establishing and perpetuating Euro-American colonialism in the last century. The missionary assumption that the society the mission is trying to change has an inferior culture—or no culture at all—has been the source of much misunderstanding and much violence. Historians and critics like Patricia Limerick (1987) and Mary Louise Pratt (1992) have outlined the alliances, both official and informal, of missionary projects with military domination and economic exploitation.[5] I am, of course, not particularly worried about dominating and exploiting the School of Engineering—they are far too rich and powerful for that;[6] but I am worried about self-righteously proselytizing from an unexamined position. And I am concerned that my students do not fall between the cracks of arguments among the disciplines, that they acquire both the skills they need to begin a professional life and the understanding to frame, historicize, and critique their institutional situations, and that I help them to do so insofar as I am able.

The Underlying Conflicts

David Russell, writing more as an historian of writing programs than an advocate for WAC, discloses several conflicts underlying WAC. He points not only to the conflict between WAC and the primarily literary mission of most English departments, but also to the conflict between WAC and the very strong "expressivist" thread of composition theory:

Perhaps more surprising [than the rift between English and WAC] is the controversy among composition specialists over whether students should be taught the conventions of specific disciplines, though this controversy is understandable given the historical divisions within the progressive tradition of writing instruction. An expressivist element in composition studies today, like its forebears in the "sentimental" progressive tradition of the 1920s, sees the teaching of disciplinary conventions as a denial of students' "authentic voice" and a rejection of the possibility of true academic community in a reformed institution, where knowledge and discourse will not be controlled by disciplinary elites. (1991, 294)

Russell lays out the conflict as being more complex than a simple dichotomy. Expressivists, working from research stemming from James Britton's findings that among three kinds of writing (expressive, poetic, and transactional), the majority of school writing is transactional, argue that writing programs should foster the development of a personal perspective and voice, rather than offering still more practice in public, disciplinary genres. Britton saw expressive writing as a means of affirming the working class backgrounds and language of his students and as a means of liberating them from the oppressive power of educational institutions and the workplaces that they served (Mahala 1991, 775; Russell 1991, 276–278).

Britton's work, however, has informed the practice of writing teachers and researchers of all persuasions; even programs like that at Michigan Tech, whose goal is ultimately to teach engineers to write, have embraced expressive writing (often under the guise of prewriting or writing to learn) as an effective means to a higher quality transactional end (Fulwiler 1986a, 27–28; Flynn, McCulley, and Gratz 1986, 160–161). Where what might be called true expressivists differ from advocates of extending expressive techniques, however, is in the conviction that personal expression is opposed to and inhibited by attention to disciplinary forms and conventions.[7] On the other hand, proponents of writing in the disciplines, like Charles Bazerman for example, may acknowledge the importance of personal growth and expressive writing but tend to see "learning to write as a dialectic between self and society" (Russell 1991, 295). For these theorists, as, according to Russell, for John Dewey himself, personal growth takes place within disciplinarity, as the student gains proficiency in and understanding of the discourses and practices of a chosen discipline (Russell 1991, 294). Thus constructivists see writing in the professions as a means to, rather than an impediment to, personal growth (Eldred 1995, 9, 19).

Some WAC practitioners, "out in the field," so to speak, like the more anthropologically oriented missionaries of expansionist Christianity—exemplified by Chinua Achebe's Mr. Brown in *Things Fall Apart*—have seen that in order to convert the "natives"—in this case the scientists and engineers—we need to understand their language, their culture, and their practices (Brantlinger 1985, 201–202). Research into disciplinary differences in discourse practices has fostered the recognition that the discourse practices of other disciplines are part of a larger disciplinary culture, the ethos of which, as I have argued elsewhere (1996), faculty in English and Composition are often profoundly ignorant and/or mistrustful of, just as other disciplines are of English. Robert Jones and Joseph J. Comprone, for example, assert, "Missionary zeal does help to establish the base for conversions. In academic institutions, however, that conversion impulse can result in concrete gains only when the desire to establish new teaching methods is substantiated by knowledge of actual, disciplinary methods and conventions and by theory based firmly in that knowledge" (1993, 64). WAC practitioners need, according to Jones and Comprone, to study the discourses and practices of the professions they are trying to impact; to become, in my extension of the religion metaphor, anthropologists as well as missionaries. But such understanding can, as the colonialist missionaries learned, blunt the fervor to convert and lead to divided loyalties—and, in the case of WAC, lead away from the expressivist values that carry such force in Composition circles.

Such anthropological work—the work, for example, of researchers like Charles Bazerman (1988), Carol Berkenkotter (1995), Alan Gross (1990), and Dorothy Winsor (1996) in the rhetoric of science and the contexts of scientific and technical discourses—demands at times that we suspend and perhaps abandon the missionary project. Such research aims less at converting students and faculty to new modes of discourse and new pedagogical practices than at examining and explaining the discourses and practices of other disciplines. It is at this point that the theoretical differences between expressivists and constructivists that could be ignored in the earlier stages of WAC threaten to become ethical differences demanding real choices; despite some common origins, the anthropologist and the missionary have different goals, different professions, and different ethics—and along with them, different codes of behavior and different conceptions of good practice. And thus, I fear, those of us who look at disciplinary writing and the development of expertise as fostering individual growth stand on the other side of a major ethical divide from those of us who see them as opposed to each other.

Ethics and Professions

The battles waged over this divide—the exchange between David Bartholomae and Peter Elbow first at the 1989 and 1991 CCCC meetings and later in *College Composition and Communication* (1995), for example, or between Mahala's critique of WAC (1991) and the letters written in response to it—are impossible to resolve. However, like others who reject the idea of an absolute, divinely ordained moral code, I am hard pressed to find an alternative to what Patricia Bizzell sees as the relativism that can be the result of relying only on the individual conscience and to the quietism that can be the result of total skepticism (1990, 671). Bizzell draws on feminist thinkers to outline an approach based on stated positionality and "the collective values of groups" (1990, 674) with whom she chooses to identify herself or to ally. In a similar vein, the professional ethicist Michael Davis defines *ethics* in terms of group consensus: *"Ethics consists of those standards of conduct that, all things considered, every member of a particular group wants every other to follow even if their following them would mean he too has to follow them"* [his italics] (1990, 25).[8]

The idea that ethics is derived from a group's consensus about ideals and practices casts some light on the conflicts within WAC, and particularly on the conflict between the missionary goals that have greater force in Composition circles and the anthropological approach that tends to carry more weight in WAC, despite their common origins. It may be useful to conceive of them as different professions, or at least, different subprofessions, with distinct values and practices. Missionaries, convinced of the truth of their own beliefs and practices, work to convert other cultures; anthropologists, at their best, work to record and preserve them (although neither missionary nor anthropologist may be completely successful at achieving these aims). Despite some crucial connections, both theoretical and historical, they are different professions. Thus, the ethics of missionaries and anthropologists may at crucial points conflict with each other. And so may compositionists steeped in the expressivist tradition conflict with the proponents of disciplinary writing.

Jones and Comprone observe that

> individuals locally involved in WAC programs often respond in oversimplifying and dichotomous ways to the question of whether WAC is a program fostering humanistic approaches to general educational reform (as embodied in the writing-to-learn and expressive-discourse movement) or a program for approaching the teaching of writing through the conventions of different discourse communities (as, for example, represented in the learning of laboratory report formats or the structure of the scientific article). (1993, 61)

And the authors call for dialogue rather than conflict between those positions. However, because, as I am suggesting, this is ultimately an *ethical* problem, a problem involving identification with different sets of professional values and different ideals of good practice, such conflict is inevitable, insofar as there are fundamental—and contradictory—differences in ideals and values between the contending positions. There are simply times when the expressivist and disciplinary writing positions do not and cannot agree, times when the consensus under which WAC was formulated falls apart.

Ethics and Ideals

That consensus is most likely to fall apart, and, in turn, the differences between disciplines to be highlighted, when WAC takes on institutional status, particularly because WAC cuts across disciplines, and thus across group practices and ideals. As WAC programs gain institutional positions in universities—marked by space and budgets and job lines—they must weigh the extent to which WAC belongs to the university against the extent to which it owes allegiance to

English departments and Composition programs. As budgets and values clash, the conflicts once ignored in favor of looking at points of contact between disciplines may well be brought out into the open. In many universities, for example, WAC programs are funded out of the dean's or provost's budget, rather than out of English department money; are located in space outside of the English venue; and are governed or at least advised by interdisciplinary writing committees representing departments across the campus (McLeod 1994, 84–85; Waldo 1993, 15). Disciplinary differences in the goals of a writing program and differences in discourse practices between disciplines can be foregrounded as WAC programs progress from concept into practice. And WAC directors sometimes must choose which group we belong to and whose assumptions we share.[9] To put the matter bluntly, at some point WAC directors must face the question of whether WAC programs should seek to teach the discursive practices of scientists, sociologists, and engineers, or to ignore or even attempt to transform them. This is an important institutional question because the answer to it determines who pays for this work, and who pays for it in turn determines the values, ideals, and practices that predominate. It is, moreover, an ethical issue because it addresses a conflict between the values of different academic disciplines (and thus of different professions) and because good practice toward one goal may run counter to good practice toward the other.

For example, the laboratory report—one of the important forms of discourse for engineers, and probably the most commonly used form of engineering "school-writing"—almost completely eschews the personal voice. The anthropologically-oriented writing teacher might seek to look for the reasons for and implications of such impersonality in this genre: the reliance on empirical and quantitative evidence, the importance of the repeatability of the experiment, the collaborative nature of laboratory work. This kind of analysis seeks to set this discourse in the larger context of the professional life of the engineer and in the socialization of novices into the profession (Winsor 1996, 10–13); it may also compare the discourse practices of different fields—different "knowledge creating communities"—and their different conceptions of persona, authority, proof, appropriate knowledge claims, and so forth (Bazerman 1988, 24). While it may distinguish successful writing in a discipline from unsuccessful and the discourse of mature practitioners from the discourse of novices (Williams and Colomb 1990, 100–103), it does not try to attach a value to different conventions or different genres on aesthetic or moral grounds. As Mark Waldo put it, in defense of disciplinary writing and the community of values that it reflects: "Physics would probably not presume to impose its goal or community on English; why then should English presume to impose its goal or community on Physics?" (1993, 24). From this point of view, all genres and all discourse practices are equal. A laboratory report or a grant proposal is no more or less good or beautiful than a poem or a novel or a work of criticism. If to be successful a report must avoid the use of "I" and "we" and all other traces of personal vision or voice, so be it.

The missionary approach sees these differences as carrying aesthetic or moral value. One way (usually "ours") is seen as better than another. In an earlier era—and there are still many people who think this way—English professors, steeped in the tradition of "belles lettres," scorned scientific and technical writing as ugly; indeed, according to Dorothy Winsor, many engineering students feel the same way (1996, 88). The passive voice, for example, a stylistic necessity in genres that avoid a personal voice, is condemned as "wordy," as are the repetitions necessary in legal writing. The more common missionary position these days, however, has more to do with ideals of the good than of the beautiful. This position is based on the conviction that not all epistemologies—and the discourse practices that derive from them—are equal. If I believe that all knowledge is situated in a social context and ultimately in the mind of its subject, if I believe that knowledge is contingent and fluid and that objectivity is therefore not possible, then I am in serious disagreement with my scientist and engineer friends who believe that an objective view of the social or natural world can be derived from empirical evidence. The differences in discourse conventions between our disciplines, then, are not merely differences in manners or conventions. The passive voice, given my conception of knowledge, is not so much "ugly" (i.e., bad style), as *wrong*, precisely because it makes a claim to objectivity. It is preferable—perhaps ethically imperative—from the expressivist perspective to state the position of the subject, to say "I think," rather than to fake a claim to a spurious objectivity.

These differences in ideals, in turn, feed into differences in pedagogical practice. For example, in *Writing Like an Engineer*, Winsor examines in great detail the growth of four engineering students as writers during and after their years in college:

> When one learns to be an engineer, one learns to participate in a community. As co-op students, the four students studied here were in transition: They were not yet engineers but they were expected to some degree to fill engineers' roles in their companies. As novices, they did not always have the power to contribute to knowledge, partly because of their low status in the corporate hierarchy, but also partly because they literally did not know how to do so acceptably. The findings of this study suggest that the four students became engineers as much through socialization while co-oping as through anything they learned at GMI. (1996, 20)

She examines the students' accounts of their growing understanding of what writing in their profession entails, and finds evidence of their development of a sense of audience and of their increased comprehension of the purposes both explicit and implicit of their writing within a corporate hierarchy. This kind of research can be incorporated into the practice of teachers oriented toward either disciplinary or expressivist writing, but in different ways.

A teacher oriented toward initiating students into the discourse of their profession might use this kind of research to help students become more proficient in perceiving hierarchies and in using the kinds of discourse that will be heard by and influential on authoritative audiences. Such teachers will work to foster what Cheryl Geisler calls "the emergence of an expert representation of the rhetorical problem space" (1994, 87) crucial to the development of professional expertise. Such an approach accepts or at least tolerates the "great divide" between professional and layperson (Geisler 1994, 88–90) and the hierarchies of power that emerge from it. On the other hand, the teacher oriented toward changing the student or the professions—the teacher with a mission— will use this research to teach resistance to or critique of institutional hierarchies and the discourses that support them. Such a teacher will reject the discourse of expertise and the professionalization it supports and look to reify and expand the student's personal knowledge. And this is where the compromises entailed in WAC really fall apart.

In an earlier article, I described an instance in which a student wrote a highly personal, self-reflective introduction to a laboratory report in his first engineering laboratory course. I describe how my response to the piece would differ in a laboratory report workshop for his engineering class—in which I would use it to introduce the conventions of a laboratory report—from my response in a composition class—in which I might help tease it into a personal narrative or a critical reflection (Bergmann 1996, 57). But the decision of how to respond to such a piece of student writing is even more complicated than the choice of venues; it depends on the immediate and long-term goals of both student and teacher,[10] and these goals may reflect different ideals and different conceptions of good practice.[11] If I am responding to the writing as an anthropologist, I will be inclined to describe and explain the discourse of engineering as an aspect of the discipline and to respond in a way that compares the student's work with expected professional performance or at least acceptable novice work. Indeed, I may even try to help the student learn to "think like an engineer"—and to write like one (in the best sense). I will reflect that the laboratory report, one disciplinary form among many, has its conventions—as the journal article in Rhetoric and Composition, or, for that matter literature, has its own—and argue that a novice needs to know and to practice what is expected in order to develop as a professional in his or her chosen field (Eldred 1995, 19). My goal will be to foster such expertise. If, however, I am going at the paper as a missionary, my goal may be to divert this student's education— or, as Elbow contends, to enrich it (1991, 137)—with practice in expressive writing or in the discourse of another discipline (my own, usually). Elbow's position is that because there are many academic discourses and those discourses themselves are not stable, we should teach students to write in "ordinary language" (1991, 149) and to understand the "principle of discourse variation" (1991, 152) as preparation for later disciplinary writing. But if I am an even more committed missionary, I may, as Bazerman suggests, *really* want to convert that student out of metallurgical engineering altogether and into a major in English (Eldred 1995, 19). I may consider the laboratory report to be ugly, boring, or even potentially evil (Katz 1992, 271), and seek to critique, change, or eliminate it or at least to enable myself as a teacher to ignore it.

Like those Christian missionaries of earlier eras who inclined toward anthropology, WAC practitioners who seriously investigate other disciplines' discourse practices face the danger of losing their ethical base and their disciplinary definition, the danger of succumbing to the relativism targeted by Gary Tate when he characterized a WAC-related approach to Composition as "shaping and fitting students to perform their appointed tasks as good little workers in the various artificial—and some would say oppressive—academic/ administrative divisions that constitute the modern American university" (1993, 320). Like the missionary in Paul Bowles' short story "Pastor Dowe at Tacate" (1986), we may that find the attempt to bridge the differences—by investigating the professional practices of, for example, engineers and adapting our practices to theirs—dissipates the missionary's faith rather than engaging the potential converts.

Ethics and Institutions

So far I have been writing as though these issues were primarily theoretical or pedagogical; but they also get played out in institutional situations in which power (read "budgets" and "turf") are at stake. WAC initiatives tend to come from relatively poor English departments and to promise a positive impact on students majoring in richer and more powerful departments like science and engineering. Because successful WAC coordinators tend to be skilled negotiators and conciliators, these differences in power are usually subsumed by cordial personal relations that obscure rather than highlight the differences between the disciplines. WAC coordinators look for these areas of agreement between disciplines, focusing on those values, ideals, and goals that departments and colleagues share, and using them as the foundation of a writing program.

As WAC programs are institutionalized, the responsibility for them (and with it the power that comes with that responsibility) tends to shift from English faculty to interdepartmental writing directors and committees. At many institutions, particularly those that focus on applied disciplines such as engineering, law, and medicine rather than on the liberal arts, the easiest and perhaps the only way to get money to fund WAC programs is to foster the claim that they will provide immediate or long-term improvement in the disciplinary writing of students and that they will foster the development of students as professionals. Faculty in psychology and economics, for example, may experiment with assignments oriented toward expressive writing, but only if they are promised that such writing will lead to better psychology or economics papers. They are not particularly interested in, and will not be willing to pay for, writing as a means of transforming those discourses or liberating students from disciplinary or institutional practices and boundaries. And many, perhaps most, faculty members tend to look at their courses as sites where they transmit knowledge to students, rather than as sites where students practice using—and perhaps even interrogating—the knowledge they have gained. Indeed, many English professors feel the same way.

WAC programs do require that faculty and administrators move away from the belief that "If faculty in the English Department were doing their job, the students would know how to write," but do not necessarily require any fundamental shift in departmental or disciplinary values or epistemologies. For example, WAC projects described in the *Journal of Engineering Education* adopt writing practices drawn from Composition and evaluate them in terms of how well they imitate the professional practices of engineers and how effectively they prepare students to write engineering reports, proposals, and so forth, in a corporate culture. (See, for example, Schulz and Ludlow 1996.) To the extent that Composition faculty, and in particular those committed to expressivism, see themselves as offering fundamental critique of or resistance to contemporary social and cultural structures and to the universities that sustain them, this fostering of the disciplinary values of other professions violates deeply entrenched professional goals. Furthermore, even though Composition faculty may entertain some suspicion of literature faculty and the traditional liberal arts when engaged in intradepartmental disputes, they are going to resist—and rightfully so—the attempts of other departments to impose their own definitions of writing and to demand that Composition courses directly address the needs of the disciplinary discourses of, for example, engineering or law or economics.

I promised no resolution to these conflicts, and I offer only my own version of the academic pluralism I tended to scorn before becoming a WAC director. Resistance and struggle is the normal state of institutional life, and resolution is a sign of institutional death. WAC is, by my account, the child of interdisciplinary investigation and consensus politics, and consensus means that we act together when we share interests. It is the WAC program's mission to preserve the consensus and maintain the compromises, in the hope, at least, of serving the students. When our interests or values conflict, however, what we call "the academy" breaks down into disciplines, and disciplines break down into subgroups; and when this happens, the ethical position of the WAC director may diverge from that of the English department or Composition program. I can only think that we have to understand and live with the disputes that we find ourselves involved in as WAC moves into the second and third stages, and as it becomes an established part of academic institutions. I hate the fights that ensue—we all do—but I am glad that they continue. Although I am not at heart an expressivist, I would not want to be in an institution or a department that did not offer a strong articulation of the expressivist position. Even when consensus and cooperation break down, and even if WAC must diverge from Composition at points where I think I need them to converge into a coherent "Writing Program," I want to be part of an institution that gives voice to both expressivist and constructivist positions. It is the questions and assertions of the people with whom I disagree that hone my conscience, that make me support what I believe, that make me continually examine the premises that underlie the programs I devise, and that provide me with a body of theory and research from which to conceive of and argue for WAC as education and not merely as training.

Acknowledgments

I owe thanks to David Coogan, my former colleague at the Illinois Institute of Technology, for his reading and commenting on this paper when it was in an early and barely readable state, and for his ongoing discussion with me of the issues it raises. And I owe thanks to Joan Mullin of the University of Toledo for reading a nearly final draft and helping me pull it into its final shape.

Notes

1. Susan McLeod (1992) cites this figure and addresses the range of programs in her introduction to *Writing Across the Curriculum: A Guide to Developing Programs.* David Russell has noted in his curricular history, *Writing in the Academic Disciplines, 1870-1970,* that WAC gained ground in response to the perceived "literacy crises" of the 1970s and 1980s, these crises themselves rising in response to the broadening of the college population during the 1960s and 1970s (1991, 275–76).

2. Susan McLeod, for example, describes the distinction between "writing to learn" and "learning to write" and proposes a definition of WAC that allows for both (1992, 3–6). The programs described in McLeod and Soven's *Writing Across the Curriculum: A Guide to Developing Programs* (1992) vary in their emphases, as do the programs outlined in Fulwiler and Young's *Programs that Work* (1990), and the projects described in Young and Fulwiler's *Writing Across the Curriculum: Research into Practice* (1986). Daniel Mahala (1991), distancing himself from issues of practice and from the position of practitioner, takes a critical stance toward WAC and exposes the theoretical weakness underlying WAC programs and argues that this inconsistency leads to bad, or at least ambiguous, practices.

3. This is part of a larger, long-standing contention in Composition circles, a contention that, for example, underlies the debates between David Bartholomae and Peter Elbow in *College Composition and Communication* in 1995, and that feeds the debates between the constructivist and process approaches to writing and writing pedagogy.

4. This is an admittedly satirical and ahistorical reading of "first wave" WAC pieces like Toby Fulwiler's "Reflections: How Well Does Writing Across the Curriculum Work?" (1986b).

5. This alliance of missionary and military surfaces in Michael Gorman's recollection of Fulwiler comparing Michigan Tech's Writing Across the Curriculum project to the Vietnam War: "Finally, Toby came up with an analogy to the Vietnam War: should we 'escalate,' or had time come to consolidate resources and withdraw gracefully. We realized that like the American military in Vietnam we had no clear idea what

sending in more troops would accomplish. We had learned that analyses, like methods, depend on goals" (1986, 40–41). This recollection also reflects the *ad hoc*, "make it up as we go along" approach typical of early WAC initiatives, such as the projects described in *Writing Across the Disciplines: Research into Practice* (McCulley 1986) and McLeod and Soven's more recent *Writing Across the Curriculum: A Guide to Developing Programs* (1992).

6. Like some of the colonial missionaries, WAC programs tend to be poor and well-intentioned, but may be supported and funded by richer and more powerful institutional forces; in the case of WAC, however, these institutional forces may be the very departments that the "missionary" is trying to convert. Therein lies the very real potential for WAC to be subverted to simplistic and catchpenny goals and practices.

7. This distinction between expressivists like Fulwiler, who use expressivist techniques without necessarily embracing expressivist ends, and proponents of truly student-centered writing (as compared with writing-centered in academic, disciplinary, or professional discourse) was made by Daniel Mahala (1991, 467), citing Lil Brannon and C. H. Knoblauch as envisioning expressivist ends rather than merely promoting expressivist techniques; in a similar vein, Russell (1991, 294) cites Kurt Spellmeyer.

8. Although Davis is addressing issues of the professionalization of technical disciplines, a similar process has occurred in the professionalization of Rhetoric and Composition over the last twenty years or so. Davis (1991) argues that codes of ethics emerge as occupations organize into professions and that codes are often recognized before they are written and formalized. While Davis' definition of the development of ethics within a profession acknowledges change, he argues that once a profession exists, any person who identifies herself as a member of that profession is bound by its ethical code.

My own sense is that professions and their ethics never become absolutely fixed; professionalization may slow changes in professional practices and ethics and may provide channels for obtaining and policing the consensus concerning ideals and values that underlies a code of ethics, but professional values, practices, and ethics are continually changing.

More cynical analysts, like the historian Burton Bledstein (1978), argue that professional ethics help eliminate competition from amateurs—those *outside* the profession. See also Cheryl Geisler (1994, 245), who persuasively argues that the academy's practice of separating the expert from the lay person and the amateur from the professional serves not to develop students' understanding, but to keep all but a chosen few from developing it.

9. For example, collaborative learning is a common part of WAC programs. Laboratory courses in engineering tend to rely on group work to a great extent, but they are also highly hierarchical. Do we consider the group work in these courses "collaborative" or not? Do we accept the hierarchy common in the discipline in order to bring writing instruction into these courses, or do we attempt to expose and disrupt it?

10. Both the missionary and the anthropologist will be affected by the student's own goals as well as the teacher's, but the anthropologist will be inclined either to stand back or to help the student fulfill them, while the missionary will seek to change them. They might also credit these goals differently. For example, this student's writing can be seen to reflect his excitement at finally being in a metallurgy laboratory and to express his eagerness to develop professional skills. Should I take this discourse at

face value as the personal narrative of an eager young novice, or should I see it as a product of coercion, and the student as being manipulated—with or without his knowledge—by parents who want him to prepare for a lucrative career and by an economy that is at best frightening in its demands for conformity to the corporate ethos?

11. Immediate pedagogical goals will also play a part in my response to this piece at this time, but the issues raised by immediate goals are issues of what will work best to achieve that long-term end. For example, if my long-term goal is initiation, I still need to consider whether this student's development as a professional would be best served by teaching him the conventions of the laboratory report at this time, or by offering him practice in expressive writing. Focusing on the generic demands and conventions of the laboratory report at this point in his education could either help or hinder his development as an engineering writer. Spending time on expressive writing rather than transactional writing could ultimately make him more proficient as an engineering writer as his career and expertise progress. Conversely, if my goal is conversion, I might find that goal best served by focusing on expressive writing. However, I might also find conversion best served by teaching the transactional writing forms of my own discipline of English. Or, still aiming for conversion, I might consider a working knowledge of the forms and conventions of engineering discourse a crucial springboard for critique of that discourse and of the epistemology and social practices it reflects.

Works Cited

Achebe, C. [1979] 1983. *Things Fall Apart.* New York: Ballantine.

Bartholomae, D. 1995. "Writing with Teachers: A Conversation with Peter Elbow." *College Composition and Communication* 46: 62–71.

Bazerman, C. 1988. "What Written Knowledge Does: Three Examples of Academic Discourse. In *Shaping Written Knowledge: The Genre and Activity of the Experimental Article in Science,* 18–55. Madison: University of Wisconsin Press.

Bergmann, L. 1996. "Academic Discourse and Academic Service: Composition vs. WAC in the Academy." *CEA Critic* 58 (3): 50–59.

Berkenkotter, C., and T. Huckin. 1995. *Genre Knowledge in Disciplinary Communication: Cognition/Culture/Power.* Hillsdale, NJ: Lawrence Earlbaum.

Bizzell, P. 1990. "Beyond Anti-Foundationalism to Rhetorical Authority: Problems Defining 'Cultural Literacy.'" *College English* 52: 661–75.

Bledstein, B. 1978. *The Culture of Professionalism: The Middle Class and the Development of Higher Education in America.* New York: Norton.

Bowles, P. [1979] 1986. "Pastor Dowe at Tecate." In *On Being Foreign: Culture Shock in Short Fiction,* ed. T. J. Lewis and R. E. Youngman, 139–57. Yarmouth, ME: Intercultural Press.

Brannon, L., and C. H. Knoblauch. 1983. "Writing as Learning Through the Curriculum. *College English* 45: 465–74.

Brantlinger, P. 1985. "Victorians and Africans: The Genealogy of the Myth of the Dark Continent." In *"Race," Writing, and Difference,* ed. H. L. Gates, Jr., 185–222. Chicago: University of Chicago Press.

Davis, M. 1991. "Thinking Like an Engineer: The Place of a Code of Ethics in the Practice of a Profession." *Philosophy and Public Affairs* (Spring): 150-167.

———. 1990. "Who Can Teach Workplace Ethics?" *Teaching Philosophy* 13 (1): 21–38.

Elbow, P. 1995. "Being a Writer vs. Being an Academic: A Conflict in Goals." *College Composition and Communication* 46: 72–83.

———. 1991. "Reflections on Academic Discourse: How It Relates to Freshmen and Colleagues." *College English* 53: 135–55.

Eldred, M. 1995. " 'Writing Is Motivated Participation': An Interview with Charles Bazerman." *Writing on the Edge* 6 (2): 7–20.

Flynn, E., G. McCulley, and R. Gratz. 1986. "Effects of Peer Critiquing and Analysis of Models on the Quality of Biology Laboratory Reports." In *Writing Across the Disciplines: Research into Practice*, ed. A. Young and T. Fulwiler, 160–75. Portsmouth, NH: Heinemann.

Fulwiler, T. 1986a. "The Argument for Writing Across the Curriculum." In *Writing Across the Disciplines: Research into Practice,* ed. A. Young and T. Fulwiler, 21–48. Portsmouth, NH: Heinemann.

———. 1986b. "Reflections: How Well Does Writing Across the Curriculum Work?" In *Writing Across the Disciplines: Research into Practice*, ed. A. Young and T. Fulwiler, 235–46. Portsmouth, NH: Heinemann.

Fulwiler, T. and A. Young. 1990. *Programs That Work: Models and Methods for Writing Across the Curriculum*. Portsmouth, NH: Heinemann.

Geisler, C. 1994. *Academic Literacy and the Nature of Expertise: Reading, Writing, and Knowing in Academic Philosophy*. Hillsdale, NJ: Lawrence Erlbaum.

Gorman, M. 1986. "Developing Our Research Model." In *Writing Across the Disciplines: Research into Practice*, ed. A. Young and T. Fulwiler, 33–41. Portsmouth, NH: Heinemann.

Gross, A. 1990. *The Rhetoric of Science*. Cambridge, MA: Harvard University Press.

Jones, R., and J. Comprone. 1993. "Where Do We Go Next in Writing Across the Curriculum?" *College Composition and Communication* 44: 59–68.

Katz, S. B. 1992. "The Ethic of Expediency: Classical Rhetoric, Technology, and the Holocaust." *College English* 54: 255–75.

Limerick, P. N. 1987. *The Legacy of Conquest: The Unbroken Past of the American West*. New York: W. W. Norton.

Mahala, D. 1991. "Writing Utopias: Writing Across the Curriculum and the Promise of Reform." *College English* 53: 773–89.

McCulley, G. 1986. "Research in Writing Across the Curriculum: Beginnings." In *Writing Across the Disciplines: Research into Practice*, ed. A. Young and T. Fulwiler, 42–48. Portsmouth, NH: Heinemann.

McLeod, S. H. 1992. "Writing Across the Curriculum: An Introduction." In *Writing Across the Curriculum: A Guide to Developing Programs*, ed. S. H. McLeod and M. Soven, 1–11. Newbury Park, CA: Sage.

———. [1989] 1994. Writing Across the Curriculum: The Second Stage, and Beyond." In *Landmark Essays on Writing Across the Curriculum*, ed. C. Bazerman and D. Russell, 79–86. Davis, CA: Hermagoras Press.

McLeod, S. H., and M. Soven. 1992. *Writing Across the Curriculum: A Guide to Developing Programs*. Newbury Park, CA: Sage.

Pratt, M. L. 1992. *Imperial Eyes: Travel Writing and Transculturation*. London: Routledge.

Russell, D. [1992] 1994. "American Origins of the Writing-across-the-Curriculum Movement." In *Landmark Essays on Writing Across the Curriculum*, ed. C. Bazerman and D. Russell, 3–22. Davis, CA: Hermagoras Press.

———. 1991. *Writing in the Academic Disciplines, 1870–1990: A Curricular History*. Carbondale, IL: Southern Illinois University Press.

Schulz, K., and D. Ludlow. 1996. "Incorporating Group Writing Instruction in Engineering Courses." *Journal of Engineering Education* (July): 227–32.

Spellmeyer, K. 1989. "A Common Ground: The Essay in the Academy." *College English* 3: 262–76.

Tate, G. 1993. "A Place for Literature in Freshman Composition." *College English* 55: 317–21.

Waldo, M. 1993. "The Last Best Place for Writing Across the Curriculum: The Writing Center." *Writing Program Administration* 16 (3): 15–26.

Walvoord, B. E. 1996. "The Future of WAC." *College English* 58: 58–79.

———. 1992. "Getting Started." In *Writing Across the Curriculum: A Guide to Developing Programs*, ed. S. H. McLeod and M. Soven, 12–31. Newbury Park, CA: Sage.

Williams, J., and G. Colomb. 1990. "The University of Chicago." In *Programs That Work: Models and Methods for Writing Across the Curriculum*, ed. T. Fulwiler and A. Young, 83–113. Portsmouth, NH: Heinemann.

Winsor, D. A. 1996. *Writing Like an Engineer: A Rhetorical Education*. Mahwah, NJ: Lawrence Erlbaum.

12

Resurveying the Boundaries of Intellectual Property

Susan M. Hunter

Intellectual property issues are inherently ethical, whether or not we understand ethics in its traditional sense, as a set of foundational principles and procedures that prescribe behavior in a community, or in a postmodern sense, as a "mode of questioning" that "always involves mediating between competing principles and judging those principles in light of particular circumstances" (Porter 1993, 218). Subject as it is, however, to historical precedent and legal codes intended to protect an individual's right to own the expression of his or her ideas as well as the public's right to have access to available knowledge, discussions of intellectual property seem always to focus on how legally to balance the proprietor's and the user's rights regarding print or electronic texts. Perhaps the terminology of intellectual property law—proprietor, copyright, fair use, public domain— and its conflating authorship with ownership (Rose 1993; Lunsford 1996) draw attention away from the inherent ethical dimension of the concept.

Perhaps because scholars and researchers in Composition studies believe that it is self-evident that intellectual property issues are ethical issues, they have not used ethics as authors in this collection use it: that is, either as a lens through which to view intellectual property or as a process of inquiry by which to examine it (Fontaine and Hunter, this volume). In their zeal for political action that would rescue intellectual property from the Romantic notion of originary authorship and align it instead with the social constructionist ideology of Composition studies, their discussions of intellectual property remain legalistic and theoretical. Composition scholars have overlooked particular sites of intellectual property within the profession itself as presenting ethical questions. The sites I am referring to may have been overlooked because legal tests such as copyright and fair use may not come to mind in the case of unpublished work; in fact, although authors do own a copyright as soon as a work is created (Conference of Editors of Learned Journals 1984, 10), the term *intellectual property* is rarely applied to texts produced in the stages along the path to publication or to students' texts regularly solicited for use in classrooms, faculty workshops, research reports, and writing textbooks. The term *intellectual property* is associated with published works. Even writing teachers may be unfamiliar with the term because it does not usually appear in discussions of plagiarism in textbooks and institutional policy statements, although the concept, as it has been constructed over the past 300 years (Lunsford and Ede 1990), is the basis for injunctions against plagiarism and the documentation conventions writing instructors teach to protect against it. Only recently has electronic discourse come into the purview of intellectual property, again as a legal issue that legislators seek to regulate by applying copyright law to it (Woodmansee and Jaszi 1995) and also as a place from which to transform the current model of intellectual property (Lunsford and West 1996). The case of unpublished written work—whether composed by an academic to submit for publication, by a student to fulfill an assignment, or by a student or academic to participate in an electronic conversation—should be investigated as a site of intellectual property where—legalities aside—we must confront the ethical dilemmas that our belief in social, collaborative theories of composing and our striving as individual authors pose.

In what follows, I briefly characterize the current discussions of intellectual property in Composition studies in order to point to some contradictory impulses or tensions these discussions imply. I then try to bring what can be learned from theoretical and legal discussions of intellectual property into the smaller, professional arena of the publication process where I believe ethical awareness or reflection can help to enact a collaborative model of knowledge making and lead to an alternate construction of intellectual property as collective and shared.

The Prevailing Concerns in Composition Studies

In the 1997 *Convention Preview,* the Conference on College Composition and Communication Intellectual Property Caucus frames the term *intellectual property* as "an array of public issues and legislative actions vital to the interests of writing and communication teachers, students, and scholars" and warns that "copyright is continuing to broaden its reach through legislation and corporate lobbying, thus promoting a paradigm of private, pay-per-view information over a robust, rich public domain" (26). Created in 1994, the Caucus now has its own listserv and Web page to support its lobbying against "pending federal legislation that threatens to increase copyright terms and extend copyright drastically in the area of electronic materials" (1997, 26). The legislation referred to here is the National Information Infrastructure Copyright Protection Act of 1995. In addition, the Caucus sponsored three sense-of-the-house motions at the 1996 CCCC Annual Business Meeting calling for (1) "models of new ownership for protecting copyrighted works to encourage broader educational use, allowing authors to retain their own copyright and add a blanket permission statement for educational use"; (2) on-line publications, including a Website for *College Composition and Communication*; and (3) the creation of a task force on intellectual property that will identify concerns and develop policies for CCCC and NCTE and "distribute those policies to the relevant legislative bodies" (Faigley 1996, 5). In addition to advocacy, the IP Caucus focuses on how recent legal rulings on such issues as fair use and copyright affect the use of coursepacks, the Internet, and electronic discourse from undergraduate writing classrooms to graduate seminars (1997, 27). The Caucus's message to CCCC members is clear: We must raise our voices as citizens and writing teachers against legislation supported by corporate lobbyists that would restrict the public domain; we must lobby to ensure the balance between public and private rights to intellectual property, to protect and extend the public domain. Those outside Composition studies might perceive this call to political action as just one more liberal-agenda item academics typically subscribe to. Insiders realize, however, that driving the Caucus's concerns are fervently-held, deep-seated beliefs about writing and knowledge-making as collaborative processes.

Ideological Underpinnings

A cluster of recent books and articles has led the field to a new awareness of the origins of intellectual property as out of step with current theories about composing and knowledge production. In these writings, the voices we hear echo those of Andrea A. Lunsford and Lisa Ede (1990) on collaborative models of writing, Mark Rose (1993) on the history of copyright, and Martha Woodmansee and Peter Jaszi (1995) on the relationship between current legal and Romantic constructions of authorship. In these articles, authors react to legal debates about authorship and ownership of electronic discourse as an impetus to reconceptualize intellectual property; they want to construct models that would value collaboration and access over the protection of proprietary authorship. For example, Rebecca Moore Howard cites hypertext as a type of discourse that destabilizes the inherited notion of intellectual property. She claims that "hypertext makes visible . . . the cumulative, interactive nature of writing that makes impossible the representation of a stable category of authorship and hence a stable category of plagiarism. . . . If there is no originality, there is no basis for literary property. If there is no originality and no literary property, there is no basis for the notion of plagiarism" (1995, 791). In "The Law of Texts: Copyright in the Academy," Martha Woodmansee and Peter Jaszi argue for bringing aesthetic and legal theory back into conversation with one another to assure that whatever regulation of networked communities gets adopted suits the needs of scholars (1995, 781). Elsewhere, Jaszi lauds "the conditions of the Internet environment . . . [because they] resemble those which prevailed at other moments of polymorphous collaboration, unrestrained plagiarism, and extraordinary cultural productivity—such as the Elizabethan stage or Hollywood before 1915" (1994, 55). Lunsford, too, predicts that Web-based publishing and electronic networks will be contested sites around which we will see "increasing efforts to establish new controls and to . . . protect . . . new forms of intellectual property as well as increasing efforts to resist such regulation . . . by . . . the explicit renunciation of property rights by some users of Internet" (1996, 269). As if in concert, these authors dismantle "the romantic-author-and-the-expression-of-his-unique-ideas-in-fixed-works paradigm that has evolved over the last 300 years" (Lunsford 1996, 272), and the evanescent nature of electronic discourse and hypertextual writing allows them to do so.

Building on these scholarly discussions of intellectual property, Andrea Lunsford and Susan West (1996) articulate most definitively thus far "the wake-up call teachers of writing have generally been slow to hear" and "just how high the stakes are for teachers of writing and reading in the national rethinking of intellectual property for a digital age" (1996, 384). Citing Derrida, Barthes, and Foucault, they locate their discussion in Poststructuralist theory by rehearsing the Poststructuralist claim that "knowledge is a cultural production, one that can never be attributed to a stable, knowable, singular agent" (1996, 391). And they illustrate this claim by representing "communicating in an electronic environment as a social activity as the necessarily collaborative process of creating and consuming information" (1996, 395). Neither the claim nor its illustration is compatible with the "fixed" standard of copyright. Lunsford and West see the transient, collaborative nature of electronic discourse as potentially transformative of traditional notions of intellectual property.

To alert writing teachers to the dangers posed by the increasing tilt in favor of protecting proprietary ownership as opposed to protecting wide access to "new" knowledge, Lunsford and West draw examples from popular media and the scientific community to demonstrate an acquisitive "society's growing preoccupation with intellectual property and ownership" (1996, 385–87). Pending legislation, the power of corporate interests, and an attitude of radical individualism, they claim, define knowledge as a marketable commodity. Further, they find teachers in contemporary writing classrooms complicit in "perpetuat[ing] traditional concepts of authorship, authority, and ownership of intellectual property" (1996, 397), in trading in knowledge as a marketable commodity. According to Lunsford and West, writing teachers can divest themselves of this complicity and participate in the transformation of intellectual property by following two empowering courses of action: (1) They can take a stand against proposed copyright legislation, and (2) they can "examine the assumptions about language that inform . . . [writing] pedagogy and decide what kind of culture . . . to promote in the classroom and . . . in cyberspace" (1996, 396). Lunsford and West seem to imply that, while writing teachers may have transformed their classrooms into student-centered, collaborative discourse communities, they have not yet done enough to transform capitalistic society, the academy, even English studies into cultures that understand the sources of knowledge as collective rather than individual.

Some Contradictory Impulses

As is often the case, arguments for radical, systemic change, such as Lunsford and West's, run the risk of being labeled foundational by their critics, and such arguments may come across to their intended readers as dogmatic and idealistic. Working within institutions that do not admit the need for proposed social and legal reform, writing teachers are hard pressed to convert dogma and ideals into policy and practice; consequently, the empowering call to action leaves its audience feeling guilt-ridden and powerless. While I, as a member of the Composition community, have been persuaded to activism and convinced to agree in heart and mind with the field's current thinking about intellectual property law, I must bring to the fore contradictory impulses in the debate that I see from my position in the profession—a position I believe to be equally as representative as James Porter's, Andrea Lunsford's, Susan West's, or any one of my reader's. These discrepancies reveal why it may be more difficult than has been suggested to rethink intellectual property.

I will begin with contradictions that Lunsford and West admit regarding the need to own texts. For example, regarding plagiarism, they take teachers and scholars to task for "hypercitation and endless listing of sources" (1996, 397), practices they associate with the need to own intellectual property as a tangible commodity. They admit that their article (with thirty endnotes and a lengthy works cited list) models this practice, although they prefer to construe notes and bibliographies as acknowledging voices in a collaborative conversation. Of course, such an intention or process of assimilating and remaking knowledge on the part of the writer is virtually impossible to document in any conventional way. In this instance, Lunsford and West imply that writing teachers continue to proselytize against plagiarism and for individual ownership of texts. But Clark and Healy note that literature—not writing—faculty are most likely to emphasize documentation format as a way to avoid plagiarism and even to deem collaboration between writers and tutors in writing centers as plagiarism (1996, 34–35; see also Roen and McNenny 1993). Again with regard to plagiarism, in note #24 Andrea Lunsford admits to the rhetorical accommodation she had to make in writing about plagiarism in the *St. Martin's Handbook* in ways that would satisfy reviewers (Lunsford and West 1996, 408). This last example suggests that the U. S. Congress, *CCC*, CCCC, a listserv on the Internet, or the writing classroom, but not a writing textbook, is a forum in which to advocate alternate models of intellectual property. Lunsford and West also claim that writing teachers have "attempted to own the space of the classroom, labeling it with individual, knowledge claims and perceiving courses as opportunities to demonstrate the teacher's expertise, rather than to facilitate collaborative learning" (1996, 398). They do not seem to recognize that this claim denies the facts of many published accounts of collaborative pedagogy in contemporary writing classrooms. Consider as just one example Donna Qualley's collaborative, interactive prose writing class depicted by Elizabeth Chiseri-Strater (1991; see also Hunter 1993).

The financial benefits of copyright and patent ownership disrupt Lunsford and West's argument as well. When they remind us that scholars in English studies regularly assign their copyright to journals and publishers (1996, 390), thereby losing future profits from granting permissions, Lunsford and West imply that scholars should not sign away this right because if scholars held onto their copyrights, they would be entitled to future profits from their intellectual labor and would be able to control the terms of how their knowledge is shared. Lunsford and West suggest this course of action at the same time that they urge authors to eschew ownership of written works as it is currently inscribed and protected by copyright. A similar conflict underlies their citing a patent case to illustrate the corporate exploitation of native knowledge. Lunsford and West figure the problem here to be that intellectual property can be owned only by "an identifiable individual or corporate 'genius' rather than an entire culture" (1996, 393). They leave readers wondering: If intellectual property law could somehow protect knowledge that belonged to an entire culture and thus allow it to profit financially from that knowledge, would intellectual property be redeemed? Would Lunsford and West be willing to claim intellectual property as a postmodern construct if a group rather than an individual benefited financially from owning intellectual property?

Even if scholarly authors were to forgo economic gain from their intellectual labors (after all, the financial stakes are not usually very high in scholarly publishing anyway), they probably would not be willing to waive the recognition and status that intellectual property bestows. Lunsford and West's argument against the current model of intellectual property, however, would deny even that benefit because it would require the overthrow of the entrenched reward system in higher education—a system that construes intellectual property as a commodity that can be evaluated and quantified. In the different system Lunsford and West imagine, a professor might have to make a case for tenure or promotion based on his or her largely untraceable collaboration in electronic discussion groups, what Lunsford and West (ironically, borrowing a term from the corporate lexicon) call "added value" (1996, 401).

The value they place on "what is added to information as it is appropriated in particular ways for particular purposes" (1996, 401) (read: hypertextual movements in texts and postings to electronic bulletin boards) highlights another logical problem with Lunsford and West's argument: their unquestioning acceptance of electronic technology as an agent of change. Print culture, they claim, is giving way to a digital culture, the nature of which just happens to coincide with postmodern notions of authoring as a disembodied function and the subject as social. Christina Haas observes that scholars in English studies tend to view electronic technology as an agent of change in order to generate enthusiasm for it (1996, 35–36; 191–93). Lunsford and West's argument partakes of this tendency (note their uncritical acceptance of studies by scholars in English studies, such as Lanham, Bolter, and Landow 1996, 396) by citing the rise of electronic technology to generate enthusiasm for another enterprise: the reconstruction of intellectual property. With such statements as "In the end, technology may decide the matter" (1996, 397), they view technology as an all-powerful agent able to transform cultural practices and beliefs. But Haas would remind them that, despite the tenets of postmodern theory, "*people* design, develop, and implement technology" and that "the view of technology as all-powerful hides this fact and so prevents users from formulating crucial questions about what technology is created, by whom, and for what purposes" (1996, 193)—and, I might add, with what intellectual property rights associated with it.

Despite these logical inconsistencies, the arguments for reimagining intellectual property are unquestionably high-minded and benevolent, trying, as they do, to tip the balance toward unobstructed access to knowledge: They value the common good over the grasping individual or corporate interest; the process of producing knowledge over knowledge as product; the self as part of a community with responsibilities to other members of the community over the self as entitled individual.

Unpublished Work, Ownership, and Ethics

I propose leaving the confines of court and legislature and the arena of the global information economy to test these values in a smaller, professional arena inside Composition studies where we *should* be able to enact the belief that knowledge is socially constructed, made and re-made in dialogue with other voices emanating from print and electronic texts. To accomplish this, I will extend the boundaries of the disputed term *intellectual property* to include unpublished work (of course, legally it already does). Unpublished work—the writing of authors, reviewers, and editors—is the site of the process that produces intellectual property, although the protection of copyright ownership is rarely invoked regarding work that is "in progress," not yet "fixed" in a publication.

The MLA Committee on Academic Freedom and Professional Rights and Responsibilities advises those involved in publishing that "As an author's work moves from manuscript to published form, it benefits from the comments, queries, and judgments of peer reviewers and copyeditors . . . [these] add value to an author's work" (1). Recall how Lunsford and West interpret the way value is added when information is added to produce something "new" in electronic networks as a "metaphor for the rhetorical process" (1996, 402). Electronic discourse and hypertext have been theorized as interactive sites of knowledge making that challenge received notions of authorship, but the publication process that involves so many texts that aim to influence other texts presents opportunities for collaborative knowledge making and ethical reflection that have remained unexamined, largely because, as I have demonstrated elsewhere, many participants in the peer review process resist seeing the process as collaborative or in need of revision (Hunter 1995a).

The path to publication in Composition studies is embedded with ethical dilemmas related to received notions of intellectual property and alternate collaborative models as well. As an editor, a reviewer, and an author, I am concerned about the responsibilities we assume when we submit our work to review for publication and when we act as referees for journals in Composition. I am concerned about the power of editors and reviewers to reconfigure—even to appropriate—an author's ideas and intentions (Hunter 1995b). Along the path to publication, we write many texts that are the expressions of our ideas, our intellectual property (e. g., proposals, abstracts, drafts, initial submissions, revisions in response to reviews). Reviewers of these texts make ethical choices in their handling of these texts that are not accounted for by the contracts and copyright laws that govern the published text. Participants in the publication process simply trust that all will "follow the rules" and treat one another fairly when they are involved in submitting and reviewing work for publication. But perhaps because the stakes in the process—professional stature and survival—are so high, the good will and trust of participants may be abused, resulting in violations of an unarticulated code of ethics we might unconsciously subscribe to or expect others to subscribe to. Those involved in the process can behave ethically by exerting what Michael Kelly calls "'ethical critique,' which requires maintaining a balance between the exercise of power and ethical reflection—'power threatens and limits reflection, yet reflection constantly challenges power'" (Porter 1993, 220–21). Most academics would agree that the issues associated with the process of editorial review are issues of power; the process of scholarly publication could benefit from ethical critique.

The editorial process for journals in Composition raises ethical questions about the ways in which reviewers and editors influence an author's intentions and ideas and about the ways in which that influence is acknowledged. Of course, because of the physical nature and stature of the published text, what has happened to shape it along the way to publication is virtually invisible to its readers, but not as untraceable as the process is on the Web. Some anecdotal evidence does exist. In *College English* in 1984, Alan Purves quoted anonymous reviewers' comments to illustrate the gatekeeper category as one of the many roles a reader can play. In *CCC* in 1990, Elizabeth Flynn wrote about her experience "Composing 'Composing as a Woman'"; she observed that "The reviewers . . . seemed to be offended by my criticisms of the field . . . so I decided to shift the emphasis of my discussion, focusing on the positive rather than the negative" (1990, 88). The publication in 1988 of anonymous reviews by *CCC* consulting readers in the first "Burkean Parlor" in *Rhetoric Review* led a reviewer to protest the publication of his words without permission or attribution as an unethical editorial practice. He wrote, "Our words melt into the intertext of the profession soon enough; some credit for having 'originated' them is only fair." But the reviewer identified as "DH" concluded that "readers' reports probably have the same status as letters" (1988, 178).

Perhaps because the documentation styles most journals and books require do not provide ways to acknowledge the many varieties of influence and collaboration that may contribute to a published work, traces of the influence reviewers exert on journal articles more and more frequently surface in the notes of the articles. Such recognition, however, may operate to thank manuscript reviewers as much for the validation their names lend to the work as for their intellectual contributions to it. Still, such credits can be said to satisfy "the ethical imperative to acknowledge those who help us think and rethink as we compose" (Roen and McNenny 1993, 12–13). More frequent acknowledgment in notes and throughout a published text could eliminate the following familiar unethical practice: An author revised a manuscript following the suggestions of one editor and resubmitted the piece to another editor, who accepted it for publication; the author did not acknowledge the suggestions of the first set of referees and the first editor. Often writers do ethically account for the social influences on their texts in forewords, prefaces, and acknowledgments, although Lunsford and Ede contend that this practice leaves collaboration "marginalized" away from "the body of the texts" (1990, 136).

In the preface to *Singular Texts/Plural Authors*, Ede and Lunsford make lengthy acknowledgments of specific people but concede, "Even as we drew up this list of those who most directly supported and influenced our work, we were aware of the scores of others upon whom we indirectly relied, and we realized that we could never make this list complete, never compile a definitive set of acknowledgments" (1990, xiv). In the "Preface" to *Revisioning Writers' Talk: Gender and Culture in Acts of Composing*, Mary Ann Cain observes that "the conversations from which this book took shape and the relationships that enriched them were . . . more than enough to remind me that I wasn't after all, imprisoned in splendid isolation but responding, initiating, talking back, listening" (1995, ix). Likewise, Elizabeth Chiseri-Strater opens her "Acknowledgments" by distinguishing her "scene" of writing from the garret: " . . . for all the isolation that writing involves, it invites a new kind of companionship. As you write . . . you feel connected to all those others like you who have tried to shape their ideas through language into a cohesive and meaningful manuscript." She goes on to mention the dissertations of friends, books by scholars who influenced her, colleagues who were "just a phone call away," and the participants in her research (1991, xi–xii). Interestingly, both Cain and Chiseri-Strater acknowledge the responses and community of their writing groups, indicating the collaborative nature of their composing processes and their attitudes toward intellectual property. By recognizing that "rich network of others with whom [writers] constantly talked and wrote" (Lunsford and West 1996, 400), Cain and Chiseri-Strater use the acknowledgment genre to portray the author as a member of a discourse community rather than a solitary genius.

These acknowledgments set forth idealized scenarios in which writers and readers worked together in ethical collaboration. Other less ideal, less ethical scenarios of the editorial process may not have been recorded in print.

For example, the following scenario could be viewed as collaborative or coercive. It involves three seasoned editors of high-profile journals in Composition studies, seven veteran peer reviewers, and an author trying to get her research about a controversial professional issue published. Instead of sending her the usual "revise and resubmit" rejoinder, the editor proposed a deal based on his own interest in the author's topic and limited space in the journal. Instead of publishing a revised version of the author's submission, the editor would coordinate a series of short pieces on the subject, supplementing and probably contradicting the author's view. Faced with the editor's proposition, what choices did the author have? She did not want to risk remaining unheard and unpublished while others wrote in opposition to her view about the topic she had alerted them to. (Although she did not know it at the time, the others in this series would be the editor and the three reviewers of her submission). So, she reduced her submission by two-thirds and became one of many voices speaking on the topic. The scenario gets even more complicated and drawn out (see Hunter 1995b), but for now, it is enough to know the following: By the time the author's perspective was published two and a half years after initial submission, it had been scrutinized by ten Composition scholars in their roles as editors and reviewers. Although finally in print, the article appeared in a context the author did not choose, a context beyond her control, a context fashioned by others. This case can be construed as being about power and access, about prestige and space. As well-intentioned professionals, the participants made choices based on their various understandings of scholarly merit and intellectual property. Did any participant in this scenario bring ethical reflection to bear on the choices that were being made about the author's intellectual property?

Reviewers and editors differ on who owns the texts generated during the editorial process. Did Purves, Flynn, and the voices in the "Burkean Parlor" have the right to quote and contend with texts by anonymous reviewers without permission from reviewers or editors? When I began doing research on the editorial process, one colleague refused to share the anonymous reviews of her work, claiming that only the editor could release those texts. Two other colleagues, on the other hand, sent me stacks of reviews they had written as anonymous consulting readers for *CCC* and *Rhetoric Review*. When he was editor, Richard Gebhardt indicated in *CCC* "that rejection letters and correspondence about referees' evaluations are confidential business between authors and editor." Only the Chair of CCCC, his publisher, would be able to release such information (1993, 7). An acquisitions editor for Southern Illinois University Press stated that the press' practice is to "behave as if peer reviews are 'works made for hire'—physically the property of the press, intellectually the property of the reviewer" (Simmons 1994).

Is it possible that few of us engage the texts of anonymous reviews explicitly in our work because they are anonymous? As such, what can these texts contribute to knowledge production in Composition studies? Proponents of blind review, like Douglas Hesse, argue that reader reports are like lore: "transitory . . . as knowledge to be consumed, taken or left, not pondered and formally acknowledged." In readers' reports he finds "practical knowledge, the experience of what will or should work . . . in this article, in this journal." Unlike McNenny and Roen or Lunsford and Ede, Hesse does not admit the reviewer as a "silent collaborator in the production of texts" who deserves to be acknowledged as such (1995, 255). But he does define reader reports as a force that shapes knowledge in the field.

At the crux of disagreements about the way reader reports should be credited and valued are the premises of the blind review method. Justified in terms of hierarchy, tradition, and professional status in a field that professes to be democratic and collaborative, blind review is advocated and employed because of the following static values it upholds. It certifies knowledge, requiring "a discipline's 'experts' [to] maintain quality control over new knowledge entering the field" (Berkenkotter 1995, 245). Anonymity in the system makes unbiased judgments possible, protecting both peer reviewers and authors from prejudice. The system we have inherited, which was begun in the sciences in the seventeenth century, is, according to its proponents, necessarily agonistic or adversarial (Bazerman 1988, 137–46; Berkenkotter 1995, 246). Editor Richard Gebhardt established blind review for *CCC* in 1986, because he believed that refereed journals in Composition studies are necessary if we are to succeed in "promotion and tenure systems that demand refereed publication" and if we are to allay the "suspicion among some faculty members that composition studies is not a 'scholarly' field" (1995, 239). The boundaries between author and reviewer that such a referee system sets up may significantly obstruct collegial interaction and the possibilities of making knowledge that collaboration among colleagues promises. If we apply such theories to the editorial process, then we see that while blind review may be in the best interests of our move toward professionalization, it is not in the best interests of a profession that puts itself forth, theoretically and politically in its scholarly discourse, as collaborative and dialogic. At the same time that we are defending collaboration as a legitimate way of advancing knowledge within the discipline, we are not recognizing the possibility of its manifestation in peer reviewing.

The case of *Dialogue: A Journal for Writing Specialists* proves that the field can support a peer review system of collaborative knowledge making. It is the editorial policy to ask prospective authors for blind submissions not so much to gain status as a refereed journal as to protect reviewers and authors from bias and intimidation during the initial reading. After the first reading, however, the policy deviates from the norm: Authors' and reviewers' identities are revealed. The editorial board members, who are the reviewers for *Dialogue*, frame their comments as a letter to the author of the article rather than as a letter to the editors, and they sign their review letters. These signed reviews are sent to the authors *and* to the reviewers of the submission. With their identities revealed, authors and reviewers may choose to communicate directly about a submission. This method of peer review may actually give reviewers more stake in the process of getting good work published—time-consuming and lacking in professional recognition as the task of reviewing is. Their names appear prominently at the end of each article they have reviewed.

Charlotte Thralls demonstrated, with a case study of the publication of a journal article, the complex voices and relationships that are "present" in published discourse (1992). According to Thralls,

> As a manuscript passes through different stages of review and revision, the dialogue that occurred among collaborative partners at any stage is retextualized in a following stage; this dialogue is then passed on to subsequent partners. The draft of an author's manuscript that reaches publication bears traces of these various dialogic partners and thus ultimately represents the entire collaborative chain. (1992, 68)

Much as Thralls describes it, *Dialogue*'s reviewing process enacts as far as possible in the printed text Bakhtin's theory that all communication involves collaborative partners who are linked through a chain of responsive reactions (Thralls 1992, 65ff.). Although it is still an imperfect method for recognizing the collaborative nature of reviewing, the alternative that *Dialogue* offers will have an impact on the way peer review evolves in journals in Composition studies. The peer review system inherited from the natural sciences has marked one stage in our field's professionalization; this reconfiguration of it could be another stage in which the ways knowledge is made and disseminated in our field are reconceptualized and the parties who are responsible at once for making knowledge and assessing it are made more visible. Many authors and reviewers are ready to rethink the conventions of peer review and, in so doing, to reimagine intellectual property as always owned in concert.

Not a Conclusion

It would be reassuring to be able to promise that bringing collaboration to the fore in the processes of print and electronic publication would give us the opportunity to resolve the ongoing conflict between intellectual property rights and collaborative authorship. But resolution is impossible; all that is possible is continually to put our professional practices and beliefs to the test of ethical reflection. Whether we consider intellectual property in a global setting or in a local, professional setting, we encounter similar obstacles in the form of people and their entrenched beliefs that would prevent our reimagining the constructs we have inherited. In whatever site it is studied, intellectual property offers numerous moments for ethical reflection that can lead to the continual evolution of our ideas about the processes of reading and writing, individual ownership, authorship, and collaboration. We need only be ever-vigilant for opportunities to foreground our ethical awareness and to question the seemingly unquestionable tenets of our time and culture.

Works Cited

Anonymous. 1988. Untitled "Burkean Parlor" Essay. *Rhetoric Review* 7: 208–10.

Bazerman, C. 1988. *Shaping Written Knowledge: The Genre and Activity of the Experimental Article in Science.* Madison: University of Wisconsin Press.

Berkenkotter, C. 1995. "The Power and the Perils of Peer Review." *Rhetoric Review* 13.2: 245–48.

Cain, M. 1995. *Revisioning Writers' Talk: Gender and Culture in Acts of Composing.* Albany: State University of New York Press.

"Caucus on Intellectual Property and Composition/Communiciation Studies." 1997. *Convention Preview.* Urbana, IL: NCTE.

Conference of Editors of Learned Journals. 1984. *Guidelines for Journal Editors and Contributors.* New York: Modern Language Association.

Chiseri-Strater, E. 1991. *Academic Literacies: The Public and Private Discourse of University Students.* Portsmouth, NH: Heinemann Boynton/Cook.

Clark, I. L., and D. Healy. 1996. "Are Writing Centers Ethical?" *WPA: Writing Program Administration 20.1/2: 32–48.*

DH. 1989. "Dear Professor Enos." *Rhetoric Review* 9: 178–79.

Faigley, L. 1992. *Fragments of Rationality: Postmodernity and the Subject of Composition.* Pittsburgh: University of Pittsburgh Press.

———. 1996. *A Letter to CCCC Members from Lester Faigley, 1996 Chair.* Urbana, IL: NCTE.

Flynn, E. 1990. "Composing 'Composing as a Woman'": A Perspective on Research." *College Composition and Communication* 41: 83–89.

Gebhardt, R. C. 1993. "Thoughts on Confidentiality and Submissions." *College Composition and Communication* 44: 7–8.

———. 1995. "Refereed Publication in Composition and *CCC." Rhetoric Review* 13.2: 238–44.

Haas, C. 1996. *Writing Technology: Studies on the Materiality of Literacy.* Mahwah, NJ: Lawrence Erlbaum.

Hesse, D. 1995. "Reader Reviews as Scholarship: A Chaotic View." *Rhetoric Review* 13.2: 254–58.

Howard, R. M. 1995. "Plagiarisms, Authorships, and the Academic Death Penalty." *College English* 57.7: 788–806.

Hunter, S. 1993. "The Dangers of Teaching Differently." In *Writing Ourselves into the Story: Unheard Voices from Composition Studies,* ed. S. I. Fontaine and S. Hunter, 70–85. Carbondale: Southern Illinois University Press.

———. 1995a. "The Case for Reviewing as Collaboration." *Rhetoric Review* 13.2: 265–69.

————. 1995b. "Making Choices Along the Path to Publication." Conference on College Composition and Communication. Washington, D. C.

Jaszi, P. 1994. "On the Author Effect: Contemporary Copyright and Collective Creativity." In *The Construction of Authorship: Textual Appropriation in Law and Literature*, ed. M. Woodmansee and P. Jaszi, 29–56. Durham, NC: Duke University Press.

Lunsford, A. A. 1996. "Intellectual Property in an Age of Information: What Is at Stake for Composition Studies?" In *Composition in the Twenty-First Century: Crisis and Change*, ed. L. Z. Bloom, D. A. Daier, and E. M. White, 261–72. Carbondale: Southern Illinois University Press.

Lunsford, A. A., and L. Ede. 1990. *Singular Text/Plural Authors*. Carbondale: Southern Illinois University Press.

Lunsford, A. A., and S. West. 1996. "Intellectual Property and Composition Studies." *College Composition and Communication* 47.3: 383–411.

MLA Committee on Academic Freedom and Professional Rights and Responsibilities. n.d. *Advice for Authors, Reviewers, Publishers, and Editors of Scholarly Books and Articles*. New York: MLA.

Porter, J. E. 1993. "Developing a Postmodern Ethics of Rhetoric and Composition." In *Defining the New Rhetorics*, ed. T. Enos and S. C. Brown, 207–26. Newbury Park, CA: Sage.

Purves, A. C. 1984. "The Teacher as Reader: An Anatomy." *College English* 46: 259–65.

Roen, D. H., and G. McNenny. 1993. "Collaboration or Plagiarism—Cheating Is in the Eye of the Beholder." *Dialogue: A Journal for Writing Specialists* 1.1: 6–27.

Rose, M. 1993. *Authors and Owners: The Invention of Copyright*. Cambridge, MA: Harvard University Press.

Simmons, J. 1994. Telephone interview. 8 February.

Thralls, C. 1992. "Bakhtin, Collaborative Partners, and Published Discourse: A Collaborative View of Composing." In *New Visions of Collaborative Writing*, ed. J. Forman, 63–81. Portsmouth, NH: Heinemann Boynton/Cook.

Woodmansee, M., and P. Jaszi. 1995. "The Law of Texts: Copyright in the Academy." *College English* 57.7: 769–87.

13

Toward an Ethics of Grading

Pat Belanoff

We academics spend a substantial portion of our time doing what we rarely talk about with any specificity: grading papers. We may seek sympathy ("I have a whole stack to grade before tomorrow morning"), moan ("Students can't write any more"), complain ("What have I done to deserve this?"), or crow ("A great class!"). But very few of us talk about an individual paper and our thought processes as we read, evaluate, respond to, and grade it. And even fewer of us theorize these activities. Why should we? In our own classrooms, we remain unchallenged in this arena, the most crucial aspect of our authority—at least in the minds of most of our students. Occasionally an aggressive student will question some one of us or even file a formal grievance. At Stony Brook, when such a grievance occurs, a committee asks for responses from the teacher and student and may call a hearing, during which both address the committee. Nonetheless, no one challenges the teacher's right to give whatever grade she considers appropriate—unless, of course, some kind of prejudice or harassment can be substantiated. As director of a large writing program, I never overturn a grade given by one of our teaching assistants (though I have the bureaucratic right to do so) on the assumption that they, as novice teachers, would suffer if their authority were undercut in this way. Thus, I always accord them the same right that regular faculty have: the right not to have their grades questioned. In truth, many faculty consider it a violation of academic freedom to have anyone other than themselves actively engaged in their classrooms in any way, most of all with their grades and grading policies. This defense of academic freedom may well be a prime factor in current motivations for circumventing and/or substantiating local grades by mandating external evaluations of various kinds at the institution, state, and national level.

I recognize that I am overgeneralizing, that there may well be departments and schools where grades are arrived at collaboratively, but I suspect that such collaborative assessment or grading occurs mainly in writing programs (particularly in those with staff largely or solely made up of graduate students and part-timers) or in departments or institutions where portfolios are being used across the curriculum in some way. Occasionally individual faculty members may agree to exchange student papers once or twice during the semester and grade each others' students. Some departments specifically meet to discuss grading policies.[1] Minus these activities, each of us communes with herself when she grades a set of papers.

What does it mean to grade in an ethical way? Traditionally, psychometricians have set up validity and reliability as ethical touchstones for grading and assessment. Validity means that our evaluation or grade does what it says it does: An A rewards good writing, and an F punishes poor writing. Reliability means that what we have asked students to do allows them to demonstrate that they can do it. For example, one paper cannot tell us whether a student writes well (Cooper and Odell 1977, xi). But these touchstones beg the question, because we still have to determine what is "good" writing and what is "poor" writing. My purpose here is to question the ethics structured by traditional stances toward evaluation and grading and to explore the ramifications of my own questioning, particularly in relation to current research and critical theory and to the encroaching threat of mass, standardized testing.[2] I will conclude by initiating a discussion of strategies for increased collaboration as a means of coping with the ethical issues surrounding grading.

The Lessons of Research

When testing through written products rather than through oral responses became the norm at the end of the last century, variability in assessment could come under critical observation.[3] Oral responses disappear with breath; judgments of them have to rely on memory. Nonetheless, such judgments were often, and continue to be in specified arenas, collaborative. Typically, for example, graduate students take at least one set of oral examinations, which are conducted by some specified number of faculty who then confer on their judgment. In most instances, the judgment is binary: pass or fail. During the process of arriving at this decision, faculty members may well change their judgments, their standards for judging, and their awareness of what is and is not a more or less crucial standard in that particular setting for that particular student. The more vexed the case, the more likely such conversations will occur. And the more vexed cases there are, the more likely standards will come under scrutiny.

In the elementary and high schools, however, almost all vestiges of assessment based on oral performance have disappeared. Harvey J. Graff has described testing practices during which the oral reading ability of 150 children was assessed in one-and-one-half hours: thirty-six seconds for each student (Witte, Trachsel, and Walters 1986, 18–21). Small wonder that educators and parents sought more reliable tests. The increased use of writing in schools led quite naturally (or so it seemed at the time) to its use for testing. Furthermore, in order to eliminate what many considered to be the "subjective" element in assessment, multiple-choice tests became increasingly popular, as did broad-based intelligence testing initiated largely during World War I.[4] Although teachers and researchers questioned the use of a multiple-choice format to assess writing ability almost from its inception, such tests continued to (and may even today) be the single most used form of testing in the United States in all subject areas. The most recent survey I know concluded that a substantial percentage of writing programs continue to use multiple-choice testing for some if not all of their decision making about placement, grading, and proficiency.[5] This, despite research that calls into question the appropriateness of such testing (Breland and Gaynor 1979). Why?

One answer focuses on the discrepancy in teachers' grades. Over the years, any number of research studies have validated what many of us have heard from students: Teachers do not agree on their grades. Some teachers have a reputation for being "hard" graders; some, for being "an easy A." Shrewd students undertake their own research to uncover which teachers belong on which side of this grade divide. How many times have all of us listened to students protest that some paper of theirs we have just graded would have gotten a better grade from some other teacher? Students are not wrong about this, though they probably also realize that the reverse is equally true, even if they are not going to tell us that. Awareness of this variability encourages the use of multiple-choice tests as the road to consistency.

Many of those who become uncomfortable about testing writing without asking students to write feel far more comfortable with holistic scoring, a form of assessment often used to "score" students' writing for placement and aptitude, and argue that readers can be "trained" to evaluate papers consistently. You and I can, they argue, participate in training sessions that will assure that we would both give substantially the same score to the same paper. Undoubtedly this is a kind of collaborative grading, but validity here seems questionable to me, both in terms of what students are asked to respond to and in terms of whether such scoring can in any way be comparable to genuine reading. But even if all of us were convinced on these issues, we are not, as a result, going to allow such practices to invade our classrooms: We will not give standard assignments under standard conditions so that "our" papers can be read holistically by a special team of trained readers. This possibility is anathema to me, as I suspect it is to most faculty.

Nonetheless, the research does not go away: No group of teachers is going to consistently give the same grades to the same papers. If we put ourselves to the test, we may discover, as Frances Zak (1993) did, that we do not even agree with an earlier version of ourselves. She put aside copies of papers she had already graded and came back to them at the end of the semester, only to discover that she graded many of them differently the second time around.[6] How many of us have the courage to chance that? I have heard teachers confess that they always have to grade papers in the same spot, as though some absolute As and Bs were hovering there to be hooked into. We want to be fair.

The best known of the professional research studies I have been alluding to is probably the one Paul Diederich did in 1974 in which he discovered that twenty percent of the papers he used for his study received every grade available from A to F—and he was using experienced teachers. But Diederich also discovered that graders agreed far more about the traits of the papers than they did about the grades—for instance, teachers may well agree that a specific paper presents thought-provoking, rich ideas but is poorly organized, or vice versa. Differences in grades then seem to depend more on the relative importance graders assign to features than to whether the features are present or absent—in other words, what feature or features does any one of us consider to be the most significant indicator of good writing? Alan C. Purves' (1992) eleven-year study of fourteen countries, four hundred schools, and 4000 high-school students, in order to pin down what qualities evaluators reward, concludes that all we can really say with any certainty is that a particular student did well or poorly on a particular task on a particular day. I would add: as determined by a particular grader or group of graders on a particular day. Generalizing any more than that moves beyond what his data uncovered.

Research such as this can cause all of us enormous discomfort if we focus on it at all. I have known quite a few professors who simply shrug their shoulders and deny the applicability of the research to their own classes and to their own grades. Somehow they seem confident that what they are doing is different from what has been looked at in the research studies. When I teach introductory Old English (which I do fairly regularly) I am—to no one's surprise—the only faculty member doing so on my campus that year. My grades cannot be compared with anyone else's in any precise way. In a sense, they are "right" because no one else seemingly is in a position to question my judgments. The existence of multiple sections of the same course (as is always true in writing programs) makes variability in grading obvious; undoubtedly that is why collaborative grading is most in evidence in writing courses. But if grades represent the student in some larger way to us, to the public, to themselves—and they do—then I need to heed the cautions implied by the research for *all* of the classes I teach. The ethics of such disregard of directly pertinent research are disquieting.

The contrast stirred up by the debate over multiple-choice, short-answer, and essay testing of writing is that between objectivity and subjectivity. And if subjectivity is feared in assessment outside the classroom, it is far more to be feared within the classroom. Unfortunately, the equating of objectivity with the ethical and subjectivity with the unfair is widespread in our culture. I would argue that subjectivity is constitutive of all tests and grading—and that this is as it should be. I would argue also that multiple-choice tests merely push the subjectivity to some other spot—perhaps less visible to both teacher and student. When subjectivity is invisible, it becomes dangerous because too many assume there is none. For example, how many of us examine in any systematic way the fit between what we do and do not question on tests, what we give special weight to, how we rate partial answers, how skilled we are at framing questions. Additionally, even on short-answer quizzes, we cannot eliminate interpretation. Still, most of us feel that such tests within the classroom are "fair"; that is, they are ethical approaches to the whole field of grading because they minimize interpretation and represent an adequate inquiry into what all students have had an equal opportunity to learn. When the situation allows, we can still do some assessment of student reading and interpretive prowess through classroom discussions, but because such judgments are a return to the dread subjectivity, most of us rely on written demonstrations as evidence of student mastery of what we teach. These written demonstrations then become the primary basis for a semester grade. Such an approach certainly appears to be more valid than multiple-choice tests. Research has thus led us to move from oral testing to multiple-choice tests to holistic scoring in large-scale assessment and to short essay tests and carefully crafted paper assignments within the individual classroom. But the ethical question, at least for me, still remains because of this untheorized belief in the possibility and value of objectivity. Current critical theory is relevant here.

The Lessons of Critical Theory

Perhaps all of this fuzziness about grading and assessment might not be so worrisome if modern critical theory did not make it so obvious that we are never, as Toni Morrison (1992) reminds, "home alone": In this case, we are never in the classroom alone. In that classroom with us have always been our experience and our education, our culturally mediated ways of viewing ourselves, our profession, and our students' and our own personal preferences. Much current theory in our discipline points to this truth from a variety of perspectives. My specific question here is how ethical is it for us to subscribe to theories relative to the interpretation of "high" and/or published texts without coming to grips on the same basis with the student texts we put grades on. A counter-argument put forth in response to this question is that student texts are not comparable to published texts. For the most part, this counter-argument contends, such texts are not literary texts. But we are on shaky ground here because the very notion that student texts might *not* be texts included within critical theory calls into question the very basis of some of these critical theories; we cannot escape our involvement by trying to categorize student writing as some specialized genre outside the scope of our theories. What might some of these theories suggest about grading strategies?

Reader-response criticism or reception theory tells us, in Jane Tompkins' words, that meaning does not inhere "completely and exclusively in the literary text" (1980, 201). This school of criticism focuses on the role "actual readers play in the determination of literary meaning" (Tompkins 1980, ix). Such an approach says that it is not in fact the text I am reading that fully controls my reactions to it. Thus, is not my grade a reflection of something other than the text in front of me? How often do I examine that "something other"? Almost all recent critical theory, no matter how it labels itself, assumes a significant role for the reader. What is the role I play as a reader of my students' papers?

As a subjective reader, critic, and interpreter, David Bleich asserts that the "essence of a symbolic work is not in its visible sensory structure or manifest semantic load, but in its subjective re-creation by a reader and in his public presentation of that re-creation" (1989, 1255). Our "public presentation of that re-creation" can be seen as the grade we put on the paper. What constructs that "re-creation"? Possibly, my almost subconscious reaction to the subject of the paper, my awareness of the student as an individual within my class who does or does not speak up, who does or does not come to see me during office hours, who does or does not remind me of someone I do or do not like. Quite possibly, whether I read a particular student's paper first or after some number of other papers that may have been superior or inferior. Quite possibly, whether I slept well the night before or ate something that is making its presence known in unpleasant ways. Quite possibly, a conglomerate of other factors that are far less visible and knowable.

Feminists focus reader-response issues on the gender of both author and reader. They see interpretation as an event influenced by gender and by social constructions of gender within specific cultural configurations. Elizabeth Flynn, after examining responses by students to short stories, concluded that there were "distinct patterns of response along gender lines" (1989, 1275). Can I claim myself immune to the influence of my own gender?[7] Deborah Tannen (1990) has extended gender-talk discriminations to many of life's social situations. Just because I am a student of her research does not make me outside of it. In my early years at Stony Brook, I recall listening to a placement-examination committee made up of all women graduate students disparage an essay that seemed to me perfectly well written and effectively structured as an argument, but undeniably arguing a point offensive to most women in the most blatant way. To what extent can we control such responses? To what extent would we want to?[8] These questions have only vexed answers for most of us. But regardless, almost all of us continue to put grades on papers because we must.

Content as well as approach concerns feminists, some of whom urge us to value personal experience in writing, to give positive weight to arguments and persuasion that are less logic-based and more overtly subjective than classical rhetoric teaches (Papoulis 1990). Farrell labels as male rhetoric the traditional form in which a thesis is stated up front, then "proved" through evidence, and finally restated as a conclusion. He speaks of female rhetoric as a more difficult-to-control form in which arguments and evidence lead the reader step by step to some conclusion manifest to a reader only at the end of the final step. Wendy Goulston agrees: "Writing, as it has been traditionally required in college, can be understood to be a 'male' establishment form"

(1987, 21). We do not need to essentialize a particular style of discourse as women's style or men's style, but we must recognize that styles themselves are gendered and that, regardless of the gender of the author and regardless of our own, we are quite likely to have our individual preferences for one or the other (or perhaps some mixture) of these modes. John Flynn, for example, speaks of his "frustration with the pedagogy of authoritarianism," a stance that he considers "feminist" (1989, 134). He concludes by describing his teacherly self as "a conservative male, working-class, Brooklyn Irish Catholic, social-democrat, feminist, environmentalist, antifascist, disabled Vietnam veteran, peace activist, and recovered cancer patient" (1989, 136). All of us bring an equally (seemingly) disjunctive set of traits to the students' papers on which we place our grades. There is a limit to how completely we can set all of this aside, or how useful we can be as readers of our students' work when we strive to set it aside. At a time when the personal is under renewed scrutiny within our own scholarship (see *PMLA*, October 1996, which is devoted to this inquiry), we cannot dismiss its influence on how we read and grade our students' papers.

Theorists who identify themselves as *social constructionists* acknowledge "the influence of social forces in the formation of the individual" (Berlin 1992, 106) and recognize that these social forces function in specific, and sometimes but not always identifiable, ways to condition gender, race, and class. My students and I are products of our individual cultures. These cultures were once more homogeneous than they currently are for most of us. To what degree do we examine the ways in which our own backgrounds have led us to grade in certain ways? I certainly began my professional life grading as I had perceived myself graded by my teachers. Perhaps, we would like to believe that our grades represent the application of some universal, external standards ("An A is an A!"), but social constructionists, new historicists, and theorists of several other stripes could point to all of the ways in which that is not true.

And, in truth, if the current plethora of anti-foundational thought has any foundational truth (always its Achilles' heel), we must conclude that there is no such thing as an "A," only the "A" we have constructed out of our own specific materials. But, of course, those are the same construction materials used by a high percentage of our colleagues. We can then argue that our "A" has validity within the context in which we apply it. I would argue, indeed, that that is its only validity. Nonetheless, we still do not agree with our colleagues on grades; even if our and their social construction ought to be similar, apparently we do not put the pieces together the same way or, at any rate, in similar enough ways to produce the same grades.

Theories subsumed under the terms *cultural studies* or *multiculturalism*, defined by Gates as the "representation of difference" (1993, 6), are perhaps more directly pertinent to grading practice than reader-response or social constructionist theories, although multiculturalists might well argue that their theories encompass these others. Be that as it may, multiculturalism cannot so easily escape the pragmatics of the classroom at the risk of negating itself, because it cannot ignore the actual presence of students from a variety of backgrounds and cultures; that is, the actual presence of "difference" as represented by actual students. Students are physically present; theories hover above us, whether we recognize them or not. The latter we can ignore; the former, we cannot. A 1982 study undertaken by Takala, Purves, and Buckmaster concludes that there is "an entity . . . called the 'national style' . . . representing existing cultural patterns of expression and thought." They link this "national style" more to the effects of schooling than to "the lexical and grammatical constraints of a language" (324). If students are not even a part of our discourse community, what do our comments and our grades communicate to them and what do they communicate to us that we must somehow grade?

But it is overgeneralizing to speak of even a "national" style—in the United States at least. In her examination of the interaction of cultural diversity and our assessments of it, Ball reminds us,

> By the year 2020, more than 50% of the students in urban educational settings will be from culturally and linguistically diverse populations. These predictions about the twenty-first century challenge educational institutions to address issues of equity for students from all backgrounds, languages, and cultures. One of the most difficult of these challenges will be to define criteria and methods of assessment that adequately reflect diverse cultural and linguistic features. (1993, 255–56)

Ball concludes that "students may be penalized for preferring text patterns that are valued in their culture but are different from mainstream academic text patterns. These text patterns are structural in nature and, therefore, are not obvious to the casual reader" (1993, 257). This research looked at a precollege population, but colleges will enroll these students soon.

One of the outcomes of the lens provided to us by multiculturalism is that we realize we have always lived in a community somewhat different from that of our students. There has always been a way that we and they speak a different language. Mary Louise Pratt calls this area "the contact zone" (1991), that area in which differences must interact if the goals and aims of those espousing the differences are to be met. The diversity of the students sitting before us forces us to recognize the differences that have always been there and to confront ourselves and our methods more and more often as this diversity becomes richer—for it will inevitably become richer, more complex, and perhaps even more individualized as these culturally diverse approaches interact through the many years of schooling students experience even before they enter my classroom. How do and can grades function in such a contact zone? I have discovered in the past that students with whom I thought I could identify culturally did not read my comments as I expected them to. How much more likely will it be that those culturally different from me and from one another will—and will understand my grades and the basis for them?

One final theoretical position needs to be acknowledged here. As Victor Villaneuva points out, a steadily increasing number of faculty members see *the*

classroom as a "political arena that aims at pointing out injustices and insti-
gating change" (1991, 249). Can we assume that our notions of social justice
and political fairness are "right," so "right" in fact that we can see our classrooms as places where students will learn to accept and act on them? And how
will we grade their productions in the classroom? Will the Christian Creation-
ist and the Marxist New Historicist and the Feminist Care-giver be subject to
the same standards? Can I set aside my views and view all of their pieces objectively? I don't think so—at least not without help, for whether I like it or
not, every time I put a grade on a paper, I authorize certain approaches and
ideas and devalue others.[9] Obviously, those teachers who hold these strong
views discuss these political, social, economic, and cultural issues with their
students, but the power structures of the classroom militate against this being
a genuine peer discussion.

I do not at all want to suggest that the incorporation of ideology into the
classroom is a recent phenomenon. Classrooms have always been enclosed
within ideologies of various kinds; currently such incorporation is more obvious simply because the ideologies are at such variance with much of past ideology. Difference has created visibility, as is its wont. But we have to admit
that this conscious espousal of ideology can distort just as much as the unconscious espousal may have in the past. As Louis Wetherbee Phelps cautions, we
need to keep in mind the rights of students and ask ourselves always "what
ethical considerations should constrain me in pursuing . . . utopian dreams?"
(1993, 48). Although Phelps is referring to the writing classroom, the ethics of
the politicization of the literature classroom are no different. I suspect there is
hardly a faculty member anywhere who has not heard a student complain that
he received a low grade because he wrote something or expressed some opin-
ion at variance with his teacher's. These students are not always wrong. Or a
student has admitted to us that in some other class (not ours, of course!), she
wrote a paper whose thesis she did not even believe, just to get a good grade.
To what extent do our grading practices put students in such positions? Patricia
Bizzell (1986) warns us to consider our ethical responsibility for the political
and social climate that surrounds our classroom and inevitably influences what
happens there. I want to include within that ethical responsibility the responsibility to subject our grading practices to the sort of reflection that can result
from conversation with our peers that helps us see the ways ideology may
color our reactions.

Perhaps the one thing that the plethora of modern critical theories agree
on most clearly is that language draws its meaning from context and that the
more contextualized language is, the more powerful it can be. It is precisely
the establishment of a common context, a common background of texts read
and information ingested, that Hirsch aims for in his controversial book *Cultural Literacy* (1987). If context determines meaning, and if I can construct the
context, I can control the meaning others derive not only from their reading,

but also from experience itself. And when I can control meaning in this way and (probably more tellingly) by handing out reward and punishment, thought control looms on my classroom doorstep.

Theory and Practice: Their Mutuality

It may be intellectually satisfying to ruminate and reflect on ideological matters such as these, but to students, grades are not ideological. Were grades merely philosophical pronouncements, with the same impact on our students' future as our preference for one writer over another, we could muse on them without limit. But grades do have an impact on our students in ways some of us may choose to ignore or even scoff at, but these ways are important to them and to their sense of their own potential. Will they be on the Dean's List? Will they be able to get into graduate school, law school, medical school? Will they end up on probation or even dismissed? Will they lose their federal or state aid? Will they get the vacation their parents promised? Maybe even a new car?[10]

Consideration of "real-life" questions such as these highlight the all too frequent chasm between theory and practice. Giroux criticizes those he labels as "progressive and radical educators" for deepening this chasm.

> One major problem facing the recent outpouring of critical discourse on schooling is that over the years it has become largely academicized. . . . [I]t has failed to recognize the general relevance of education as a public service and the importance of deliberately translating educational theory into a community-related discourse capable of reaching into and animating public culture and life. In effect, critical and radical writings on schooling have become ghettoized within the ivory tower. (Giroux and McLaren 1989, xiii)

I would alter Giroux's statement slightly for my purposes here and substitute "textuality" for "schooling": "the recent outpouring of critical discourse *on textuality* . . . has become largely academicized." Additionally, I would take Giroux's argument a step farther, for this ghettoization exists within institutions of higher education and even within individuals in those institutions. The theoretical and the practical are often kept quite separate. At a public forum in which I participated recently, one of the faculty member participants said quite clearly that he did not see a connection between research and teaching. And in an essay concluding *Contending with Words*, John Sosnoski states, "It is instructive, though not surprising, that this volume contains no theses on grading" (1991). He slightly atones for this lack by suggesting the development of criteria for different groups of students that take into account the value of their differences, but he does not extend this awareness to those making whatever judgments are made. Ethics demand that we recognize our own situatedness just as we recognize that of the students we teach and the texts we read, whether to enjoy, to analyze, to teach, or to grade.

The Impetus for Standardization

One logical conclusion to the argument I have been advancing is advocacy of external testing and assessment, the imposition of judgments by someone other than the classroom teacher. The argument would run something like this: "If classroom teachers cannot grade fairly, find some other way of grading." At the elementary and high school levels, external standardized assessment has become the avenue for leveling the playing ground. If everyone takes the same test at the same stage of their academic career, students, administrators, parents, and public officials will have a logical basis for comparison. And so we have a plethora of tests. According to a report of the National Commission on Testing and Public Policy, entitled *From Gatekeeper to Gateway: Transforming Testing in America*, "Mandatory testing consumes some 20 million school days and the equivalent of $700 to $900 million in direct and indirect expenditures annually" (1990, x). The summary conclusion of this study is that "Current testing, predominantly multiple choice in format, is over-relied upon, lacks adequate public accountability, sometimes leads to unfairness in the allocation of opportunities, and too often undermines vital social policies" (1990, ix). It would appear as though this study, supported by the Ford Foundation, has not had much effect on public policy, because calls for national testing have accelerated over the past seven years in conjunction with the establishment of national standards in a variety of disciplines. In fact, this report sees the standards movement as leading to "the full development of everyone in our society" (1990, 1) and advocates a testing system that will serve as a "gateway" rather than a "gatekeeper." The preparers of this report never speak of ethics, though they do refer fairly often to "ideals of fairness and equal opportunity" (1990, ix) and to the need to be sensitive to tests that "disproportionately deny opportunities to minorities" (1990, xi).

This report sets forth a list of factors that influence test scores: text anxiety, test sophistication, test-taking habits, attitudes toward tests, test directions, noise level of the testing environment, language of the test, native language of the test-taker, cultural background of the test-taker, special coaching, and even not having eaten breakfast (1990, 7). A reasonable—and ethically responsive—conclusion to an analysis such as this would be to recommend the discontinuance of multiple-choice tests, but despite this report's awareness of the implications of the items on its own list and despite their seemingly incisive criticism of current testing procedures, the framers of this report never advocate the discontinuance of multiple-choice tests but consider them "a legitimate part of many assessment programs" (1990, 27). How can they come to such a conclusion? One reason would seem to be that they sincerely believe that there can be a test that can eliminate the effects of the factors on this list. Such a test would need to eliminate context altogether. All students have "attitudes toward tests"; all students have a native language and a cultural background. And will I turn away at the door those who have not eaten breakfast?

Or will I feed them? What if some students perform better on an empty stomach? How will I know which ones to feed and which ones to reschedule because they unwisely ate breakfast? We must come back to what our theories have taught us: Language use is contextual because it is context that provides needed meaning. I can only wonder about the ethics of recommendations made by those who ignore their own findings.

Recent research studies have been examining the unproven hypothesis that the reason why American students lag behind students of other advanced countries, as evidenced by the results of the tests given by the National Assessment of Education Progress, is that the stakes for students taking these tests are low and that this lack of a meaningful outcome for the individual test-taker results in poor motivation and poor achievement. One of these studies (Kiplinger and Linn 1995/1996) concludes that raising the stakes somewhat does not appear to affect motivation or achievement. Another study, however, demonstrates that providing financial rewards to students results in better test scores. The researchers conclude that "NAEP very likely underrepresents students' knowledge and ability, and we would attribute part of the cause to low motivation. More accurately, then, we would say that NAEP shows what students know and are motivated to show us" (1995/1996, 155). I confess to being horrified by this approach and its implications. The authors themselves do not appear to be horrified (if monetary rewards for school achievement had been repugnant to them at the start, I suppose they would never have undertaken this study); they say merely that "providing financial rewards for performance may be neither practical nor desirable" (1995/1996, 154).[11]

Standardized tests, which bear little relevance to classroom activities, are unethical, but they will tend in the long run to shape what occurs in the classroom. As Grant Wiggins notes, "Tests themselves teach" (1988). What is not tested tends to disappear from the classroom. Thus, standardized tests lead to standardization of classrooms—a strange outcome for a country that prides itself on individualism! Despite this tendency, contexts can never be controlled to the point of creating some sort of vacuum in which all students would take the same test completely uninfluenced by anything other than the knowledge in their heads. Nor would I want to exercise such control even if it *were* possible. Knowledge cannot be usable *unless* it is connected to context. Who wants all fourth graders to be doing exactly the same thing, using the exact same materials, guided by teachers who have been cloned from some prototype? Should all school buildings and all classrooms look exactly alike also: same pictures on the wall, same books in the library, same clothing code? I think of such a situation as "mall" education. But short of such standardization, students can never be "equally" prepared to take any given test. This is not where the inequity lies; the inequity lies in attempts to create this even playing ground, when we know it can never be.

My condemnation of external testing has been aimed at testing on the national level. But statewide tests and institutionwide tests are vulnerable to exactly the same criticism. What students know and what they can do with that knowledge will always be conditioned by the environment in which they learn and are graded. Thus, grading and assessment must always be linked to what students do in the classrooms they are actually in. If external assessment is not linked to what students do in the classroom, it is obviously unfair.

Many in the assessment field subscribe to my position but believe that a national testing system that focuses on the "3 Ps"—performance, portfolios, and products—can eliminate the inequities evident in multiple-choice, standardized testing. Madaus lays out the reasons why such testing directed from a national center raises exactly the same equity issues as any other kind of national testing, for he recognizes that no system can produce just measures "until policymakers put in place appropriate national delivery standards for social, health, family, and educational resources and support systems" (1993, 12). Ethics is not an issue solely of "the nature of the test per se" or of "item and test bias"; equity issues must be looked at "from a much broader perspective" (1993, 11). Even delivery standards are not enough. "We also need national systems that implement those delivery standards equitably across states and districts and within districts across schools." Madaus concludes his historical examination of the technology of testing by discounting the claim that any test can reform schools. "Although testing can assist in reform efforts, the nation cannot test its way out of its educational problems." This is indeed the master inequity: that somehow testing is the solution to our educational problems. Madaus and I agree that "it is the teachers, not tests or assessments, that must be the cornerstones of reform efforts" (1993, 23). It is my faith in teachers as the only legitimate reformers that moves me to propose collaboration. And it is my fear that thoughtless grading and assessment may lead to increased external testing that moves me to propose collaboration strongly.

Albert Shanker tells us what we all know, even if we do not particularly want to face it: "All A's are not equal" (1994).[12] Can we say that an A at Suffolk Community College is equal to an A at Yale? To a C? To an F? Is Virginia Woolf a "better" writer than Sandra Cisneros? As literary critics, we have learned that this is essentially a pointless question, though all of us certainly have our own judgments on these issues. Might it not be equally pointless to seek to equate grades assigned at disparate institutions with disparate student bodies, faculty, and educational missions?

Whatever we say to defend our individual grading procedures may not be under direct attack in the current criticism of higher education and its standards, procedures, and costs, but it most certainly is under indirect attack in the form of increasing talk at the state and national levels about the need for standards and standardized assessment to determine how well our colleges and universities "are doing." Calls for national testing reflect the public's concern about the quality of education; the results of these national tests then confirm the existence of problems (Haney, Madaus, and Lyons 1992, 126). A study undertaken by the Policy Information Center of the Educational Testing Service concludes that eleven percent of the graduates of four-year colleges and twenty-one percent of the graduates of two- and four-year colleges cannot produce a written explanation of an extended argument (Shanker 1994). What does this all mean? Does it mean that I as a college teacher am not doing my job (especially because my specialized field is Composition and Rhetoric); does it mean that few of us are doing our jobs well; does it mean that students are underprepared when they enter my institution—or just stupider than they used to be? Could it possibly mean (horror of horrors!) that I am inflating my grades? I ask myself all of these questions, but perhaps the question I should be asking is whether the tests upon which these conclusions are based have any validity for me and for my students at my institution now.

Within the current climate, however, this is not a popular or politically wise stance to assume. To the public, it naturally appears like a cop-out. "Sure," they say, "blame the tests instead of yourselves!" Too often we are too quick in our refusal to take public complaints seriously. I believe that if we do not confront the ethical issues posed by research and by current theories, we may well deserve public condemnation. Those who pay the bills have the right to expect us to be thorough and consistent in our procedures—particularly when those procedures are directly pertinent to educational outcomes. Charles B. Harris (1993) has warned us about the unpleasant potential of standardized tests to invade our once-protected classrooms. We need to avert such an outcome by opening our grading closets and making this space more public. Protecting this space only confirms the public in its belief that external assessment is essential.

Negotiated and Shared Grading

At the precollege level, some institutions are experimenting with including parents as part of evaluation and grading teams. At the high-school level, some schools are asking students to create interdisciplinary portfolios, which are then graded by teams of teachers from all departments. Some colleges are designing similar systems for their undergraduates. And the New School for Social Research has developed a system of evaluation for some of its graduate students which sets up oral "conversations" to which students may invite friends, family members, and others.[13]

Undoubtedly, at least at the outset, shared grading will create more work, but at least part of that additional time will be offset by spending less time grading our own students' work. And both we and our students will become better at what we do. But we do not need elaborate systems to grade collaboratively. The least irksome and yet still productive system is simply to trade three or four papers with a colleague who is teaching the same class or a similar one. Doing this in groups of three or four can provide even greater benefits. Participants can agree on categories for these papers: Perhaps they should all be problematic papers in some way; perhaps they could consist of one very good paper, one very poor paper, and one so-so paper. The intent is not to learn how to give the same grades as a colleague; the intent is to think about one's own grades in a context in which they matter greatly. If knowledge is socially constructed, then our knowledge of what an A or an F is has also been socially constructed. I am simply advocating that the social construction of our standards become overt.

A move of this same nature is occurring even within the field of psychometrics. Guba and Lincoln (1989) recommend what they call "fourth generation evaluation," in which evaluators discuss among themselves a suitable evaluation for a particular performance. They recommend that all stakeholders, whoever they may be in a specific situation, join in this negotiation. Stakeholders here could thus include the students themselves. Guba and Lincoln consider it crucial that negotiations involve both those who are embedded in the context from which grow the materials to be evaluated and those who stand outside of this immediate context. Such an argument suggests the usefulness of including in collaborative grading someone who is outside the class—perhaps even outside the discipline—perhaps even outside the institution. Pamela Moss advocates "hermeneutic" evaluation as "one of several possible strategies of serving important epistemological and ethical purposes" (1994, 5). She sees such evaluation as the search to understand the "whole in light of its parts," and as a way to keep final judgments open as one interprets and reinterprets evidence. Those engaged in such evaluation would work collaboratively to create a transparent "trail of evidence leading to the interpretations [scores or grades], which [would] allow users to evaluate the conclusions for themselves" (1994, 7). Moss reminds us that many of the judgments that most affect our professional lives are derived through such processes: Hiring committees and tenure and promotion committees all work collaboratively to make their decisions. Few of us want to be judged by one other person through a process that is not examined by any one else. Is it ethical to judge our students in that way when we eschew it for ourselves?

One possible remedy for variations in grading might seem to be the development of a departmental grading policy complete with agreed-upon standards. Time spent in the development of such a policy is undoubtedly time well spent, but ultimately it proves most valuable to those involved in the development and of little value to those who were not involved but who are obligated to use it. One recent study of elementary and secondary teachers provides some startling information about assessment practices and grading in light of systemwide policies:

> Only about one half of the teachers surveyed indicated that they were aware of their districts' policies on grading; most were not aware of the assessment practices of their colleagues. Many teachers seemed to have individual assessment policies that reflected their own individualistic values and beliefs about teaching. (Cizek, Fitzgerald, and Rachor 1995/1996, 159–60)

The authors of this study also reported that there were teachers who reported that they "knew formal policies for grading existed, but they chose to ignore them" (1995/1996, 172). If such reactions occur in the precollege class-room, we can be sure they are even more embedded at the college level, where most faculty consider themselves independent contractors. If departments de-vote time to collaboratively creating a grading policy and standards, they must also apply those policy and standards collaboratively if they genuinely wish to create a realistic context for students across their classes. Furthermore, even the creation of a policy should not be undertaken in the absence of examples of student writing. Because grades are contextual, grading policies cannot be developed apart from the object of the grades, for the texts we construct in our heads are not the texts students produce.[14]

Two final issues remain. The first has to do with the purposes of various kinds of evaluation. Whose interests does evaluation serve? Much national testing does not serve students at all, and even young students know that. One study of students in grades six to nine, cited by Kiplinger and Linn, reports that "nearly half [of those taking the test] thought taking achievement tests was a waste of time; almost one third wanted to get the achievement test over with more than they wanted to perform well; and over one fifth saw no good reason to try to do well and reported that they did not try very hard" (1995/1996, 114). Many of the tests produce information only on systems, not on students.

Surely the purpose of testing has to be more than the accumulation of so-called data about the status of achievement in particular locations. Testing and grading need to serve as a gateway, not as a gatekeeper (to borrow the terms of the Report of the National Commission on Testing and Public Policy), a gateway into both improved learning and improved teaching. For me, the ini-tiation of such improvement is the natural product of shared grading. The shared context in which grades are collaboratively determined spills over into the classroom. Armstrong notes, "Going from classroom to classroom can sometimes seem to students like entering a different world with different rules for reading, different norms for acceptable discourse, and different assump-tions about literature, culture, and the status of texts" (1991, 16). Although he does not discuss grading, Armstrong concludes as I would: "Teachers can bet-ter help students relate the worlds of their different classes if we have a com-plex, deep, nonpolemical understanding of one another's assumptions, methods, and aim and how they affect our teaching." I would add "and how they affect our grading." We need to put grading in its place as an aid to im-proving our classrooms. Students take the tests and write the papers. They have the right to experience them as learning experiences.

The final issue for me here is one of morality. How does morality, tradi-tional and otherwise, fit in here? Should schools be in the business of incul-cating moral and ethical standards? "Education . . . includes moral growth—preparation of the mind to make the best judgments for the good of society. It takes both aspects of education, moral and intellectual, to be fully educated" (Johnson 1984, 99). To what extent do we grade on the basis of the perceived moral or ethical quality of what we read? I remember once receiv-

ing a personal experience narrative in which the writer described an evening
of driving drunk and throwing bottles through the windows of houses. As we
had our conference on this paper, it was all I could do to keep from telling him
I thought he should be in jail. I was a beginning teacher, and it never occurred
to me to ask whether he was describing a real occurrence. That possibility
never surfaced as we talked. I, of course, wanted him to revise and insert some
moral learning of some sort into it. I do not know whether I said that directly
or tried to lead him to it. And, frankly, I do not remember at all whether he
did revise or what grade I put on the paper. What remains fresh in my mind is
my own moral outrage. Did the grade I gave him reflect my outrage? Should
it have?

Classical rhetoric foregrounds the moral and ethical qualities of rhetori-
cians. As Johnson notes in her analysis of the role of ethos in classical rhetoric, "In *Georgias* and *Phædrus* the nature of ideal truth and absolute goodness
are central issues in Plato's argument for reformed oratorical practice; the reality of the speaker's virtue is presented as a prerequisite to effective speaking
. . . the role of rhetoric is defined as the instruction of ideal truth" (1984, 99).
Quintilian, in *Instituto Oratoria*, defines his goal as the "education of the perfect orator" (Johnson 1984, 103). For him, the most important quality of an
orator is "intrinsic moral virtue," and he asserts that moral character can be
learned. If so, can we assume it can be taught? But what is the difference between indoctrination and teaching? Viewed from one side, teaching is always
indoctrination to some degree. Viewed from another side, teachers should not
leave values in the hallway. If we believe this, how do we grade student work
that seems to undercut "goodness." To be fair or ethical to students, we need
to put our own truths under a searchlight periodically. We cannot, for the most
part, uncover our own assumptions without help from others. This is a further
reason for collaboration grading. We have to be on guard about both our own
grading methods and our response to the ethical stance of what we grade.

Increasingly, I read and hear a concern for values in education. An an-
nouncement for the upcoming conference sponsored by the NCTE Assembly
for Research is one example:

> [A]s we edge ever closer to a new millennium, talk of measurable goals and
> standards is eclipsing more fundamental questions: How to prepare a new
> generation for the challenges of a diverse democracy? How to define our
> notions of goodness—in the educative process, and in the social order that
> contains and shapes it? . . . [W]e'll talk of ways we might join forces for the
> common good—teachers, teacher educators, parents, researchers, and com-
> munity members. (1996)

What is potentially frightening here is that each of us might feel empowered to base our judgments on our individual moral systems rather than on the
"common good." We can know what that "common good" is only if we arrive
at it collaboratively and maintain it (or alter it) collaboratively.

Conclusions

I do not want to be read as saying that there is no such thing as an A. Of course there is. My contention is that an A is always the result of tacit and perhaps unconscious interactions with texts and students and papers and colleagues over a number of years. Making this process explicit discharges our ethical obligation to examine our standards in the context in which they currently function. When the A is given in a setting in which standards and grades have been shared and discussed and thus reached in a collaborative context, that A is as objective as an A can ever be. A plethora of subjective reactions is the only way to even come close to the objective. Is this not what courtroom trials and juries are based on? And is this not why we seek second and third medical opinions? And why do we allow and even encourage diversity of judgment on "high" literary texts and deny that to student texts? Surely, it would be more ethical to convey to students the reality that readers do not agree on texts.

As Edmund Gordon, Emeritus Professor at Yale University (1993), has observed, "The core of equity in assessment lies in deep attitudes and values regarding the social purposes of assessment. In the past, the central purpose of assessment has been to sort and rank students according to presumed inherent abilities—in effect to create winners and losers." Personally, I would like to find some way to keep that from happening, but in the current climate, I am not sanguine about that sort of change. And because I am not, I write to urge all of us to join periodically in conversations with others about specific student-produced texts in order to examine our grading practices in light of what research has taught us and what our theories say about texts and contexts. I cannot say this better than Grant Wiggins:

> The most tangible signs of value in schools, the "coin of the realm"—the grades and scores we give on students' tests and papers—remain untouched by the work of reform under way around us. Perhaps that should not surprise us. Anthropologists know that often the most important and revealing behaviors in a culture are the least noticed, so much are they a part of the habits and rhythms of life. (1988, 21)

Writing instruction has moved from being "authoritarian, teacher-centered current-traditional" to "process-centered" and "more student-centered, more collaborative, and more aware of diversity." But grading has for the most part not moved; it continues to be authoritarian and teacher-centered—but it could at least be more collaborative.

Nel Noddings (1984) emphasizes that ethics is a one-on-one issue, involving our relationships to individuals in specific situations. Ethics cannot be turned into generalities. Our theories about texts, their interpretation, and their influence are too often frozen in a world of generalities, generalities often created by the very theories we hold so dear in most corners of our professional life. To be ethical in that professional life, we need to bring these theories into our classrooms and fully consider what they might reveal about our interpretations of our students' texts and the grades that result from those interpretations. But I also urge that we do not lightly dismiss the looming possibility of external evaluation. If standardized tests become the norm, our classroom grades might well become meaningless. If we can begin to be more open, more public, more collaborative in our grading, we will be serving ethical purposes and, at the same time, deflecting from our doorway the standardized specter, bearing its own bag of ethically questionable practices.[15]

I have only touched on the issues surrounding collaborative grading and suggested only a few ways to begin; I invite others to explore these possibilities more fully. The research we must listen to and the theories we hold so dear are generalities that we can and should, if we are ethical beings, turn into "everyday use" when we face an individual student one-on-one as a reader of his or her paper who has the obligation to grade it.

Notes

1. To my knowledge, the only time collaboration has occurred recently at Stony Brook (outside of the Writing Program's portfolio system) was an outgrowth of a charge of plagiarism. Because the student continued to deny the charge, the grievance committee sent the questioned pieces of writing to several faculty members, asking them to present their individual conclusions about the possibility of plagiarism. I assume that the committee then resolved these collective responses in some way and came to its own conclusion. It is perhaps instructive (ironic?) that a collaborative decision such as this is made in a situation where legal repercussions hover in the background. Another colleague reported to me that he had shared grading with another faculty member when they taught the same course. At one point in the semester, they simply gave the same assignment and graded each other's papers.

2. By *theory*, I intend mainly theories of interpretation. The need for a new theory for assessment itself is set forth thoroughly and forcefully by Huot. His stance, I believe, complements mine, but he comes to the subject from a slightly different, but certainly equally valuable, direction.

3. See Madaus for a concise summary of the ways in which technology has intersected with forms of testing.

4. Stephen Jay Gould's (1981) exposure of the lack of scientific procedures in the administration and interpretation of the Army Alpha and Beta intelligence testing during World War I is unsettling, particularly in view of the fact that these tests served as the basis for the widespread use of intelligence tests in the schools for decades.

5. Eighty-four percent of responding schools used multiple-choice examinations for admission; sixty-eight percent for exemption; seventy-five percent for placement; forty-two percent for proficiency; and forty-five percent for graduation (Murphy and Carlson).

6. Frances Zak, dissertation, Stony Brook

7. A relevant aside: Recently, Cizek, Fitzgerald, and Rachor (1995/1996), in a survey of the grading practices of elementary and secondary school teachers, uncov-

ered the disturbing fact that a far higher percentage of female respondents in comparison to male respondents (45.2 percent to 18.5 percent) used publishers' tests rather than self-developed tests for major assessments (165). I can only wonder briefly for the nonce whether these figures would turn up if postsecondary teachers were surveyed and what the significance would be. Do women have less confidence in themselves as test constructors and interpreters, or do they have a greater respect for community in contrast to isolated and individualistic standards? Or both?

8. Periodically, I distribute anonymous essays to my students and ask them to decide whether they were written by males or females. When I last did this, two-thirds of the students correctly identified the gender of each writer.

9. For a full discussion of the "social history" of grading and of the reasons why it can never be apolitical, see Boyd, "The Evolution of Grading Student Writing, 1870–1920: Pedagogical Imperatives and Cultural Anxieties."

10. A recent letter to *The New York Times* (Schwarzbach 1995) makes this issue graphic. The writer undertook research on the relevance of scores on the Graduate Record Examination to success in graduate school. He concludes, "Based on the statistics published by the Educational Testing Service, the institution that administers the test, I . . . found that the success of students, once they made it to graduate school, had little correlation with their score on the exam." When he sent copies of his research with his graduate school applications as explanation for why he had not taken the GRE, he was not accepted. In the following year, he took the test and was accepted.

11. In the process of these studies, their authors set forth a whole array of reasons why tests do not represent students' knowledge fairly. Those reasons that struck me the most strongly include exclusion from tests of students who might do poorly and pull down the overall class or school ratings, the use of old tests, and "instructional activities aimed at increasing test scores—*without concomitant increases in students' conceptual learning*" (Kiplinger and Linn 1995/1996, 122) [emphasis is mine]. I find myself wondering whether teachers, administrators, parents, and the public just want high scores and care little about whether those scores actually reflect the level of achievement by individual students.

12. It is a constant marvel to me that Shanker is such an outspoken support r of external standards, for which surely one of the strongest reasons is that teachers cannot be trusted to maintain high standards without an external prod and help from "higher" authorities. I would expect that he, as a union leader, would have more faith in the professionalism of his members.

13. At a recent NCTE conference on reflection, Cynthia Onore reported on just such a practice at the New School in New York City.

14. For an interesting analysis of collaborative work, see McClure *et al.*, "None of Us Is as Smart as All of Us." This study concludes with a discussion of "the importance of free, informed, collegial dialogue in promoting change" and links that discussion to the development of standards of evaluation.

15. Madaus, in his criticism of national testing, analyzes the ways in which technology contributes to increased standardization. Exploration of this issue would have extended my article beyond allowable limits, but this is an area, too, that has the potential to be an ethical morass.

Works Cited

Armstrong, P. 1991. "Deprivatizing the Classroom." *ADE Bulletin* 99 (Fall): 13–19.

Ball, A. F. 1993. "Encorporating Ethnographic-Based Techniques to Enhance Assessments of Culturally Diverse Students' Written Exposition." *Educational Assessment* 3 (Summer): 255–81.

Berlin, J. A. 1992. "Composition Studies and Cultural Studies: Collapsing Boundaries." In *Into the Field: Sites of Composition Studies*, ed. A. R. Gere, 99–116. New York: MLA.

Bizzell, P. 1986. "Foundationalism and Anti-Foundationalism." *Pre/Text* 7: 37–56.

Bleich, D. 1989. "Feelings About Literature." In *The Critical Tradition*, ed. D. H. Richter, 1254–70. New York: St. Martin's.

Breland, H. M., and J. L. Gaynor. 1979. "A Comparison of Direct and Indirect Assessments of Writing Skill." *Journal of Educational Measurement* 16 (Summer): 119–28.

Cizek, G. J., S. M. Fitzgerald, and R. E. Rachor. 1995/1996. "Teachers' Assessment Practices: Preparation, Isolation, and the Kitchen Sink." *Educational Assessment* 3: 159–79.

Cooper, C. R., and L. Odell. 1977. *Evaluating Writing*. Urbana, IL: NCTE.

Diederich, P. 1974. *Measuring Growth in English*. Urbana, IL: NCTE.

Estrin, E. T. 1993. "Alternative Assessment: Issues in Language, Culture, and Equity." *Knowledge Brief* 11: 1–8.

Farrell, T. J. 1979. "The Female and Male Modes of Rhetoric." *College English* 40: 909–21.

Flynn, E. A. 1989. "Gender and Reading." In *The Critical Tradition*, ed. D. H. Richter, 1271–84. New York: St. Martin's.

Flynn, J. F. 1989. "Learning to Read Student Papers from a Feminine Perspective, II." In *Encountering Student Texts,* ed. B. Lawson, S. S. Ryan, and W. R. Winterowd, 131–37. Urbana, IL: NCTE.

From Gatekeeper to Gateway: Transforming Testing in America. 1990. Boston College: National Commission on Testing and Public Policy.

Gates, H. L., Jr. 1993. "Beyond the Culture Wars: Identities in Dialogue." *Profession* 93: 6–11.

Giroux, H., and P. McLaren. 1989. "Introduction: Schooling, Cultural Politics, and the Struggle for Democracy." In *Critical Pedagogy, the State and Cultural Struggle*, ed. H. A. Giroux and P. McLaren, xi–xxxv. Albany: State University of New York Press.

Gordon, Edmund. 1993. "Human Diversity, Equity, and Educational Assessment." Paper presented at 1993 CRESST Assessment Conference.

Gould, S. J. 1981. *The Mismeasure of Man*. New York: Norton.

Goulston, W. 1987. "Women Writing." In *Teaching Writing: Pedagogy, Gender, and Equity*, ed. C. L. Caywood and G. R. Overing, 19–29. Albany: State University of New York Press.

Guba, E., and Y. Lincoln. 1989. *Fourth Generation Evaluation*. Newbury Park, CA: Sage.

————. 1996. "Guest Column. Four Views of the Place of the Personal in Scholarship" and "Forum." *PMLA* 111.5: 1063–79; 1146–69.

Haney, W. M., G. F. Madaus, and R. Lyons. 1992. *The Fractured Marketplace for Standardized Testing*. Boston: Kluwer Academic.

Harris, C. B. 1993. "Mandated Testing and the Postsecondary English Department." *Profession* 93: 59–67.

Hirsch, E. D. 1987. *Cultural Literacy: What Every American Needs to Know*. Boston: Houghton.

Johnson, N. 1984. "Ethos and the Aims of Rhetoric." In *Essays on Classical Rhetoric and Modern Discourse*, ed. R. J. Connors, L. S. Ede, and A. A. Lunsford, 98–114. Carbondale: Southern Illinois University Press.

Kiplinger, V. L., and R. Linn. 1995/1996. "Stakes of Test Administration: The Impact on Student Performance on the National Assessment of Educational Progress." *Educational Assessment* 3: 111–55.

Madaus, G. F. 1993. A National Testing System: Manna From Above? An Historical/ Technological Perspective." *Educational Assessment* 1: 9–26.

McClure, R. M., and J. Walters, with L. Bietau, D. Daws, and L. Grosvenor. 1993. "None of Us Is as Smart as All of Us." *Educational Assessment* 1 (Winter): 71–89.

Morrison, T. 1992. *Playing in the Dark: Whiteness and the Literary Imagination*. Cambridge, MA: Harvard University Press.

Moss, P. A. 1994. "Can There Be Validity Without Reliability?" *Educational Researcher*, March, 5–12.

Murphy, S., and S. Carlson, with the Members of the CCCC Committee on Assessment. Draft report.

Noddings, N. 1984. *Caring: A Feminine Approach to Ethics and Moral Education*. Berkeley: University of California Press.

Onore, C. 1996. "Roundtales: Seeing Ourselves and Seeing Ourselves as Others See Us." Learning and Literacies Conference, National Council of Teachers of English, Albuquerque, NM.

Papoulis, I. 1990. "'Personal Narrative,' 'Academic Writing,' and Feminist Theory: Reflections of a Freshman Composition Teacher." *Freshman English News* 18.2: 9–12.

Phelps, L. W. 1993. "A Constrained Vision of the Writing Classroom." *Profession* 93: 46–54.

Pratt, M. L. 1991. "Arts of the Contact Zone." *Profession* 91: 33–40.

Purves, A. C. 1992. "Reflections on Research and Assessment in Written Composition." *Research in the Teaching of English* 26 (February): 108–22.

Schwarzbach, D. 1995. "Where Questioning Graduate Admissions Tests Will Get You." *New York Times,* 12 April, A9.

Shanker, A. 1994. "All A's Are Not Equal." *On Campus* 14.3 (November): 5.

Sosnoski, J. J. 1991. "Postmodern Teachers in Their Postmodern Classrooms: Socrates Begone!" In *Contending with Words: Composition and Rhetoric in a Postmodern Age*, ed. P. Harkin and J. Schilb, 198–219. New York: MLA.

Takala, S., A. C. Purves, and A. Buckmaster. 1982. *Evaluation in Education*. New York: Pergamon.

Tannen, D. 1990. *You Just Don't Understand*. New York: Ballantine Books.

Tompkins, J. P. 1980. "An Introduction to Reader-Response Criticism." In *Reader-Response Criticism: From Formalism to Post-Structuralism*, ed. J. P. Tompkins, ix–xxvi; 201–32. Baltimore: Johns Hopkins University Press.

Villaneuva, V. 1991. "Consideration of American Freireistas." In *The Politics of Writing Instruction*, ed. R. Bullock and J. Trimbur, 247–62. Portsmouth, NH: Boynton.

Wiggins, G. P. 1988. "Rational Numbers." *American Educator* (Winter): 20–25.

———. 1993. *Assessing Student Performance: Exploring the Purpose and Limits of Testing*. San Francisco: Jossey-Bass.

Witte, S. P., M. Trachsel, and K. Walters. 1986. "Literacy and the Direct Assessment of Writing: A Diachronic Perspective." In *Writing Assessment: Issues and Strategies*, ed. K. Greenberg, H. Wiener, and R. Donovan, 13–34. New York: Longman.

Zak, F. 1993. "An Inquiry into Response to Student Writing." Dissertation. State University of New York at Stony Brook.

Zak, F., and C. Weaver, eds. 1998. *The Theory and Practice of Grading Writing: Problems and Possibilities*. Albany: State University of New York.

Contributors

Pat Belanoff is Associate Professor of English and past Director of Writing Programs at the State University of New York at Stony Brook. She is a member of the College Steering Committee of NCTE and Chair of the CCCC Assessment Committee. She is coauthor (with Betsy Rorschach and Mia Oberlink) of *The Right Handbook*. She has also coedited (with Marcia Dickson) *Portfolios: Process and Product* and (with Peter Elbow and Sheryl Fontaine) *Nothing Begins with N: New Investigations of Freewriting*.

Linda S. Bergmann is Associate Professor of English and Director of Writing Across the Curriculum at the University of Missouri–Rolla. In 1992, she was a fellow in the summer workshop of the Center for the Study of Ethics in the Professions at the Illinois Institute of Technology. She has published articles on writing in *The Journal of Teaching Writing*, *CEA Critic*, and *Perspectives on the Professions*, as well as studies of the rhetoric of nineteenth-century science and exploration and of the relationship between public and private writing.

Olivia G. Castellano is Professor of English at California State University, Sacramento, where she teaches courses in composition, creative writing, and Chicano literature. Author of four books of poetry, as well as essays on Chicano literature, she has received a number of awards for teaching and for her work in developing programs for bilingual/bidialectal students of writing.

Frances V. Condon is Director of the Writing Center at Siena College in Loudonville, New York, and she is a Ph.D. candidate in English at the State University of New York at Albany. Her fields of study include composition theory, critical theory, and critical pedagogy. In addition to her scholarly work, she is a playwright and poet.

Paul Connolly is John D. & Catherine T. MacArthur Professor of English and Director of the Institute for Writing and Thinking at Bard College. He is the author of *Building Family: An Act of Faith* (Abbey Press, 1982), editor of *On Essays: A Reader for Writers* (Harper & Row, 1981) and *New Methods in College Writing Programs: Theories in Practice* (MLA, 1986), and coeditor with Teresa Vilardi of *Writing to Learn Mathematics and Science* (Teachers College Press, 1989).

Devan Cook is an Assistant Professor of English at Lindsey Wilson College in Columbia, Kentucky. Her poems have appeared in *Buffalo Spree*, *NewCollage*, and *Poetry Motel*. In addition, she has an article in *Writing on the Edge* and a chapter (with Darrell Fike) in *Elements of Alternate Style: Essays on Writing and Revision*.

Sheryl I. Fontaine is Associate Professor of English and Coordinator of Composition at California State University at Fullerton. She coedited *Nothing Begins with N: New Investigations of Freewriting* (Southern Illinois University Press, 1991) and *Writing Ourselves into the Story: Unheard Voices from Composition Studies* (Southern Illinois

University Press, 1993). She and Cherryl Armstrong Smith are coauthors of *Shoptalk for College Writers* (Harcourt Brace, forthcoming)

Janet C. Fortune is Assistant Professor of Education at Berea College in Berea, Kentucky. Her primary research interests focus on spirituality as a guide for establishing classroom relationships and for defining the democratic classroom. She taught grades 5 through 12 for thirteen years in public and private schools before entering higher education. Her essay "Democracy in Education: A Foxfire Experience" appears in *Democratic Teacher Education.*

Richard Fulkerson is Professor of English and Director of English Graduate Studies at Texas A & M University–Commerce. He has published widely in rhetoric and composition and serves on the CCCC Executive Committee. Most recently, he has written *Teaching the Argument in Writing* (NCTE, 1996).

Marguerite H. Helmers is Assistant Professor of English and Director of Composition at the University of Wisconsin, Oshkosh, where she teaches criticism, cultural studies, and writing courses. She has written *Writing Students: Composition Testimonials and Representations of Students* (State University of New York Press, 1994).

Susan M. Hunter is Associate Professor of English and the Director of the master's program in Professional Writing at Kennesaw State University. She coedited *Writing Ourselves into the Story: Unheard Voices from Composition Studies* (Southern Illinois University Press, 1993) and *The Place of Grammar in Writing Instruction: Past, Present, Future* (Boynton/Cook, 1995). She is a founding and current editor of *Dialogue: A Journal for Writing Specialists.*

Cherryl Armstrong Smith is Associate Professor of English at California State University, Sacramento, where she teaches courses in composition, teacher education, and poetry writing. She has published numerous articles and book chapters on composition pedagogy and also publishes poetry. She and Sheryl I. Fontaine are coauthors of *Shoptalk for College Writers* (Harcourt Brace, forthcoming).

William E. Smith is Associate Professor of English and past director of Composition at Western Washington University in Bellingham, Washington. He was editor of *WPA: Writing Program Administration* from 1983 to 1988. Smith has served as a WPA at five universities since 1975. He is coauthor of two composition textbooks and several articles on the teaching of writing.